TIME AND SPACE IN LITERACY RESEARCH

"This important volume sets the grounds for reframing literacy education as a means for the institutional construction and reorganization of space and time.... [It] shows how place and time shape and influence, enable and constrain peoples' cultural practices with texts, whether in formal institutional or community and family settings."

Allan Luke, Emeritus Professor, Queensland University of Technology, Australia, from the Foreword

"*What could have been lost* is a phrase that is fitting for what [this] book does for the literacy community: it saves memories and preserves agency in elegant and eloquent ways. . . . The front story of every chapter is to develop and enhance accounts of time and space in literacy research, and the back story is how we become and change as researchers across time and space. *This* is the story that intrigued me. . . . Time and space, as they are seen in nuanced and inflected ways in the book, expose fundamental truths about life and learning."

Jennifer Rowsell, Brock University, Canada, from the Afterword

Literacy researchers interested in how specific sites of learning situate students and the ways they make sense of their worlds are asking new questions and thinking in new ways about how time and space operate as contextual dimensions in the learning lives of students, teachers, and families. This timely, significant book provides a conceptual framework for extending existing conceptions of context and provides unique and ground-breaking examples of empirical research. Offering a richer and more nuanced understanding of learning, knowing, being, and becoming, these investigations inform questions related to history, identity, methodology, in-school and out-of school spaces, and local/global literacies. An engaging blend of methodological, theoretical, and empirical work featuring well-known researchers on the topic, *Time and Space in Literacy Research* offers the literacy education community invaluable insight into the current state of the field.

Catherine Compton-Lilly is Associate Professor, University of Wisconsin, Madison, USA.

Erica Halverson is Associate Professor, University of Wisconsin, Madison, USA.

TIME AND SPACE IN LITERACY RESEARCH

Edited by
Catherine Compton-Lilly
Erica Halverson

Routledge
Taylor & Francis Group

NEW YORK AND LONDON

First published 2014
by Routledge
711 Third Avenue, New York, NY 10017

and by Routledge

2 Park Square, Milton Park, Abingdon, Oxon OX14 4RN

Routledge is an imprint of the Taylor & Francis Group, an informa business

© 2014 Taylor & Francis

The right of Catherine Compton-Lilly and Erica Halverson to be identified as authors of this work has been asserted by them in accordance with sections 77 and 78 of the Copyright, Designs and Patents Act 1988.

Library of Congress Cataloging-in-Publication Data

Time and space in literacy research / edited by Catherine Compton-Lilly,
    University of Wisconsin Madison, Madison, Wisconsin, Erica Halverson,
    University of Wisconsin Madison, Madison, Wisconsin.
        pages cm
    Includes bibliographical references and index.
    1. Language arts.   2. Context effects (Psychology)   I. Compton-Lilly,
Catherine.   II. Halverson, Erica.
LB1631.T55   2014
428.0071'2—dc23   2013044742

ISBN: 978-0-415-74987-9 (hbk)
ISBN: 978-0-415-74988-6 (pbk)
ISBN: 978-1-315-79582-9 (ebk)

Typeset in Bembo
by Apex CoVantage, LLC

Printed and bound in Great Britain by TJ International Ltd, Padstow, Cornwall

CONTENTS

ACKNOWLEDGMENTS

This book exists because of a group of smart, generous, and dedicated teachers, graduate students, and professors who came together in Madison, Wisconsin, for three chilly days in February 2011. We need to thank not only the presenters at that conference but also all the attendees who brought their ideas, insights, and questions to that forum. We would especially like to acknowledge Mariana Pacheco, our conference co-chair who was instrumental in developing the mission of the conference and the program that resulted from that mission. In addition, this conference and thus this book could not have been possible without the dedication and efforts of an amazing team of doctoral students who helped to organize and host the conference. You are all in our hearts as this book comes into being.

The weekend when the conference was held coincided with the early days of the *Wisconsin Uprising*. While union protestors and public workers, including teachers, protested restrictions on collective bargaining rights in the streets surrounding the state capitol in Madison, a mile away at the university a group of educational researchers met to talk about time and space. As described in the introduction to this book, timespace is a way to talk about context and the situations that surround children's and teachers' lives. In our own ways, we were also exploring social justice, human rights, and economic equity. The university and the capital were simultaneously spaces of conversation, struggle, and new possibilities.

We acknowledge both the intellectual work of the academics who contributed to the conference and the organizational action of the people in the streets. Ultimately, we work toward the same goals.

We would particularly like to thank Naomi Silverman, our editor at Routledge. Naomi not only has brought an astounding range of books into existence but has also been recognized as a brilliant mentor who has helped many scholars to find their voices and to find an audience. We thank her for all her help and assistance.

Finally, we would each like to thank our families and friends for their endless support as we drafted, revised, revisited, and reworked our contributions to this volume, and as we collaborated and communicated with chapter authors. In particular, Cathy would like to thank Todd and Carly Lilly—her heart and her soul. Erica would like to thank Cathy for the opportunity to come along for the ride; it's always great to learn from your colleagues!

FOREWORD

On the Taming of Space

This important volume sets the grounds for reframing literacy education as a means for the institutional construction and reorganization of space and time. As Catherine Compton-Lilly and Erica Halverson's introductory essay explains, many of these studies draw upon the sociohistorical and sociocultural theories of Vygotsky and colleagues to show how literacy as a human technology mediates spatial and temporal contexts. These studies of teaching and learning focus on the reflexive relationship between technologies of inscription—handwritten and print, visual and digital—and the material and imagined spaces where they are used. One of the effects of the long-standing definition of literacy as an internal, cognitive process has been to treat it as a universal, cross-contextual, "autonomous" entity (Street, 1984). *Literacy Research in Time and Space* shows how place and time shape and influence, enable and constrain people's cultural practices with texts, whether in formal institutional or in community and family settings. Turning to schools, we see how lived and imagined spaces and histories are represented and constructed through the mediating codes of communications systems and affiliated ideologies. The core premise here follows on from a half century of foundational work in economics and communications theory by Lewis Mumford and Harold Innis through the pioneering anthropological studies by Jack Goody and recent critical social geography by David Harvey, Edward Soja, and others: that communications media and their systems of representation enable the reshaping and redesign of spatial and temporal relations—with economic and social, cultural and cognitive effects.

Yet the lineage of the work described earlier, stretching back to Vygotsky and Luria, is premised on a profoundly Western, Eurocentric view of material and cognate relations to space, of dialectical and onto/phylogenetic relations of time. It is not incidental that Goody's prototypical study of the cultural evolution of literacy was entitled *The Domestication of the Savage Mind* (1977), reference to Levi-Strauss intended. It is this complex relationship between Western literacy, Enlightenment science, and the affiliated quest for the rational mastery and control of space and time that I want to query in these brief, prefatory comments. My aim is to underline a theme that runs across these chapters: that Western literacies have and continue to have profound consequences for relationships of colonialism and empire, ideology and local knowledge, and, ultimately, power.

I am currently reading the novelist and biologist Andrea Barrett's (2002) elegant fictional accounts of the emergence of Western science. In *Servants of the Map*, Barrett follows the 1863 Nepalese trek of Max Vigne, a British surveyor with the "Grand Trigonometrical Survey of India." Writing to his wife, Clara, at home in England, he describes the work of a mapmaker:

> As I fill in the blank spaces with the bends and curves of a river valley, the dips and rises of a range, the drawing begins to resemble a map of home. For company I have the handful of porters who've carried the equipment, and one or two of the Indian chainmen who assist us—intelligent men, trained at the Debra Dun in the basics of mapping and observation. Some know almost as much as I do and have the additional advantage of speaking the local languages as well as some English. When we meet to exchange results with those who work on the nearby peaks and form the rest of our group, the chainmen gather on one side of the fire, sharing food and stories. In their conversations a great idea called "The Survey" looms like a disembodied god to whom they—we—are all devoted. Proudly they refer to both themselves and us as "Servants of the Map." (Barrett, 2002, p. 33)

This is an incredibly vivid picture—of the mapmaker using pen and ink, drawing and designing, defining and representing the heretofore unknown (i.e., *terra nullius*), uncharted territory for science and, indeed, for empire. Through his recount, we see his understandings of the Sherpas upon whose local knowledge and expertise his very survival depends and of the Indian colonial subjects who serve as "chainmen" and "triangulators" to the project.

The aim of the mapmaker is accurate cartography. The "natives" here are part of the process, both as objects in the cartographer's letter to that place called "home" and as technological assistants, "servants" to the "disembodied god" of Western scientific exploration. This is about a *taming of space*—and the use of the map to compress, represent, and claim mastery over space.[1] Through this synchronic drawing of place, science supplants Indigenous connections between spirit and land, intergenerational histories and local knowledges—in effect displacing the ownership and mastery of the "natives" (in this case, Nepalese Sherpas). The cartographer's work is done through the technology of print/

visual drawing literacy—a taxonomy of space that was contemporaneous with Darwin's, Huxley's, and others' cataloguing of the biosphere. It was hardly a stretch, Torres Strait Islander scholar Martin Nakata (2007) explains, for European scientists and soldiers to extend this cartography of Indigenous lands first to the scientific observation and taxonomic classification of Indigenous peoples and then to pathologization and genocide.

Barrett succeeds in capturing the complexity and the naiveté of this Western scientific/imperial project. It is about the remediation of space and time, such that local Indigenous place and spirit, healing, history, and language are either ignored or misrecognized—and literally written over by Western taxonomic description. By Western scholars' naming, cataloguing and categorizing, and, quite literally, redrawing the world, the unknown becomes the known, the unwritten becomes written, and the local is repossessed as part of the grander project of science and empire. As Freire continuously reminded us: reading and writing the word—in this case, drawing and naming space and place—are about reading and writing the world (Freire & Macedo, 1987). At the same time, both for Barrett's characters and so many colonial personae portrayed in literature, this reading and writing of the cultural and geographic "other" has effect of displacing writers' senses of "home"— to the point where the prospects of return to a site of colonial origin fade.

A half century ago, the Canadian economist Harold Innis (1950, 1951) explained the nature of the relationship between communications technologies on space and time. Documenting the history of Canada's westward expansion, Innis describes the elaboration of transportation and communications infrastructure through Hudson's Bay outposts, the river portage system used by Simon Fraser and fur traders, and, later, the Canadian Pacific railroads and telegraph. This was part of a compression of time and space requisite for colonial settlement, the exploitation of natural resources, the expansion of trade and capital, and, indeed, the competitive expansion of empire.

Innis goes on to explain how different communications media have specific bias, that is, what we now term technological affordances that enable and constrain the expansion and compression of time and space. At the University of Toronto, *Innis Town Hall* is a cultural venue that now features concerts, cinema, and multimedia events. It was Innis's work that inspired a young Wordsworth scholar named Marshall McLuhan (1962) and, later, the developmental psychologist David Olson (1977) to, respectively, anticipate the emergence of new multimediated forms of communication and to describe the developmental acquisition of print literacy. Both Toronto scholars spoke of the distinctive "bias of communication" of writing, speech, and electronic media.

Literacy was and remains a key technology for the expansion, manipulation, and reconstruction of temporal and spatial relations. As a technology, it has profoundly ambivalent and ambiguous effects. While autonomous models of literacy treat it as of universal value and epistemological and cultural power, the effects and consequences of literacy depend upon both their spatial and their temporal contexts, the relationships of power and knowledge therein, and how they act to normatively reorganize the spatial and temporal experience of the literate (Luke, 1996).

Yet, however we reconstruct it, the standpoint of Innis's project was itself centered in Anglo/European place and time, written and imagined from the urban heart of English Canada. While he could begin enumerating the "biases" of dominant media of communications and their macroeconomic and sociopolitical consequences, he could not begin to envision or map the consequences of Western "civilization," empire, and modernity for Canadian First Nations peoples. A half century later, that work is finally under way.

I am currently working with Indigenous scholars at the University of Calgary whose work documents and interprets the consequences and possibilities of literacy for Canada's First Peoples. The Cree/Métis scholar Phyllis Steeves (2010) writes eloquently about the uses of literacy in Indigenous education, referring to Western literacy as "genocide's silken instrument." Steeves begins from the established case that European education and its affiliated approaches to literacy education have been part of a systematic attempt to eradicate Indigenous ways of knowing and being, asserting these "distinct and valued knowledge systems" continue to be under siege. Working from the orb-like image of a spider's sticky web, her work is a powerful critique of current bids to define "Aboriginal literacy" as an expansion of that web. Historically, the willful subordination and desecration of Indigenous places and histories, cultural resources and languages was but a first step, as recent work by the Cree/Métis scholar Lyn Daniels (2013) on residential schooling documents. Steeves's key argument is that current efforts to add "Aboriginal Literacy" to a (taxonomic) catalogue of multiple or plural literacies is an extension of that same historical project. She surmises that the risk is of a further "expansion of the concept of literacy harmful to the well being of Aboriginal peoples" (p. 53).

The Métis scholar Yvonne Poitras Pratt (2011) offers a complementary picture of the powers of digital media when enlisted as part of a larger cultural agenda of decolonization. Working in the community of Fishing Lake, Alberta, Poitras Pratt undertook an ethnographic study of the uses of digital technology among multiple generations in a Métis community. Poitras Pratt's work demonstrates the potential of digital technologies as a means for recovering and reinstating cultural narratives, traditional knowledges and world views—the same cultural resources that Steeves and Daniels show had been systematically suppressed and overwritten through schooling and Western literacy. But even when enlisting new technologies as part of a strategy for "giving back" to these communities, the outcomes are something more than literacy education or "voice," which remain saddled with the baggage of empire and genocide, as Steeves maintains. Poitras Pratt concludes: "Looking back, our digital storytelling workshop—however chaotic and haphazard—constituted an act of sacred exchange" (p. 213). Part of that exchange is about the reinstatement of Indigenous place and cultural memory.

I began these brief comments with a critique of the Western, Enlightenment scientific and political project as constituting a *taming of space,* an erasure of local knowledge and history. My case was that writing, drawing, imaging, and inscription are key media in that project—whether it entails mapping the Himalayas, measuring the crania of Torres Strait Islanders, or demanding that children in residential schools exchange Indigenous language, tradition, and kin for the proper White gifts of Christianity, reading, and writing. The chapters in this volume document how literacy education always entails a normative coding of space and time, both enabling and disenabling. That coding is always itself located in temporal and spatial relations of power.

The educational questions and possibilities raised by Phyllis Steeves, Lyn Daniels, and Yvonne Poitras Pratt are about those ways of seeing and experiencing, imagining and healing time and space, place, kin, spirit, and history that have been written out of schooling and social science. Do we write and draw, teach and learn as cartographers or as locals? Where and when do we read and write, draw and design? Literacies—whether singular or plural—are not neutral technologies for defining space and time. And with nothing less than survival on the line, whose versions of space and time are framed matters now more than ever.

Allan Luke
Lennox Head, New South Wales
Australia

Note

1 With acknowledgment to the University of Toronto philosopher Ian Hacking's *The Taming of Chance* (1990).

References

Barrett, A. (2002). *Servants of the map.* New York: Norton.

Daniels, L. (2013). Colonial education policy's repetitive effects: Bridging history with memory. Manuscript submitted for publication.

Freire, P., & Macedo, D. (1987). *Literacy: Reading the word and the world.* New York: Bergin & Garvey.

Goody, J. (1977). *The domestication of the savage mind.* Cambridge: Cambridge University Press.

Hacking, I. (1990). *The taming of chance.* Cambridge: Cambridge University Press.

Innis, H. (1950). *Empire and communications.* Toronto: University of Toronto Press.

Innis, H. (1951). *The bias of communication.* Toronto: University of Toronto Press.

Luke, A. (1996). Genres of power? Literacy education and the production of capital. In R. Hasan & G. Williams (Eds.), *Literacy in society* (pp. 303–338). London: Longman.

McLuhan, M. (1962). *The Gutenberg galaxy.* Toronto: University of Toronto Press.

Nakata, M. (2007). *Disciplining the savages: Savaging the disciplines.* Canberra, ACT: Aboriginal Studies Press.

Olson, D. R. (1977). From utterance to text: The bias of language in speech and writing. *Harvard Educational Review, 47*(3), 257–281.

Poitras Pratt, Y. (2011). *Meaningful media: An ethnography of a digital strategy within a Métis community.* Unpublished doctoral dissertation, University of Calgary, Calgary.

Steeves, P. G. (2010). *Literacy: Genocide's silken instrument.* Unpublished doctoral dissertation, University of Alberta, Edmonton.

Street, B. (1984). *Literacy in theory and practice.* Cambridge: Cambridge University Press.

INTRODUCTION: CONCEPTUALIZING PAST, PRESENT, AND FUTURE TIMESPACES

Catherine Compton-Lilly

Some might worry that the constructs like *time* and *space* are too abstract, too intellectual, or too philosophical to be the subject of a book about education or literacy. Why focus on time and space when educators should be concerned with children and teachers? Rather than lofting into transcendental conversations about time and space, some would argue that we should be getting back to the basics to identify best practices for instruction. Over the past 20 years, these arguments have been particularly influential in terms of educational policies. Educational practices and movements based in the work of a range of scholars—from Madeline Hunter (1982) to E. D. Hirsch (Hirsch, Kett, & Trefil, 2002)—and a more recent barrage of educational policies (e.g., No Child Left Behind, Reading First, Race to the Top) have offered practical, classroom-based solutions to solve the literacy challenges faced by American students. However, these solutions have consistently failed to change long-term trajectories for students.

One reason for the failure of these massive movements may be their inability to capture the complexity of human learning, human nature, and being human. This edited volume offers one, admittedly partial, solution to this dilemma. By attending to time and space, we highlight significant and essential dimensions of being human via the spatial and temporal dimensions of experience. As Vygotsky (1978/1933) noted in the early decades of the past century, the relationships between human beings and their social environments are central to understanding human learning: "The internalization of socially rooted and historically developed activities is the distinguishing feature of human psychology" (p. 57). Thus, the spaces and times in which people act and interact, alongside the social relationships that transpire within those contexts, are significant considerations for learning. Significantly, the work of Vygotsky and others (Barton & Hamilton, 1998; Cole, 1996; Gee, 1996; Heath, 1983; Rogoff, 2003; Street, 1995) has contributed to an understanding of literacy as a social, cultural, and historically defined set of practices that include and extend far beyond an individual decoding written text.

Alas, human literacy learning cannot be addressed by implementing a particular educational practice—universal content that every child should know, test-score benchmarks, or particular reading programs. Attending to the unique dimensions of being human and learning within time and space demands complex answers, negotiated understandings, intellectual challenges, and sophisticated and nuanced attention to children and their families, communities, identities, and social, economic, cultural, and historical backgrounds. The chapters in this volume attest to the power of exploring the times and spaces of children's lives and literacy practices to explore the multiple, hybridized, personal, social, and unique literate practices that engage students and provide opportunities for literacy learning.

Context as Entailing Temporal and Spatial Dimensions

Over the past century, scholars have increasingly argued that *context* matters in terms of how people make sense of their worlds and become literate (Berliner, 2002; Duranti & Goodwin, 1992; Hanks, 1996; McHugh, 1968; Perinbanayagam, 1974; Rex, Green, & Dixon, 1998; Thomas, 1927; van Dijk, 2006). However, these same scholars have grappled with how context is defined and which dimensions of experience are significant (Duranti & Goodwin, 1992). Thomas (1927), drawing on anthropology and sociology, described context as involving both time and space. He described situational analysis as involving the temporal culmination of life-course experiences while simultaneously highlighting the role of physical environments. Similarly, McHugh (1968) described situations as involving "emergence" and "rela-tivity." He defined "emergence" as "the temporal dimension of activity wherein past, present, and future are analytically distinct and at the same time inextricable for they are not correspondingly distinct in their influence upon concrete behavior." Relativity is a spatial construct that "characterizes an event in its relationship to other events across the boundaries of space" (McHugh, 1968, p. 28).

While these early conceptualizations referenced both time and space, more recent discussions of context have focused on the ways language is situated within social settings and among participants (see Duranti & Goodwin, 1992; Hanks, 1996; van Dijk, 2006). For example, Duranti and Goodwin (1992) described four dimensions of context: (1) a setting or the social/special framework; (2) a behavioral environment, including the ways actors use bodies and behavior to frame and organize talk; (3) language as a context for ongoing interaction; and (4) the extrasituational context that extends beyond local talk and includes relevant background knowl-edge. Cobb and Bowers (1999) argued that both cognitive and situated learning theories are grounded in conceptualizations of context that are metaphorically entrenched in notions of location. Other theorists have focused on language. Van Dijk (2006) defined context as "mental constructs of relevant aspects of social situations—influence what people say and especially **how** they do so" (p. 165). Other researchers have attended to the role of context in reading texts.

Rex and her colleagues (1998) distinguished types of context related to texts: context within texts, contexts surrounding texts, and macro contexts that extend beyond texts (i.e., political, institutional, cultural, and social contexts). This reading of text and context has been complicated by scholars who highlight the ways temporality is embedded in texts. For example, Ricoeur (1983, 1984) explores in great depth how temporality is taken up in narratives. He notes that the "temporal character of human experience" (p. 3) is echoed in narrative plots, maintaining that the "circle of narrativity and temporality is not a vicious but a healthy circle" (p. 3) when texts reference familiar understandings, invite us into new poetic realms, and support our reconfiguration of the known and the text. Thus, the reading of narrative involves not only the temporal unfolding of the story but also our own pasts and meaning-making resources.

A collection of essays edited by Leander and Sheehy (2004) has been critical in extending conversations about context, time, and space. The essays in this book explore what the authors refer to as a "transdisciplinary spatial turn" (p. ix). These explorations have provided entry for exploring new insights and envisioning new ways of thinking about frameworks, theories, and practices. While Leander and Sheehy's collection highlights spatial dimensions of experience, temporality penetrates many of the chapters as researchers explore the time frames that define the experiences of participants and the timespaces that are created by educational policies and practices. In addition, time is inherently present in the chapter authors' discussions of identity construction and explorations of the ways historical literacies intertwine with current practices.

In this text, we strive to retain and highlight the complex nature of context by highlighting the ways space and time intersect in the space/moments that people occupy. As Sztompka (1993) explains, both space and time are universal dimensions of social contexts; as he argues, time requires being, and being must occur within a space (e.g., physical, digital, conceptual, social); all spaces have a duration, which implies that all spaces have a past, present, and future through which events and activities are connected across time. While at times the authors in this volume pull time and space apart in order to examine the nature and effect that various dimensions of time and space have on educators, children, and classrooms, the volume as a whole highlights the interconnectedness and unavoidable situatedness of simultaneously living in both time and space. In the following sections, we explore four theoretical conceptualizations of timespace: chronotopes, the space of time and the time of space, rhizomatic spaces, and the sociolinguistics of globalization.

Chronotopes and Timespace

Bakhtin (1981) applied the construct of chronotope to explore the literary worlds created by authors. Specifically, Bakhtin explored how various literary motifs, including the nature of change in novels, created different chronotopes or genres of novels. More recently, chronotope has been taken up by educational researchers to investigate interactions within times and spaces that inform students' understandings of their literacy experiences in school and at home (Compton-Lilly, 2010), the ways researchers and teachers characterize students (Brown & Renshaw, 2006), and interactions occurring within classrooms (Bloome, Beierle, Grigorenko, & Goldman, 2009; Matusov, 2009). Analyzing data using a chronotopic lens allows scholars to investigate how time and space work together to shape the participation structures experienced by teachers and students. The concept of chronotope has been used to explore how particular ways of being in the world are formed at the intersection of past experience, ongoing activity, and future goals that shape expectations for students as they move through school (Brown & Renshaw, 2006). Thus, chronotope is an explanatory construct that invites educators to explore how time and space intersect in daily experiences and how those experiences are taken up, made sense of, and ultimately matter in teachers' and students' lives.

The Time of Space and the Space of Time

Wallerstein (1997) argued that timespace is a single dimension that is central to being human. Specifically, Wallerstein identified five types of timespace that affect our understandings of experiences:

1. Episodic Geopolitical TimeSpace involves the time and space of immediate experiences in which the here and now are critical to understanding.
2. Cyclio-Ideological TimeSpace invokes longer spans of time. Meanings are constructed by a local group of people in reference to what are understood as typical experiences.
3. Structural TimeSpace expands the scope of relevant context. This form of timespace highlights the historical systems that have been constructed and accessed to understand experience.
4. Eternal TimeSpace moves beyond the meanings imposed by historical ways of being. Eternal TimeSpace is both timeless and spaceless. What is understood is considered universal—it always has been and always will be.
5. Finally, Transformational TimeSpace highlights the unique contributions and profound effects of particular acts or events. These are the experiences that change the ways the world is understood and explained.

In short, Wallerstein maintained that all phenomena within timespace are ultimately social, constructed, and subject to the power structures and accepted histories that frame people's understandings of phenomena.

Wallerstein (1997) was concerned with the multiple, nuanced, and intersecting cleavages that exist temporally between past and present and spatially between powerful Western countries and the rest of the world. These cleavages highlight differential degrees of power, relationships with science, education, and culture, and inequitable economic resources. Thus, in Wallerstein's framework, timespace operates as a lens that can reveal fractures across timespace that matter for people in various times and spaces.

Rhizomatic Spaces

Rhizomes (Deleuze & Guattari, 1987) are organic networked spaces in which relationships and dimensions, including time and space, intersect or do not intersect, in parallel, random, or perpendicular manners that can be obtuse, fragmented, and even marginalized from dominant constructions and ways of being. Like metaphorical botanical rhizomes, a rhizome is a creeping underground growth that can sprout in any direction at any time, defying prediction and complicating design. This chaotic and improvisational growth makes rhizomatic structures difficult to contain and eradicate. As a theoretical concept that is useful to education, a rhizome is a space that embodies multiple forces co-constructing the various identities of students and teachers, the unpredicted outcomes of carefully planned lessons, and the spur-of-the-moment learning opportunities that emerge at a particular time in a particular classroom (Leander, 2006). Such spaces cut across the borders of space, time, and technology, affecting and revising practices in neighboring contexts. In educational contexts, an understanding of rhizome opens up possibilities and potential learning opportunities.

The Sociolinguistics of Globalization

Blommaert (2010) builds on Wallerstein's analysis to propose a revised sociolinguistics—one that is ostensibly dynamic and continuously sensitive to cultural, social, political, global, and historical influences. Arguing for linguistic analyses that change, shift, and morph and that are sensitive to local contexts and situations, Bloommaert maintains that sociolinguistics across global spaces are never static. Thus, a constantly changing and global sociolinguistics requires the inextricable merging and entanglement of time and space. While previous paradigms often limited language and linguistic analysis to bounded and nameable grammatical structures and vocabulary, this conceptualization not only highlights linguistic movement across physical/globalized spaces but also recognizes the inequitable value of particular languages and language practices within local spaces and across globalized networks. As Blommaert (2010) notes, indexical scales grant more worth to some language forms than others, converting "linguistic and semiotic differences into social inequities" (p. 6). These "orders of indexicality" (p. 6) are always connected to the times and spaces within which linguistic interactions occur. For example, Blommaert (2010) argues that the worth of any particular language practice could be momentary, local, and situated, valued only in a brief and localized timespace; conversely, its worth could be treated as timeless, translocal, and widespread, bestowed with the capacity to transcend time and space and influencing others over globalized spaces and long periods of time. Blommaert

(2010) argues that recognizing the ways language, literacy, and other practices are located within time and space provides insights into equity and social justice across globalized spaces.

These conceptualizations of time run counter to traditional conceptions of time as linear and space as flat. As Jenkins (1999) has argued, "the past doesn't exist outside of historians' textual constructive applications" (p. 2). This has led to the "collapse of metanarratives" (p. 5) or easily accepted pervasive accounts of history. Ermarth (2001a, 2001b) agreed; she proposed that the disruption of existing historical accounts creates "openings for new, possibly even more enabling definitions of identity and sequence, for new kinds of relationships with the past" (2001a, p. 207). To Ermarth, "Postmodernity re-introduces diversity, even contradiction, back into the process of identification" (p. 209). Truth, fact, and history are all called into question. Not only does this recognition define what can be known and what can be taught, but it also highlights the merging of time and space in human learning and knowing. For example, Facer and his colleagues (2004) are exploring the affordances of gaming technologies in which children are physically involved in simulations that situate children within times and spaces, as actors in lived scenarios—for example, lions hunting on the African savannah. In a very different example, Meacham (2012) compares times when children are learning abstract reading strategies to times when children are genuinely and personally involved with text. They note that genuine involvement involves a conversational framework, interruptions, affective responses, and a sense of being fully present. In contrast to linear and controlled academic interactions, these forays disrupt how time and space are typically used and experienced in classrooms, suggesting that meaningful learning may entail distinct temporal and spatial relations with texts and among participants.

Time and Space as Context: What Next?

Recognizing timespace as embodying context is merely a first step. The recognition and appreciation of the many ways time and space constitute context is a larger question. By recognizing the various dimensions of time and space, we reveal opportunities for investigation, conceptualization, understanding, and questioning. Exploring various manifestations of temporal and spatial dimensions of context entails possibilities for rethinking the complexities that accompany literacy learning and schooling. In this volume, chapter authors explore a wide range of temporal and spatial dimensions, including memory work, collective memory, timescales, cultural historical activity, hybrid spaces, and Third Spaces. The descriptions that follow provide a brief overview of constructs that will be explored in greater depth in chapters throughout this volume.

Memory Work

As people make sense of their worlds, their experiences and the tensions they have encountered in their lives, they rewrite memories of important events that contribute to the way they construct their identities and the stories that support those identities (Grbich, 2007, p. 100). The ultimate purpose of memory work reaches beyond a simple explication of self to explore how we have become who we are, the constraints on our possible identities, the role of perceived agency in identity construction, and how identities might shift in the future (Liamputtong, 2009). Ricoeur (1980) describes the narrative time of memories as nonlinear and looping back on themselves, disrupting linear conceptions of time. Individual memories disrupt public time and the *grand narratives* that operate in our lives. Disrupting taken-for-granted conceptions of time and space makes it possible to mount epistemological challenges to Western, often racist constructions of identity and selfhood.

Collective Memory

Collective memory has been conceptualized as a tool that groups of people use to situate themselves and others within time and space (Wertsch, 2002). Wertsch distinguishes collective memory from history by emphasizing that collective remembering is the act of narrating events that happened in the past for a particular purpose in the present (e.g., understanding current literacy instructional practices, defining self, problematizing the failure of student of a particular group of students).

Zerubavel (2003) explores the relationship between collective memories and timescapes of the past. He explains how the collective memories of groups impact actions and beliefs in the present. This work transcends a focus on personal recollections, foregrounding the ways we operate as *social beings*. Zerubavel argues that it is through the acquisition of a group's memories that people come to identify with a collective past and thus acquire a social identity.

Timescales

Time becomes salient when researchers and educators attend to meaning making. Lemke (2000) explicates the notion of timescales to explore the simultaneous occurrence of events within multiple scales of time (e.g., seconds, hours, days, seasons, years, decades, life spans, eras). In other words, his work focuses in the dialogic relationships between processes that occur slowly over long periods of time and those that occur within minutes or seconds. As Falchi and Siegel argue in chapter 5, semiotic meaning is "an effect not simply of accumulating shorter timescales into a longer one but of the longer timescale giving meaning to a shorter timescale activity" (this volume, p. 86). Understanding the relations among timescales allows researchers and educators to understand how "moments add up to lives" (Lemke, 2000, p. 273).

Cultural-Historical Activity Theory

Cultural-historical activity theory highlights how teachers and students are politically, historically, and socially positioned within activity systems related to reading, writing, understanding, and schooling. In short, it is concerned with analyzing human activities that are ongoing within the times and spaces of people's lives. Cultural-historical theories recognize how the structures that accompany school and literacy experiences situate students and teachers within existing cultural contexts and position them in terms of pre-existing labels, expectations, and accepted cultural models (Engeström, 1998). Within activity theory, the individual acts through sets of established rules, using available tools, participating in existing divisions of labor, and engaging with community expectations related to reading, writing, and acting. Timespace is invoked as people operate within environments and social histories with their respective individual purposes and social relationships in sight.

Hybrid Spaces

Hybridity theories explore how various established practices can be tapped to contribute to unique meanings and novel understandings; these hybridizations occur as people draw on resources, insights, and practices across times and spaces. Remixing, involving multimodal meanings that draw upon diverse cultural and linguistic experiences, allows new insights and ways of understanding to emerge. While hybridity has been applied to artifacts and understandings that emerge at the margins, dividing groups of people and their respective ways of viewing the world, it has also been used to explore the affordances of digital technologies. Hybridity invites opportunities for students and teachers to redefine and re-create themselves, thus acquiring novel insights and understandings, as well as new ways of acting, interacting, creating, and being competent (Parker, 2010).

Third Spaces

By challenging static conceptualizations of the world that rely on bifurcation and dichotomy (e.g., universal/specific; global/local; autonomous/ideological; strength/deficit), Third Space scholars in literacy studies (Gutiérrez, 2008; Moje et al., 2004; Pahl, 2002; Kostogriz, 2004) have posited new perspectives. They draw on the work of Bhabha (1994) and Soja (1996), suggesting that spaces exist between and amid dichotomous positionings and that these spaces can serve as pedagogical and curricular resources that students can use to fashion transformative experiences and spaces to nimbly, knowingly, and strategically negotiate school literacy (Gutiérrez, 2008). Researchers and educators can draw upon and foster Third Spaces to craft times and spaces that welcome and support students.

As these brief descriptions suggest, there are a range of theoretical tools that that literacy researchers are using to conceptualize and explore temporal and spatial dimensions of literacy learning in classrooms, schools, and online spaces. In the chapters that follow, we invite readers to join us into an exciting foray of understandings related to time and space that has the potential to contribute to refined insights as well as recognition of the complexities that accompany literacy learning.

A Tour through TimeSpace in Literacy Research

In the opening section of this volume, "TimeSpaces and the Past in Literacy Research," we present chapters that explore how operating in the timespaces of the present always draws on the past as people make sense of the present while simultaneously dreaming, envisioning, and conceptualizing possible futures. Four chapters explore the ways the timespaces operate for literacy researchers, families, and students. These chapters demonstrate how the past lives on—although in revised and modified forms—through ways of being and thinking in the present.

In chapter 1, Johnny Saldaña describes "memory work," as a qualitative research technique that explores how and why the past has shaped one's present condition in psychological, sociological, political, and cultural ways. Saldaña explores his memories of learning and teaching across time and space and how the past and present involve interwoven influences and affects. A beloved high school English teacher, Ann Whitehouse, is the through-line for 40 years of Saldaña's student and professional careers, and this chapter—presented through flashback, flashforward, and flashsideway vignettes—pays homage to the power of teachers to serendipitously yet significantly chart a student's life-course trajectory.

Also drawing on life experiences, Juan Guerra identifies and describes life in the "Neither/Nor" to reveal figural representations of literacy, space, and identity. He focuses on navigational tools that disenfranchised students can use nimbly and self-reflexively to move from one space to another and within and across varied spaces. Guerra uses this analysis to describe the modalities of memory that play crucial roles as students navigate various spaces and make sense of their worlds.

Kate Pahl examines the spaces of family time and school time as resources for meaning making in homes, schools, and communities by drawing on talk, oral storytelling, gesture, film, photography, writing, and reading. In particular, she explores the relationships between individual and shared subjectivities and people's identities-in-practice. Drawing on accounts of a Pakistani family and students in a local elementary school, Pahl argues that by focusing on time and space it is possible to isolate and describe the singularity of the moments that relate to meaning making. Rather than viewing time as "uniformly flowing without regard for individuals or the actions they take" (Springgay, Irwin, & Kind, 2008, p. 88), Pahl understands time as shaped by memories and subjectivities that provide tools for challenging epistemologies that dominate and contain subjectivities (Dillabough 2009; Ricoeur 1980).

In chapter 4, Grigorenko, Beierle, and Bloome explore the process of collective remembering in classrooms by examining how students and teachers think about themselves and others in time and space. Within any group and as part of the process of acting as a group, past events are brought to bear in present contexts through public narrativization. Conceptions of the past and their application to the present and the future provide interpretive frames for examining interactions in classrooms. The authors contend that such rememberings are an inherent part of the social construction of learning in classrooms. They report on the collective memories that operate in one language arts classroom (Bloome, Beierle, Goldman & Grigorenko, 2009).

Section 2 of this volume, "TimeSpaces and the Present in Literacy Research," highlights how researchers, teachers, and students operate in the temporalized spaces of the present. While these studies look across a vast range of spaces—a high-needs public school, a local LGBTQ center, African American discourse communities, and high school English classrooms—they all reference the actions and understandings of people in the present and how the present, albeit informed by the past, feeds into possible futures.

In chapter 5, Lori Falchi and Marjorie Siegel explore the role of multiple timescales in defining and disciplining young writers. They apply Lemke's (2009) notion of timescales to examine the ways school literacy in the space of a high-needs public school disciplined young children's writing and defined some of them as "struggling" writers. Young children in public schools are under pressure to produce more in less time and increasingly are held accountable for that work. While the "cultural flows" present in New York City affect "the scope of time and space" (Lam, 2006), schools often operate as if literacy development occurs in a lockstep manner with predictable stages. Even in writer's workshop classrooms, which many consider a progressive pedagogical space, literacy learning is defined and regulated through time. In particular, Falchi and Siegel look beyond the curricular constructs of neat scope and sequence linear time to consider the child's time and experience of texts and writing at school.

Mollie Blackburn and Caroline Clark explicitly ask, "How do *moments* add up to *lives?*" (Lemke, 2000, p. 273). In particular, they are interested in how moments mediated by LGBTQ-themed texts add up to the lives of queer and ally youth. The project described in chapter 6 focuses on a long-term book discussion group that emerged from an ongoing teacher inquiry group focused on combating homophobia and heterosexism in classrooms and schools through literature and film. The Pink TIGers brought queer and ally students, typically from their Gay Straight Alliances, to the local center for LGBTQ youth to select, read, and discuss LGBTQ-themed books. Blackburn and Clark focus on processes related to queer and ally identities. In particular, they examine places in the transcripts where short timescale processes produced effects in much longer timescale activities and vice versa (Lemke, 2000, p. 280). Thus, they work to understand how youth, across multiple timescales and timespaces, were be(com)ing gay, lesbian, and ally together through reading and discussing LGBTQ-themed literature in queer-friendly spaces.

In chapter 7, Bryan Crandall explores the importance of listening to adolescent voices that are too often ignored in secondary school literacy research. As he maintains, youth can teach us how they reinvent their literacies in unique timespaces and how they use literacies as tools for navigating complex technologies. This analysis draws on a six-month ethnographic case study that was designed to learn about writing from the perspectives of eight African male English-language learners enrolled in 9th- through 12th-grade English classes. As Crandall argues, the voices of youth arriving as part of the global diaspora of the 21st century can no longer be ignored in secondary English classrooms.

sj Miller closes this section by drawing together several themes presented in the book and exploring their significance. He argues that contexts are specific spaces/places, accentuated by time, within particular geographies. Spaces/places are not fixed or static; they shape and orient peoples' values, thoughts, behaviors, beliefs, and identities, just as people shape spaces/places and ascribe meaning to them. Miller argues that the interrelatedness between person and place offers teachers opportunities to make meaning about how evolving geo-histories could be recast as nonlinear and as nonhierarchical counternarratives. Such a recasting has the potential to challenge the way dominant narratives have been interpreted and have traditionally marginalized people on the basis of social categories connected to race, ethnicity, gender, gender expression, age, appearance, ability, national origin, language, spiritual belief, size (height and/or weight), sexual orientation, social class, economic circumstance, environment, ecology, culture, and the treatment of animals. Miller explores how the recasting of literacy events can turn classrooms into "real-time" experiences that have the potential to generate agency for students through a retelling of history.

Section 3, "TimeSpaces and the Future in Literacy Research," focuses in particular on how our futures are connected to various technological advances that inspire students and point researchers in new directions. These chapters explore how new technologies not only offer new possibilities as representational tools that students can use to tell their stories but also challenge researchers, teachers, and students to rethink what counts as literacy.

In chapter 9, Bass argues that children, adolescents, and emerging adults are leading the way in using new technologies as tools for representation. She maintains that the ability to create, re-create, and make meaning from processes and products afforded by these new digital media technologies has disrupted the esteemed field of literacy studies, leading scholars to ask: What counts as literacy in the 21st century? To explore these issues, she explores temporal and spatial dimensions of creation within youth media arts organizations. In particular, she focuses on processes of remixing and hybridity accessed by young artists.

Although literacy researchers in the sociocultural and sociocognitive traditions have long pointed to the necessity for students to have the opportunity to construct meaning through classroom discussions that address authentic questions, build on other students' ideas, and incorporate multiple perspectives on a given topic, such discursive interactions continue to be rare in secondary English classrooms. In chapter 10, James Chisholm examines the usefulness of a temporal language lens for making sense of talk as students completed (a) traditional, (b) inquiry-based, and (c) multimodal tasks. He argues that this analysis reveals the dynamic and dialogic nature of English classrooms and challenges the privileging of preferred meanings and texts.

In chapter 11, Kevin Leander and Beth Aplin draw on an ethnographic study of the digital literacy practices of youth that explores how two youth use digital literacies—including Web logs, instant messaging, and Web-based access to school materials—to alter, extend, transform, and manipulate the space-times of their lives. They inquire how these youth use digital literacies to produce and organize space-time in school and at home and in making school-home relationships. The chapter concludes with recommendations for a new imagination of online literacy practice in school that takes into account the changing experiences of literacy and space-time.

Finally, Lisa Schwartz, Silvia Nogueron-Liu, and Norma González argue that one way to challenge the time and space restrictions that are placed on Latino and immigrant youth is to capitalize on the affordances of youth digital and multi-modal meaning-making (Hull, Zacher, & Hibbert, 2009; Ito et al., 2010) and on Latino students' funds of knowledge (González, Moll & Amanti, 2005). Within this perspective, it is possible to challenge deficit narratives about Latino students' academic identities, to examine the potential of collaborations that mobilize community resources within and across contexts in relation to learning, literacy, and identity, and to shed light on the complexities of Latino students' negotiation of multiple languages and literacies in physical and virtual, in-school and out-of school spaces. This chapter is an example of the mobilization of knowledge, as researchers have moved themselves across their own social fields, coalescing and merging their work at critical junctures and weaving among theoretical frameworks.

Figure 0.1 begins to capture contextualizations within time and space. In this diagram we treat timespace as intersecting vortexes that enter sites of meaning

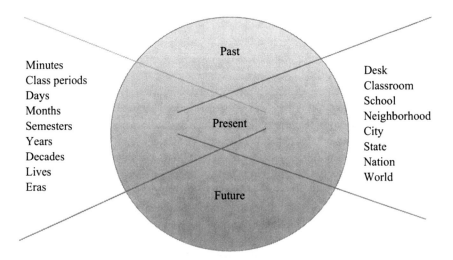

FIGURE 0.1 A Diagram of TimeSpaces in Schools

construction. Meaning construction in the present is always negotiated in relation to our interpretations of the past and our expectations for the future. The spaces and times of school experiences are multidimensional with the immediate present—which might entail sitting at one's desk during a third-period science lesson—that is always experienced as a point of time within a larger temporal frame (e.g., a semester, a life) and a larger spatial landscape (e.g., community, nation, world). Each chapter in this edited collection works within sites that involve temporal and spatial negotiations. The chapters in Part One highlight timespaces of the past. In Part Two, chapter authors focus on timespaces in the present, and in Part Three we consider the timespaces of the future. Regardless, all of the chapters locate students, researchers, educators, and learners within timespaces that recognize and grapple with the complexities that accompany learning and schooling. It is our hope that by complicating context through attending to time and space we can begin to acknowledge the complexities that surround not only teaching and learning but also humanity and life.

References

Bakhtin, M.M. (1981). *The dialogic imagination: Four essays.* London: University of Texas Press.

Barton, D., & Hamilton, M. (1998). *Local literacies: Reading and writing in one community.* London: Routledge.

Berliner, D. C. (2002). Educational research: The hardest science of all. *Educational Researcher, 31(8),* 18–20.

Bhabha, H.K. (1994). *The location of culture.* London: Routledge.

Blommaert, J. (2010). *The sociolinguistics of globalization.* Cambridge: Cambridge University Press.

Bloome, D., Beierle, M., Grigorenko, M., & Goldman, S. (2009). Learning over time: Uses of intercontextuality, collective memories, and classroom chronotopes in the construction of learning opportunities in a ninth-grade language arts classroom. *Language and Education, 23(4),* 313–334.

Brown, R., & Renshaw, P. (2006) Positioning students as actors and authors: A chronotopic analysis of collaborative learning activities. *Mind, Culture and Activity, 13(3),* 247–259.

Cobb, P., & Bowers, J. (1999). Cognitive and situated learning perspectives in theory and practice. *Educational Researcher, 28(2),* 4–15.

Cole, M. (1996). *Cultural psychology: A once and future discipline.* Cambridge, MA: Harvard University Press.

Compton-Lilly, C. (2010). Considering time: In the field of family literacy and in the lives of families. In K. Dunsmore & D. Fisher (Eds.), *Bringing Literacy Home* (pp. 306–331). Newark, DE: International Reading Association.

Deleuze, G., & Guattari, F. (1987). *A thousand plateaus.* Minneapolis: University of Minnesota Press.

Dillabough, J. (2009). History and the making of young people and the late modern youth researcher: Time, narrative and change. *Discourse: Studies in the Cultural Politics of Education, 30(2),* 213–229.

Duranti, A., & Goodwin, C. (Eds.). (1992). *Rethinking context: Language as an interactive phenomenon.* Studies in the Social and Cultural Foundations of Language, No. 11. Cambridge: Cambridge University Press.

Engeström, Y. (1998). *Cognition and communication at work*. Cambridge: Cambridge University Press.

Ermarth, E. D. (2001a). Beyond history. *Rethinking History, 5*(2), 195–215.

Ermarth, E. D. (2001b). Agency in the discursive condition. *History and Theory, 40*(4), 34–58.

Facer, K., Joiner, R., Stanton, D., Reid, J., Hull, P., & Kirk, D. (2004). Savannah: Mobile gaming and learning? *Journal of Computer Assisted Learning, 20*(6), 399–409.

Gee, J.P. (1996). *Social linguistics and literacies: Ideology in discourses* (2nd ed.). London: Taylor & Francis.

González, N., Moll, L.C., & Amanti, C. (2005). *Funds of knowledge: Theorizing practices in households, communities, and classrooms.* New York: Teachers College Press.

Grbich, C. (2007). *Qualitative data analysis: An introduction.* London: Sage.

Gutiérrez, K.D. (2008). Developing in the third? A sociocritical space. *Reading Research Quarterly, 43*(2), 148–164.

Hanks, W. F. (1996). Language form and communicative practices. In J. Gumperz & S. Levinson (Eds.), *Rethinking linguistic relativity* (pp. 232–270). Cambridge, UK Cambridge University Press.

Heath, S. B. (1983). *Ways with words: Language, life and work in communities and classrooms.* New York: Cambridge University Press.

Hirsch, E. D., Kett, J. F., & Trefil, J. (2002). *The new dictionary of cultural literacy: What every American needs to know.* New York: Houghton Mifflin Harcourt.

Hull, G., Zacher, J., & Hibbert, L. (2009). Youth, risk, and equity in a global world. *Review of Research in Education, 33*(1), 117–159.

Hunter, M. (1982). *Mastery teaching.* El Segundo, CA: TIP Publications.

Ito, M., Baumer, S., Bittanti, M., Boyd, D., Cody, R., Herr-Stephenson, B., et al. (2010). *Hanging out, messing around, and geeking out: Kids living and learning with new media.* Cambridge, MA: MIT Press.

Jenkins, K. (1999). *Why history? Ethics and postmodernity.* Routledge: London.

Kostogriz, A. (2004). Rethinking the spatiality of literacy practices in multicultural conditions. Annual conference of the Australian Association for Research in Education, Melbourne. Retrieved February 15, 2014, from www.aare.edu.au/04pap/kos04610.pdf

Lam, W.S.E. (2006). Culture and learning in the context of globalization: Research directions. *Review of Research in Education, 30,* 213–237.

Leander, K. (2006). Mapping literacy spaces in motion: A rhizomatic analysis of a classroom literacy performance. *Reading Research Quarterly, 41*(4), 428–460.

Leander, K., & Sheehy, M. (2004). *Spatializing literacy research and practice.* New York: Peter Lang.

Lemke, J. (2000). Across the scales of time: Artifacts, activities, and meanings in ecosocial systems. *Mind, Culture, and Activity, 74*(4), 273–290.

Lemke, J. (2009). Multimodality, identity, and time. In C. Jewitt (Ed.), *The Routledge handbook of multimodal analysis* (pp. 140–150). New York: Routledge.

Liamputtong, P. (2009). *Qualitative research methods* (3rd ed.). South Melbourne: Oxford.

Matusov, E. (2009). *Journey into dialogic pedagogy.* New York: Nova Science Publishers.

McHugh, P. (1968). *Defining the situation: The organization of meaning in social interaction.* Indianapolis, IN: Bobbs-Merrill.

Meacham, S.S. (2012). Temporality and textual engagement in a middle school English Language Arts classroom. *Journal of Linguistic Anthropology, 22*(3), 159–181.

Moje, E., Ciechanowski, K., Kramer, K., Ellis, L., Carrillo, R., & Callazo, T. (2004). Working toward a third space in content areas literacy. *Reading Research Quarterly, 39*(1), 38–70.

Pahl, K. (2002). Habitus and the home: Texts and practices in families. *Ways of Knowing Journal, 2*(1), 45–53.

Parker, J. (2010). *Teaching tech-savvy kids: Bringing digital media into the classroom, grades 5–12.* Thousand Oaks, CA: Corwin.

Perinbanayagam, R. S. (1974). The definition of the situation: An analysis of the ethno-methodological and dramaturgical view. *The Sociological Quarterly, 15*(4), 521–541.

Rex, L., Green, J., & Dixon, C. (1998). What counts when context counts?: The uncommon "common" language of literacy research. *Journal of Literacy Research, 30*(3), 405–433.

Ricoeur, P. (1980). Narrative time. *Critical Inquiry, 7*(1), *On Narrative* (Autumn 1980), 169–190.

Ricoeur, P. (1983). *Time and the narrative,* vol. 1. Chicago: Chicago University Press.

Ricoeur, P. (1984). *Time and the narrative,* vol. 2. Chicago: Chicago University Press.

Rogoff, B. (2003). *The cultural nature of human development.* Oxford: Oxford University Press.

Soja, E. (1996). *Thirdspace: Journeys to Los Angeles and other real-and-imagined places.* Malden, MA: Blackwell.

Springgay, S., Irwin, R. L., and Kind, S. (2008). A/R/topographers and living inquiry. In J. G. Knowles & A. L. Cole (Eds.), *Handbook of the Arts in Qualitative Research* (pp. 83–92). Los Angeles, California, London: Sage.

Street, B. (1995). *Social literacies: Critical approaches to literacy in development, ethnography, and education.* New York: Longman.

Sztompka, P. (1993). *The sociology of social change.* Oxford: Blackwell.

Thomas, W. I. (1927). *Situational analysis: The behavior patter and the situation.* Papers and Proceedings from the Twenty-Second Annual Meeting of the American Sociological Society, (pp. 1–13). Chicago, IL: University of Chicago Press.

Van Dijk, T. (2006). Critical discourse analysis. In D. Tannen & D. Schiffrin (Eds.), *The handbook of discourse analysis* (pp. 352–371). London: Wiley-Blackwell.

Vygotsky, L. (1978/1933). *Mind in society: The development of higher psychological processes.* Cambridge, MA: Harvard University Press.

Wallerstein, I. (1997). The time of space and the space of time: The future of social science. Retrieved June 6, 2013, from www2.binghamton.edu/fbc/archive/iwtynesi.htm

Wertsch, J. (2002). *Voices of collective remembering.* Cambridge: Cambridge University Press.

Zerubavel, E. (2003). *Time maps: Collective memory and the social shape of the past.* Chicago: University of Chicago Press.

SECTION 1

Timespaces and the Past in Literacy Research

"Flashback"

We open Section 1 by foreshadowing a bit of chapter 1. In chapter 1, Johnny Saldaña engages the reader in a "flashback" into his past. He tells stories of the places he has traveled and the people he has met, including his former high school English teacher, Ann Whitehouse. This concept of flashback aptly captures our everyday experiences as we find ourselves remembering and contemplating the past as we work to make sense of the present. The chapters in section 1 highlight these timespaces of the past, including the lessons we learned at home, in school, and in communities. Experiences across childhood and youth inform the people we become. Interactions in classrooms from yesterday and last month affect the ways we make sense today. The spaces of family and school create contexts that children move across as they also move through time. Both time and space are recursive as our minds move back and forth between the present and the past and as we occupy spaces previously occupied in different ways on different days. These are the timespaces explored in this first section.

1

THANK YOU, MRS. WHITEHOUSE: THE MEMORY WORK OF ONE STUDENT ABOUT HIS HIGH SCHOOL ENGLISH TEACHER, FORTY YEARS LATER

Johnny Saldaña

Flashback, fall 1960, Austin, Texas: I'm in first grade. The teacher is not in the classroom, but a few of us students are. I see on top of my teacher's desk—a sacred temple to a six-year-old—a copy of our math textbook. But hers was different from ours. It was almost twice as large and had "Teacher's Edition" printed in big letters on the front cover. What is this? I thought. I picked up the book and flipped through its pages. It had the same content as our books, but the answers to all the math problems were included—in red ink. This was so cool! One of my art projects was to take a sheet of lined notebook paper, fold it in half, and fold it again as if to make a small book. I drew a copy of the cover of our math book on the front page with pencil and proudly wrote along the side "Teacher's Edition." Inside the booklet I included some simple addition problems, but I also included the answers—in red ink. Back in 1960, red ink pens were not so common to children—they were the province of teachers and other professionals. But, because my father did his own business accounting, he had red ink pens at home for me to play with. I proudly showed my creation—not to my teacher but to my first-grade friends. They were so impressed with what I made that they asked me to make them a Teacher's Edition, too.

Flashsideway: I didn't know it at the time but, fifty years ago, that was my earliest memory of fascination with being a teacher.

Flashforward, the 1980s, Tempe, Arizona: I can't remember the specific year, but it was most likely within that decade. I'm a university professor in theatre education at Arizona State University, ordering textbooks for my Methods of Teaching Theatre class. One of the standard titles on my recommended list was a well-known textbook for high school students. I wanted future educators to know what most high school theatre programs adopted as a core textbook for adolescents. But one year, I thought, instead of just the textbook, maybe I should order the

Teacher's Edition of it for my university students. So, that's what I ordered. The university bookstore contacted me a few months later, stating that the publisher was reluctant to ship those books because the Teacher's Edition was authorized only for full-time secondary school teachers, not pre-service education majors. Why? I asked them. Security reasons, they said. The Teacher's Edition of the textbook has the answers to standardized tests they composed for classroom use.

Flashsideway: "Memory work" originated in Europe in the 1980s as a form of feminist participatory action research. One's personal past is individually and then collectively examined with others to recall moments of oppression that formed gender socialization. The agenda of memory work is therapeutic and emancipatory. One's memories of actions, motives, and emotions are key experiences that form the construction of one's present identity. Ultimately the purpose of memory work is the exploration not of "Who am I?" but rather of "How did I get to be this way and, if necessary, how can I change?" (Liamputtong, 2009, pp. 130–131).

Flashback, fall 1960: I was taught by and grew up on Dick and Jane readers:
Oh, oh, oh.
See Spot run.
Oh, Puff. Funny, funny Puff.

Flashforward, the 2000s: In my 50s, I am on avid searches for Dick and Jane books in antique stores and online sites. I find a few titles from my childhood that evoke memories of "Yes, this is one I actually read!" Scott Foresman: I even remembered the publisher. The books had a distinctive look; they had *style*. It was a world of children. They were all the perfect White nuclear family, but race or ethnicity didn't matter to me back then. The words were big, the pictures were colorful, the workbooks were fun. I was learning how to read. And in my adult searches for these collectable items, about $15 to $125 each depending on the condition, I bought old cover-worn copies of *We Look and See* and *Guess Who?* and, yes, the Teacher's Edition of *Fun with Dick and Jane*.

Flashsideway: Memory work is the rewriting of memories of past oppression in order to find liberation. As we go through life, we experience "important events and their memories and the reconstructions of these form a critical part of the construction of self" (Grbich, 2007, p. 100). We trace back to find out how our selves became who we are—how we've been socialized. We transform ourselves as a result of this. The individual attempts to find significant themes. We look not only for what is present but also for what is missing.

Flashback, fall 1967, eighth-grade English: Our teacher was crazy. We were scared to death of her. I did my best to please her just to keep her from yelling at me as she often did to others. One day I sat down in class before the bell rang and opened my three-ring notebook, getting solidly prepared for class. The teacher walked up to me with a frown on her face, literally yanked my notebook away from my desk, took it up to hers, and slammed it down. I was stunned, and she offered me no explanation for why she had done it. She was crazy. Everyone at school said so.

Flashsideway: Don't worry. This chapter is not some trauma-filled purging or exorcising of personal demons. On the contrary, it's an upbeat success story, yet tinted with just enough genre variety and occasional tension, humor, and revelation of juicy stuff to keep you engaged.

Flashforward, fall 1969, high school sophomore English: The teacher was a pleasant enough woman, beautiful penmanship on the chalkboard, but not a very good instructor. She would frequently venture off into tangents with stories about her husband and family. The content was weak, and classes were generally boring. I remember very, very little about them, except for reading *Julius Caesar*—yawn—and John Steinbeck's *The Pearl*. Latin American characters—oh yeah, I could relate. Simple, beautiful language, like poetry. And the literary *elements:* symbolism, irony, foreshadowing. Now this was literature! I would read it over and over again throughout the next decade. I even constructed English tests for myself about the novel to show how well I knew it. And I put the answers in red ink.

Flashsideway: For memory work, once a theme has been chosen for exploration, memories are recalled and written down by the individual. The originators of the method advise writing one's memories in the third person to provide a sense of detachment and bird's-eye perspective. But I choose to employ writing in the first person since I'm working on my own rather than with a collective. I write in the first person to take deep ownership of my memories.

Flashforward, spring 1978: I took a graduate-level anthropology course in folklore because the subject sounded really interesting. I had taken a course in children's literature the semester before and immersed myself in reading folk tales from around the world. But I was way over my head in that seminar with the anthropology majors, and I lasted only about five weeks before I withdrew. But I learned a lot. We were coding African stories' motifs. And it was there that I learned the concept of what a motif was. I got up to speed by reading Stith Thomson's books on the subject and found it to be a very intriguing literary element.

Flashsideway: The filmmaker Jean-Luc Godard is credited with saying, "Every story should have a beginning, a middle, and an end. But not necessarily in that order."

Flashback, spring 1972, high school senior English: We were studying dramatic literature of late-19th- and early-20th-century Great Britain, and our teacher was trying to discreetly explain the notoriety of Oscar Wilde. After some skirting around the issue, one of the school thugs blurted out, "You mean he was a *homo?*"

Flashforward, the late 1970s: I've moved away from home, and I'm coming to terms with my own sexual identity. I bought a paperback copy of Walt Whitman's *Leaves of Grass*. Read it cover to cover, looking for "those" passages. Found them, savored them—and underlined them in red ink.

Flashsideway: We study the personal to get to the historical, social, political, and cultural. I present a hybrid form of time study in this address—a qualitative mixed-methods genre of memory work, autoethnography, and longitudinal qualitative research (Saldaña, 2003). As the anthropologist Clifford Geertz (1983) mused, "Life is just a bowl of strategies" (p. 25). Life is adaptation, and I am a notorious adaptor. I take what is necessary for me and reshape and blend it to suit my own purposes.

Flashback, summer 1971: I took the first semester of high school senior English during summer school, just to get ahead of my program of study. We had an import teacher from another high school that term—admittedly and frankly an old, bitter queen of a man. We read *Hamlet,* as most seniors will in that course. A hard play, especially for a high schooler, to digest. But this teacher asked us to read the entire play on our own rather than guiding us through it one act at a time for whole-class discussion. On the first day we discussed the Shakespearean work the teacher asked me, "Johnny, what's the theme of *Hamlet?*" I remember being taken aback and feeling the need to say something—anything—lest it appear that I hadn't read the play. I cannot remember what I said to him in front of the class, but I know I said something—a desperate fledgling answer. But the teacher's sarcastic reply, almost forty years later, will never be forgotten. He said, "Well, that's very interesting, Johnny. What a shame it doesn't have a damn thing to do with the play."

Flashforward, the 1980s through 2000s, Methods of Teaching Theatre class: When we study the teaching of dramatic literature, I tell my students that story, and I encourage them to never ask someone what's *the* theme of a play. Instead, I encourage them to ask their students to look for those lines in the play that strike them as the most interesting, and why.

Flashsideway: Holstein and Gubrium (2000), in *Constructing the Life Course,* conceptualize that

> The life course and its constituent parts or stages are not the objective features of experience that they are conventionally taken to be. Instead, the constructionist approach helps us view the life course as a social form that is constructed and used to make sense of experience. . . . The life course doesn't simply unfold before and around us; rather, we actively organize the flow, pattern, and direction of experience in developmental terms as we navigate the social terrain of our everyday lives. (p. 182)

Flashback, fall 1970: As a beginning high school teacher and presumably on a low or modest salary, Mrs. Ann Whitehouse, my junior-year English teacher, would wear the same outfits frequently throughout the year. There were two in particular that I remember: a bright orange and cream-white polyester pants suit (well, that *was* the fashion at the time) and a dark-blue knee-length dress flecked with gold motifs. The dark-blue dress in particular was remembered because it was a bit low cut at the top—somewhat scandalous for a female high school teacher in 1970. But Mrs. Whitehouse looked *stunning* in those outfits. Add her long brunette hair, sparkling eyes, pleasant smile, and bright red lipstick, and she was *pretty.*

Flashforward, the 1980s: I go through my beiges, tans, and browns phase.

Flashforward, the 1990s: In midlife crisis I go through my tight jeans, Harley T's, and leather phase.

Flashforward, the 2000s: I go through my blacks and whites and grays phase. A graduate student once asked me, "Johnny, why do you always dress in blacks and whites and grays?" I sincerely replied, "I guess it's like a uniform, a sense of professionalism." But I learned later, on my own, that that was not the real reason.

Flashsideway: There are five categories of memories for memory work. The first is *accretion*—how memories accumulate meaning over time; the second is *condensation*—how meanings intensify and become simpler over time; the third is *secondary revision*—how we create retrospective narratives to fit with present needs; the fourth is *repression*—material that is forgotten or pushed to the unconscious; and the fifth is *melancholia*—an inability to let go of what is lost—a form of hyper-remembering (McLeod & Thomson, 2009, pp. 26–27).

Flashback, summer 1971: Remember senior English, bitter old queen, the theme of *Hamlet?* Before that, we read *Beowulf.* Not just excerpts from it, the whole poem. Couldn't figure out what was going on; hated it.

Flashforward, fall 1973: University sophomore English. We had to read *Beowulf* again. Still couldn't figure out what was going on; hated it.

Flashforward, the mid-1990s: Me in my forties and in midlife crisis. For some strange reason, felt compelled to reread *Beowulf* on my own. *Loved* it! Knew *exactly* what was going on!

Flashsideway: I've always been good at recalling memories from childhood through the present day. In theatre, this is actually part of actor training—sense memory and emotional recall, two tools of the trade that help an actor imaginatively reconstruct from his own experiences believable circumstances on stage when portraying a fictional character.

Flashback, fall 1970: Mrs. Whitehouse was giving us instructions and deliberately and gleefully used the word "ain't" as if she had just uttered an obscenity. The class mockingly gasped and "oohed" in wicked delight.

Flashforward, spring 1971: We were reading O. Henry's short story "The Cop and the Anthem," and Mrs. Whitehouse explained to us the what the term "goose egg" in the story meant and read the line aloud in an Irish dialect.

Flashforward, a summer in the late 1980s: I discover that the teacher's voice, my voice, needs to be performative in order to communicate effectively with students.

Flashsideway: McLeod and Thomson (2009) wisely note that "The language of social science is not always best suited to express the subtleties of temporal processes, and for this reason we employ literary examples along the way" (p. 15). Thus, to study time and change, writers can creatively incorporate genre, metaphors, symbols, and motifs.

Flashback, fall 1970: In the high school hallway, I was walking to my next class, and I saw Mrs. Whitehouse walking briskly toward her classroom. She moved with speed, with confidence, with *style.*

Flashsideway: Life has motifs, those recurring elements that pop up now and then in serendipitous times and places. I employ motifs in my original playwriting and even in my academic writing. I feature Motif Coding in my book, *The Coding Manual for Qualitative Researchers* (Saldaña, 2009). I explain that a *motif* is "the smallest element in a tale" that has something unique about it, such as characters, significant objects, and single incidents of action (Thompson, 1977, pp. 415–416).

Flashback, fall 1970: In Mrs. Whitehouse's class, we had to read an American novel on our own time, and since I liked *The Scarlet Letter* I picked another Hawthorne novel, *The House of the Seven Gables*. My, what a lot of exclamation points it had! But what a story! I was telling all my friends, "You have *got* to read this book!" I told Mrs. Whitehouse, "This should be required reading for an English class!"

Flashforward, the 1990s: I am a peer reviewer of article manuscripts for professional journals, and I wrote in my comments that a particular author had used far too many exclamation points in her writing.

Flashsideway: In memory work, McLeod and Thomson (2009) advise, "We're not uncovering the nature of the event but the meaning that the event had for us then and now" (pp. 23–24).

Flashback, fall 1970: Mrs. Whitehouse was smiling, as she often did, as she told us about the works of Herman Melville, such as "Bartleby the Scrivener" and *Moby Dick,* at which the class clown smirked and asked, "Moby's what?" Mrs. Whitehouse kept smiling and, without missing a beat, ignored the remark and moved on with her lecture.

Flashforward, summer 1975: I took a summer school class in early American literature at the University of Texas at Austin for my English Education minor. I can't remember the professor's name; I simply recall that he was an elderly, bearded, gentle soul of a man. Over the course of six weeks we were to read an American literature anthology of approximately 1,000 pages plus a few American novels—including *Moby Dick*. And I immersed myself in this country's literary heritage and came to class each day ready to excitedly discuss these works with that kind and amiable man. In *Moby Dick,* though, there's that rather awkward and inference-laden passage about Ishmael's hand in the barrel of whale sperm from the chapter titled "A Squeeze of the Hand," which the professor read aloud:

> Squeeze! squeeze! squeeze! all the morning long; I squeezed that sperm till I myself almost melted into it; I squeezed that sperm till a strange sort of insanity came over me; and I found myself unwittingly squeezing my co-laborers' hands in it, mistaking their hands for the gentle globules. Such an abounding, affectionate, friendly, loving feeling did this avocation beget; that at last I was continually squeezing their hands, and looking up into their eyes sentimentally; as much as to say,—Oh! my dear fellow beings, why should we longer cherish any social acerbities, or know the slightest ill-humor or envy! Come; let us squeeze hands all round; nay, let us all

squeeze ourselves into each other; let us squeeze ourselves universally into the very milk and sperm of kindness.

And I so wanted to blurt out to my English professor about Melville: "You mean he was a *homo?*"

Flashsideway: After the memories' social meanings have been constructed, they are thematically organized and theorized.

Flashback, fall 1970: We had mint-green-colored vocabulary workbooks, and we had to research the definitions on our own for about fifteen new words each week. On vocabulary days, Mrs. Whitehouse would call on students randomly to present the definition of a word. And if you didn't have your homework completed, you would get a mark in her grade book. One day, she called on a particular student—not exactly the smartest one in our class—to give the definition for the first word on the list. "I don't have it," he said. Mrs. Whitehouse reached for her grade book and proceeded to put a mark in it as she asked, "You didn't do your homework?" The student raised his vocabulary workbook to show her: "I have the definitions for the other fourteen words, I just don't have the first one." Mrs. Whitehouse looked puzzled and asked, "Why don't you have the first one answered?" The student replied, "Well, I work backwards by starting at the bottom and working my way up to the top, and I ran out of time and didn't get the last one—or the first one—done." There was a brief pause of silence in the room as we all basked in that rather surrealistic moment. Mrs. Whitehouse stared at him with a confused look, shook her head, laughed, and erased the mark from her grade book.

Flashsideway: What is the accretion of these memories?

Flashback, fall 1970: Mrs. Whitehouse would occasionally read poetry to us, as most every English teacher will do. She read aloud Walt Whitman's "Young Grimes" and told us ahead of time it was one of his early attempts and a fairly shaky poem, not his best, and so she read it with slight tongue-in-cheek glee:

> When old Grimes died, he left a son—
> The graft of worthy stock;
> In deed and word he shows himself
> A chip of the old block.
> In youth, 't is said, he liked not school—
> Of tasks he was no lover;
> He wrote sums in a ciphering book,
> Which had a pasteboard cover.

But I will never forget her reading of Whitman's "O Captain! My Captain!" During the first two verses, her eyes were riveted to the book. I could tell she wasn't performing for us; she seemed to be genuinely moved by the poem's power:

> O Captain, my Captain! our fearful trip is done;
> The ship has weathered every rack, the prize we sought is won;

The port is near, the bells I hear, the people all exulting,
While follow eyes the steady keel, the vessel grim and daring:

But O heart! heart! heart!
O the bleeding drops of red,
Where on the deck my Captain lies,
Fallen cold and dead.

Flashsideway: I believe that there is pattern and purpose to everything. Like that old bitter queen of an English teacher might have asked me, "Johnny, what's the theme of your existence?" I'm afraid that after I give an answer, he'll reply with, "Well, that's very interesting, Johnny. What a shame it doesn't have a damn thing to do with your life."

Flashback, fall 1970: We were about to read *The Adventures of Huckleberry Finn,* required reading those days in junior English just a year before Austin's mandatory school bussing and integration. But everyone knew the book had the "n" word in it. Only back then Texans didn't call it the "n" word; we said it out loud. Mrs. Whitehouse, in her discreet way, forewarned us that the word would be read throughout the novel and told us, "It's a word you needn't be embarrassed by; it was used frequently during the time the book was written."

Flashforward, the 1990s through 2000s: I model how to teach monologue reading to my Methods of Teaching Theatre class, and I use a selection from Jane Wagner and Lily Tomlin's one-woman show, *The Search for Signs of Intelligent Life in the Universe.* I tell my students, "You're going to read the word 'lesbian' in this monologue and it's a word you needn't be embarrassed by; it's not a derogatory slur, it's a clinical term."

Flashsideway: If there's a direct link between past and present, it's because I've constructed it as such. I'm a weaver, an integrator of disparate threads. I was trained as a costumer, so I sew. I put things together, and I repair them. It's a male thing: Fix things if they're broken. Find the solution. Find the answer.

Flashback, spring 1971: It was either a Bret Harte or Stephen Crane short story we had been reading, and Mrs. Whitehouse explained to us the symbolism and foreshadowing in the tale: sunrises and the east represented birth, while sunsets and the west represented death.

Flashforward, summer 1975: One day my university American literature professor asked the class why we thought a writer would choose to set the death-related action of a story in the west. One student thought it was related to this obscure literary reference about an ancient culture's soldiers marching off toward the west to their defeat, to which the teacher said, "Okay." Then I told him what Mrs. Whitehouse taught us about the east and west, and sunrises and sunsets, and birth and death, to which he smiled and said, "That's right." Then it occurred to me: I'd bet anything that Mrs. Whitehouse had this professor as a teacher, too.

Flashsideway: My life has a through-line because I've constructed it as such. There's pattern and purpose to everything because that's what I believe. There's symbolic meaning because I've attributed it. I am the symbol for myself and of myself, representing and hiding who I really am.

Flashback, spring 1971: We had small-group reports to make to Mrs. Whitehouse's class, and my contribution was how to read and voice Emily Dickinson's poetry. I read aloud some of her verses to show the class that it was to be spoken not in artificial sing-songy fashion but as free verse with parsed thoughts, paying careful attention to the punctuation as clues for when to stop and flow. I showed them the wrong way first and, like Mrs. Whitehouse, spoke it with that Whitmanesque "Young Grimes" attitude:

> Be*cause* I *could* not *stop* for *Death*—
> He *kindly stopped* for *me*—
> The *Carriage held* but *just* Our*selves*—
> And *Immortality.*

And then I showed the class the right way to read Dickinson's poetry:

> If I can stop one heart from breaking,
> I shall not live in vain;
> If I can ease one life the aching,
> Or cool one pain,
> Or help one fainting robin
> Unto his nest again,
> I shall not live in vain.

Flashforward, the 1990s through 2000s: In my Methods of Teaching Theatre class, I teach the mechanics of voice. All my students have heard of pausing, but virtually no one's heard of parsing. I explain it to them and demonstrate with a reading from *Macbeth.*

Flashsideway: I played the clarinet in high school band, and I loved the complexity of the keys, found beauty and intrigue in the codes of its music instruction manual notation. I even made up foreign-language written alphabets because the beauty of symbol was so intriguing. It was the code I was after. I was not just in pursuit of meaning, I was in pursuit of symbol—something else, something different, something that captured the essence and essentials of what something was and is. The act of decoding is about mysteries to be solved, but encoding is deep dark secrets to savor and sometimes to strategically keep hidden from others.

Flashback, spring 1971: We were to have read a short story by Ernest Hemingway for the day, and when we walked into Mrs. Whitehouse's classroom the word "juxtaposition" was written in large letters across the chalkboard. This was the literary element we were to learn and notice in a particular passage from

Hemingway's story. I can't remember the short story's title, but I will never forget the "juxtaposition" of ideas.

Flashforward, the 1990s through 2000s: When I lecture on methods of teaching dramatic literature, I use scenes from Tennessee Williams's *The Glass Menagerie* as an exemplar. I list on the board the literary elements found most often in his plays, such as symbolism, irony, foreshadowing, motif, and juxtaposition.

Flashsideway: Why *do* I always dress in blacks and whites and grays?

Flashback, spring 1971: It was mystery day. Each student in Mrs. Whitehouse's class was given a copy of Edward Arlington Robinson's poem "How Annandale Went Out," and we were asked to read it on our own and to answer a series of questions about it:

> They called it Annandale—and I was there
> To flourish, to find words, and to attend:
> Liar, physician, hypocrite, and friend,
> I watched him; and the sight was not so fair
> As one or two that I have seen elsewhere:
> An apparatus not for me to mend—
> A wreck, with hell between him and the end,
> Remained of Annandale; and I was there.
> I knew the ruin as I knew the man;
> So put the two together, if you can,
> Remembering the worst you know of me.
> Now view yourself as I was, on the spot—
> With a slight kind of engine. Do you see?
> Like this . . . You wouldn't hang me? I thought not.

And after first reading this poem silently I thought, "What the hell?" For 30 minutes as a class we each sat in silence trying to decode and decipher the mystery of this poem. All of us were lost and confused, but after the independent study time Mrs. Whitehouse talked us through the poem one line at a time. And when she told us that the "engine" was a syringe for euthanasia I thought, "What the hell?" I left frustrated that day that I couldn't figure out what the poem meant. *Me!* But, I was Mrs. Whitehouse's best student! I was a junior in high school, and I knew *everything!*

Flashsideway: Red ink. The answers. There's a personal need for things to stand out—to bring forward what is important, salient, to capture the essence and essentials. I've been coding all my life—not reducing data but distilling it, condensing it, symbolizing it.

Flashback, spring 1972: I cheated on one of my senior weekly English exams. I was a teaching assistant that semester and had access to the textbook room for some of my responsibilities. I knew that our senior English teacher used the standardized tests from the Teacher's Edition of our textbook, so I peeked at the answer key for our upcoming test. Today, I'm afraid of "getting caught" in so many ways. We all have deep dark secrets—I'm convinced of that. Just as in 1st grade when I looked at the answers in the Teacher's Edition of the math textbook, here I was in 12th grade looking at the answers for a standardized quiz. That was the first and only time I ever cheated in school.

Flashsideway: The significance of the Teacher's Editions: I like answers. I want answers. I need answers. I hate unanswered questions. In research, I grow easily frustrated at the string of unanswered questions that sometimes comes at the end of an article. Every time I read this series of questions the researcher is too lazy to answer on his or her own, I think, "Why are you asking *me* this, don't *you* know?" I state that, in your writing, if you don't have an answer, don't ask the question. And I know some of you don't want to hear that. But to me, if you can't come up with answers or, at the very least, educated guesses to the questions you ask, then you have no business calling yourself a researcher. It's not the questions that are interesting; it's the answers that are interesting. It's the answers that are profound.

Flashback, spring 1971: We had a short-answer quiz on a piece of literature, and our answers were to be just one to two sentences in length. But I wanted to impress Mrs. Whitehouse with how much I knew and how much I cared. So my short answers were not just one to two but three to five sentences in length. I gave her what she wanted and more! My test paper was returned the next day—a good grade as I recall—but in red pencil she had crossed out my extended passages and wrote "extra" next to the irrelevant portions. "Extra."

Flashforward, the 1990s through 2000s: I am a promoter of simplicity, elegance, of finding the essence and essentials. Get to the point, already—my time is short. Death will be stopping for me.

Flashsideway: Mrs. Whitehouse embodied, symbolized, all that I loved about *teaching*, not of learning. She symbolized what I wanted to become, though I only vaguely knew it at the time. She unknowingly planted in my soul a seed that would grow, after a few years of my own personal journey, into a rebirth of teaching, a renaissance within myself of discovery; that my voice was not always right but that it was important; that after my own fumbling trial and error in the classroom, realizing that she got it right and that I could, too. I would reflect during my early career, "Gee, I wish I could be as good a teacher as she was." And then one day it hit me—I *could*. I could become who she was by nothing harder than simple replication of her pedagogy—her techniques, her mannerisms, her language, her organization, her patterns, her *style*. And I did, and I am, and I hope I will be until I retire. Even my death will be highly organized—the will's in a safe, the contingency info for my partner's up to date, and my memorial service, according to my last wishes, will have *style*. Yes, Ms. Dickinson, death will stop for me, too, but only at the specific intersection where I tell him to pick me up.

Flashback, the 1990s through 2000s: When I read my students' dissertations, I prefer to review them on hard copy, not reading them on a computer monitor with that electronic "comment" function. I use red pen to point out the grammatical errors and to make recommendations for revision. Red pen is better than gray carbon pencil. Red pen will ensure that the students see my notes on the black and white of their documents. Red pen says, "Hey, look here. Fix this—it's broken."

Flashsideway: Style. It's one of the most elusive processes in art, yet it's something all artists strive to accomplish. It's simple to define but very slippery to achieve. If you want to discover the meaning of your life, then closely examine the *style* of it.

Flashback, spring 1971: I was in theatre at the time and had fallen in love with the plays of Anton Chekhov. And Mrs. Whitehouse allowed me to perform a monologue I had memorized from *The Cherry Orchard* as a final class presentation. It was an American literature class, but she allowed me to make a presentation of something from Russia—something I was passionate about. She even wrote in my report card for that six-week reporting period that I had done an "excellent" job with it.

Flashforward, spring 1976. For part of my student teaching practicum in Texas, I am assigned to teach an English class called "Paragraph Writing" at my high school site. Back then, "Paragraph Writing" was code for "the remedial students who really need a lot of help with their composition and writing skills." I remember a breaking-in period in which I had to gain the confidence of the Hispanic gang members and redneck cowboys in the class, but we eventually got along. Yet my personal success story was tutoring and encouraging a young African American woman to write not what she thought I wanted to read but what was truly in her mind and in her heart. Her grades rose that semester from Cs to As. And I told her how proud I was of her *excellent* work.

Flashsideway: Think back, remember deeply, write it down, cut and paste, create the categories, look for patterns. If you're lucky and if you're open, themes will emerge and disparate threads will be woven together. But don't connect the dots; connect the *motifs.*

Flashback, May 2009: A PhD student whose dissertation I supervised was graduating, and we were excitedly waiting for the ceremony to begin. She had been in my research class a few years back and felt she could finally ask me: "Johnny, why *do* you always dress in blacks and whites and grays?" I looked at her, smiled, felt she had earned the real answer; so I told her, "I dress in blacks and whites and grays because sometimes I feel as if there's no color in my life. Except for red ink, of course."

Flashsideway: Never underestimate the power of one teacher. Never forget that what you say and do in the classroom—every single day—has the potential for lifelong impact. Don't you *dare* take teaching for granted. Teaching is meticulous craft. Teaching is an art form. It is *enduring* art.

Flashback, the middle of spring 1971, close to the end of the school year: I loved Mrs. Whitehouse so much for junior English that I wanted her for senior English, too. I told her after class one day, "You know, the junior class is pretty big, and I don't think the senior English teacher can handle all of us by herself next year." "Really?" she said. "Yeah," I replied and stated as a bold hint, "You should teach a section of senior English, too."

Flashforward, the end of spring 1971: Students learn through the grapevine that Mrs. Whitehouse will not be returning to our high school next year.

Flashforward, summer 2010: I keep my high school yearbooks stored in my bedroom's chest of drawers. As I wrote this keynote address, I remembered that I had them and went searching for what I might find. In the 1971 edition on the faculty pages, Mrs. Whitehouse's picture is in it—looking a bit too serious for some reason. But I did ask her to sign my yearbook for me, and she wrote me this message:

> Johnny,
>
> You don't need my good wishes. I know you'll do well. It has been a pleasure to know you. You'll make a fine teacher.
>
> Ann Whitehouse

Flashback, November 11, 2009: I initiated a Google and Facebook search for "Ann Whitehouse" and came across a listing of an English faculty member at Austin Community College. I e-mailed to the truncated address:

> Ms. Whitehouse,
>
> I'm searching for a former high school English teacher of mine. By chance, are you Ann Whitehouse who used to teach junior/11th grade English at Wm. B. Travis High School in Austin, Texas during the early 1970s? Thank you.
>
> Johnny Saldaña, Professor
> Arizona State University
> School of Theatre and Film

Flashforward, November 12, 2009: An e-mail reply from Ann Whitehouse:

> Yes, Johnny, and in my mind's eye I can see your face, looking up at me and smiling. I've been teaching a long long time, but when I read your name on the subject line, you and our English classroom at Travis High came into focus. Look at you! Fill me in on the journey that took you to ASU teaching in the School of Theatre and Film. Thanks for writing. . . .

Flashforward, today: Thank *you*, Mrs. Whitehouse, for accepting me just as I was; for instilling in me not just an appreciation but a love of American literature; for showing me the power, the grace, the *style* of excellent teaching; and for making me be the best teacher I try to be today. It took me 40 years to tell you this, and for that I am truly sorry. For maybe there was a time earlier in your life when you really needed to hear what I'm saying now. But now you know. Like Emily

Dickinson, you have not lived in vain. You have serendipitously and significantly influenced a human life, and the lives of those I've taught, and the lives of those they teach now.

O Captain . . . My Captain . . .

References

Geertz, C. (1983). *Local knowledge: Further essays in interpretive anthropology.* New York: Basic Books.

Grbich, C. (2007). *Qualitative data analysis: An introduction.* London: Sage.

Holstein, J.A., & Gubrium, J.F. (2000). *Constructing the life course* (2nd ed.). Dix Hills, NY: General Hall.

Liamputtong, P. (2009). *Qualitative research methods* (3rd ed.). South Melbourne: Oxford.

McLeod, J., & Thomson, R. (2009). *Researching social change.* London: Sage.

Saldaña, J. (2003). *Longitudinal qualitative research: Analyzing change through time.* Walnut Creek, CA: AltaMira Press.

Saldaña, J. (2009). *The coding manual for qualitative researchers.* London: Sage.

Thompson, S. (1977). *The folktale.* Berkeley: University of California Press.

2

INVOKING MODALITIES OF MEMORY IN THE WRITING CLASSROOM

Juan C. Guerra

Over the past 12 years, I have been working to identify and describe navigational tools that historically underrepresented students in colleges and universities can use nimbly, self-reflexively, and tactically to move *from* one physical space to another and *within* social spaces as well.[1] In what follows, I examine those spaces and describe *the modalities of memory*, an as-yet unacknowledged tool that I believe plays a crucial role in how students navigate them. Braidotti's (1994) description of a figuration—which she defines as a politically informed account of an alternative subjectivity designed to help us "learn to think differently about the subject, invent new frameworks, new images, new modes of thought" (p. 2)—provides a way to conceptualize both the tools and the varied physical and social spaces that students are likely occupy under these circumstances. Because this figurative mode functions according to what she calls "the philosophy of 'as if'"—"as if some experiences were reminiscent or evocative of others" (p. 5)—a figuration has the potential to open up, "through successive repetitions and mimetic strategies, spaces where alternative forms of agency can be engendered" (p. 7). How figurations work will become apparent in my discussion and examination of what I am calling the modalities of memory.

Before unpacking the figuration at the heart of this essay, I first present *Life in the Either/Or, Life in the Both/And*, and *Life in the Neither/Nor* as alternative metaphorical conceptions for the three approaches to language and cultural difference now commonplace in the field as scholars and researchers work to overcome what Kostogriz (2004) has described as the space-place dichotomy in our conceptions of literacy. I then use the work of Deleuze and Guattari (1987) on rhizomes and of Camus (1955) on the myth of Sisyphus to describe how space functions in the context of Life in the Neither/Nor. Along the way, I analyze two autobiographical passages from my lived experience to demonstrate how disenfranchised students in our schools can reconfigure the social spaces they occupy by using the modalities of memory to navigate and negotiate the various rhetorical and discursive challenges they face in the course of their everyday lives. My goal is to provide examples of how we can equip students with the tools they need to negotiate the cumbersome circumstances they encounter in school as a consequence of the nontraditional experiences they bring with them from their home communities.

From Third Space to Life in the Neither/Nor

In the 1980s, Heath (1983) and Street (1984) delegitimized the autonomous and conservative ideological assumption that it was possible to live in an either/or world, that is, that it was possible to formulate a space in which people's ability to use the modalities of reading and writing could be assessed on the basis of objective standards that imagined social and cultural assets and deficits. As a consequence of their important contributions, we found ourselves in a more comfortable space that privileged context and situatedness and supposedly valued difference equitably. In time, legitimate critiques emerged that suggested the inherent limitations of this new position. So what really happens, critics asked, when you find yourself in a both/and world where equal value is supposedly granted to the cultural capital accumulated locally by the disenfranchised in our society? Despite efforts to equate sameness and difference, they answered, we end up valuing a set of social practices that have tremendous currency in the local communities inhabited by the disenfranchised but limited currency in the larger, more global communities by whose standards these individuals will eventually come to be assessed and will likely be found wanting. As Brandt and Clinton (2002) pointed out in their groundbreaking essay, "Limits of the Local: Expanding Perspectives on Literacy as a Social Practice," the new ideological paradigm that emerged to contest the autonomous model of literacy ended up veering "too far in a reactive direction, exaggerating the power of local contexts to set or reveal the forms and means that literacy takes" (p. 338).

As we have all struggled with the untenable bifurcation of the oral and the literate, the universal and the specific, the global and the local, and the autonomous and the ideological, several scholars in literacy studies (Gutiérrez, 2008; Kostogriz, 2004; Moje et al., 2004; Pahl, 2002) have posited new perspectives of a Third Space based on the work of Bhabha (1994) and Soja (1996). Although she was not aware of Bhabha's or Soja's work when she formulated her ideas, Gutiérrez's (2008) conception of a Third Space is very similar to their more theoretical, postcolonial iterations. Unlike Bhabha and Soja, however, Gutiérrez is interested in formulating a pedagogical and curricular tool kit that "nondominant" students can use to fashion a transformative sensibility that will serve as the crucible for collectively nurturing the historical agency they need to nimbly, self-reflexively, and tactically navigate and negotiate the terrain of any given social space.

In Gutiérrez's view, migrant students in the program she studied used syncretic *testimonio,* a hybrid form of critical autobiography and *testimonio,* to tell "stories of movements across borders, across both new and familiar practices" that call "our attention to an important and unresolved dilemma in the learning sciences":

> How do we account for the learning and development embodied by and through movement, the border and boundary crossing of students who migrate to and throughout the U.S.? What new capacities and identities are developed in this movement? To what extent do these capacities and identities travel and shift across settings? And what new educational arrangements provoke and support new capacities that extend students' repertoires of practice? (p. 150)

I will return to Gutiérrez's work in my concluding remarks when I offer some of my own suggestions for how educators can use what we have learned from our conceptions of the Third Space and Life in the Neither/Nor to develop tools that address the needs of historically underrepresented students.

While the concept of Third Space has provided us with a lens for understanding alternative contexts beyond the binary systems that inform how we typically construct the world around us, it still has inherent limitations as a theoretical tool because it continues to be constrained by how we conceptualize and imagine space when we use it. Williams (2003), for example, describes how an easy kind of "essentializing and naïve approach to the nature of hybridity and resistance has been embraced by multiculturalist thinking." In such instances, "the idea of a 'Third Space' has been employed to describe a benign and ultimately progressive and positivist multicultural synthesis, [what I have been referring to as a both/and world], that creates a new culture of pluralistic tolerance" (p. 600). I certainly don't want to suggest that we should stop using the term "Third Space"; I do, however, want to suggest that it may be worth our while to consider a slightly different figuration that more directly removes itself from our commonplace understanding of how space functions in our daily lives.

Arguably the most salient characteristic of the first two theoretical perspectives I mentioned earlier—Life in the Either/Or and Life in the Both/And—is their unrelenting binary rigidity and stability. Whether we are locked in the midst of the black and white, the right and wrong of the former, or the synthetic/integrated quality of the latter, every one of us is able to navigate and negotiate these terrains without much trouble because they both call on our agility with and our awareness and recollection of highly prescribed ways of being. In the conservative conception of Life in the Either/Or, we have little need to worry about the complexity of the social networks we traverse because everyone pretty much knows (or should know) his or her place in the broader matrix that has been laid out for them to follow. In this context, we typically invoke what Bourdieu (1977) calls doxa, Giddens (1991) calls practical consciousness, and psychologists call working memory (Sulzen, 2001) as we follow the habitual patterns of our preformulated lives. In their work, Deleuze and Guattari (1987) describe this "first type of book [as] the root book," which they contend is firmly grounded in the linear and hierarchical logic of the root-tree (p. 5).

Navigation is ever more challenging in Life in the Both/And, if only because we have a more varied array of different choices to make. Here, we are positioned by a liberal conception to combine contrastive patterns into new formulations, but in time these new formulations also become rigid, stable, and habitual. This reflects a different kind of essentialism-in-the-making. In the "radical-system, or fascicular root," Deleuze and Guattari note,

> the principal root has aborted, or its tip has been destroyed; an immediate, indefinite multiplicity of secondary roots grafts onto it and undergoes a flourishing development. . . . [But] whenever a multiplicity is taken up in a structure, its growth is offset by a reduction in its laws of combination. (1987, pp. 5–6)

In other words, while a situated and multicultural frame of reference at first blush suggests that we have overcome the rigidity of a binary system, we soon discover that it's an illusion. The truth is we are still locked within a comparative frame of reference that is difficult to disrupt; we are still prisoners of a multiplicative process constrained by a totalizing unity.

Life in the Neither/Nor, on the other hand, is measured by its never-ending fluidity, instability, and unpredictability. As such, it resembles a fragmented, discontinuous, and disorienting space that the disenfranchised—postcolonial subjects in Bhaba's (1994) language—must learn to navigate and negotiate. It also mimics Deleuze and Guattari's notion of a rhizome (1987), which, because it "has no beginning or end," becomes a particularly fascinating terrain. Deleuze and Guattari are not so much interested in the either/ors or the both/ands that mark the endpoints. What really intrigues them is the middle, what they refer to as "between things, interbeing, *intermezzo*," the "coming and going rather than [the] starting and finishing." This middle, they contend,

> is where things pick up speed. Between things does not designate a localizable relation going from one thing to the other and back again, but a perpendicular direction, a transversal movement that sweeps one and the other away, a stream without beginning or end that undermines its banks and picks up speed in the middle. (p. 25)

What happens in this kind of middle, what they call a rhizome and I call Life in the Neither/Nor, awakens within each of us a *nomadic consciousness*[2] that requires a dynamic set of nimble, self-reflexive, and tactical capabilities (Braidotti, 1994, p. 23; Guerra, 2004, p. 19).

Although I suspect that Deleuze and Guattari would be put off by its binary, transcendental, and existentialist characteristics, for me their discussion of a rhizome brings to mind Camus's (1955) description of Sisyphus rolling a stone up a mountainside again and again for all eternity. In many ways, the act of pushing the stone up the mountainside figuratively reflects Life in the Either/Or and Life in the Both/And. The act describes the perceived futility of everyday life as each of us goes through the phases that make up much of our lived experience on this earth, phases so automatic that we have only to rely on our doxa, practical consciousness, or working memory—on our habits of mind—to get through them.

What interests Camus, and what I find useful in conceptualizing Life in the Neither/Nor, is what Sisyphus does on the way down the mountainside as he prepares once again for the futile task that awaits him. Says Camus:

> It is during that return, that pause, that Sisyphus interests me. A face that toils so close to stones is already stone itself! I see that man going back down with a heavy yet measured step toward the torment of which he will never know the end. That hour like a breathing-space which returns as surely as his suffering, that is the hour of consciousness. At each of these moments when he leaves the heights and gradually sinks toward the lairs of the gods, he is superior to his fate. He is stronger than his rock. (1955, p. 121)

And because Sisyphus is able to reflect on his condition, "the struggle toward the heights is enough to fill" his heart. In these moments, Sisyphus is engaged in "coming and going rather than starting and finishing." One, Camus concludes, "must imagine Sisyphus happy" (p. 123).

In my view, the building block that makes a heightened consciousness in Life in the Neither/Nor even possible is what I referred to earlier as the modalities of memory, that precious navigational tool that Sisyphus calls on as he walks down the mountainside. I should note that shortly after I first "coined" this term in the course of preparing this essay, I did a Google search to see if anyone had used it before. It turns out that Wallach and Averbach (1955) first used it in an article in *The American Journal of Psychology*. In their study, they reached two conclusions: first, that "there are memory modalities just as there are sense modalities" (p. 249), and second, that "the conception of memory modality is essential in the study of recognition" (p. 250). Building on prior research and theoretical work, Sulzen (2001) has since developed a model of modality-organized cognition (see Figure 2.1) that describes a set of first-level modalities directly related to our senses (auditory, gustatory, haptic, kinesthetic, olfactory, and visual) and a set of second-level modalities (emotional/affective, linguistic, and spatial) that extends recognition beyond our senses and makes use of our memory.

Together, this set of second-level modalities, what I am calling modalities of memory, informs how we perceive and interpret, then act in the world. It's important to keep in mind that these internal memories—which bring together the past, the

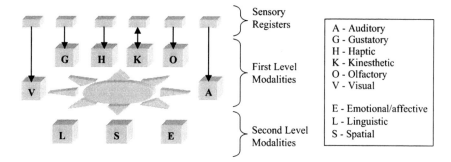

FIGURE 2.1 Modality-Organized Cognition

Reprinted from James Sulzen (2001), "Modality Based Working Memory."

present, and a possible future in dreamlike fashion—as Kotre (1995) reminds us, "don't sit inertly in our minds the way they do on an audiotape or the shelves of a library. They are constantly refashioned" (p. 37). As Vivian (2010) concludes in his study of *Public Forgetting,*

> we activate the fickle and nomadic character of memory whenever we discuss our memories with others, whenever we preserve them in writing, images or sound, thereby ensuring that our memories subsist in more than one place and form, in multiple "inheritances" or "forms of enactment" at once. (p. 126)

This discussion about our internal modalities of memory should remind us that the external modalities of sense we discuss with our students in our work as educators are not simply things out there in the world that we use in the production and reception of knowledge. In different ways, each is also represented in and is a syncretic part of our ever-changing and emerging sense of a bodily self, of our evolving and conditional capabilities as historical agents caught in the flux of time. What I would like to do now is to share two autobiographical passages to illustrate how I believe the modalities of memory make it possible for us to function in the social, cultural, discursive, material, and imagined worlds that we occupy in Life in the Neither/Nor, especially when it comes to our ability to navigate and negotiate these and other spaces in a heightened state of consciousness.

Identity as Lived Experience, or the Body Remembers

No doubt each of us can remember moments in our lives when we felt very much like Sisyphus trudging up that mountainside pushing a weighty stone, as well as those exquisite moments of heightened consciousness when we discovered on the way down that same mountainside, and later remembered many times over, the linguistic and cultural experiences that shaped our provisional identities in ways we could have never imagined possible. In an effort to present some data that I can analyze and interpret using the theoretical schema I just outlined, I want to share publicly for the first time two autobiographical passages from my own synathetic *testimonio* that describe key moments in my life informed by a legal document that has haunted me for more than 50 years. Gutiérrez (2008) describes syncretic *testimonio* as a hybrid form of critical autobiography and *testimonio* "situated in the subjective particularity and global and historical reality in which people co-construct their understanding of the social world and of themselves" (p. 149). My goal here is to illustrate how modalities of memory can shape and reshape our identities as our memories themselves are shaped and reshaped not by who we are but by who we are continuously becoming. Hall (1996) puts it this way:

> Though they seem to invoke an origin in a historical past with which they continue to correspond, actually identities are about questions of using the resources of history, language and culture in the process of becoming rather than being: not "who we are" or "where we came from," so much as what we might become, how we have been represented and how that bears on how we might represent ourselves. (p. 4)

In the pre-civil rights summer of 1959, when I was 9 years old, I rode my bike from the housing project in the Mexican part of my hometown of Harlingen, Texas, across the railroad tracks to the White part of town to try out for Little League baseball. A White coach who saw me trying out thought I had the skill to make it on his team, so he came over and asked if I could bring him my birth certificate to prove I was old enough to play. I went home immediately and excitedly told my mother I needed something called a birth certificate to prove my age if I wanted to play baseball. My mother hesitated for a moment, suspicious about why anyone would need what she obviously considered one of the most important documents in her possession, then told me she would give it to me the following day.

The next day after I reminded her I needed my birth certificate, my mother left the room for a few minutes, came back with a white envelope, and told me not to share it with anyone but the coach. I said okay, got on my bike, and took it to the baseball park, where the coach removed my birth certificate from the white envelope, glanced at it, then gave it right back to me. "Okay," he said, "I'll see you here at our first practice on Monday." After I took the envelope and thanked him, I got on my bike and started home. Probably more out of curiosity than anything else, I stopped on my way home, leaned the bike against a tree, sat on the ground, and took the birth certificate out of the white envelope.

The birth certificate was an ordinary piece of blue paper, folded several times over, with information printed and typed on it. As I felt the piece of paper between my fingers, I noticed it had a lifted seal on the left-hand edge with a signature over it. I also noticed and became curious about the information typed in the first series of boxes listed next to CHILD. First name: Juan. Middle Name: Cruz. Last Name: Guerra. The middle name caught me by surprise because I had never heard that word uttered in my life. The next set of boxes listed next to FATHER had question marks in them. My mother's name was typed into its respective boxes. First name: Teresa. Last name: Guerra. I had known for some time that the individual who lived with my mother, my two older Mexican-born sisters, my three younger siblings, and me was not my father—he had told me that himself—but I had never been told and had never asked who my birth father was or what had happened to him.

At the very bottom left-hand corner, in a box numbered 21, I came to a final section that had a strange-sounding word with a question mark after it: Legitimate? Typed in the box this strange word occupied, I found another word in capital letters: NO. Not knowing what to make of it, I folded the document, put it in the envelope, and headed home on my bike. Along the way, I pondered the blank space where my birth father's name should have been and the word NO in the box numbered 21. When I got home, my mother immediately took the white envelope from me and asked if anyone else but the coach had looked at it. "No, *mami*," I lied. I then went to my bedroom, took out a dictionary and looked up that strange word. Legitimate: "Being in compliance with the law. Genuine. Authentic. Born of legally married parents."

Because I was a monolingual Spanish speaker who had never read, written, or heard a single word of English until the first grade, almost three years before the birth certificate incident, I'm not sure how much I can trust my recollection that I actually took out a dictionary and looked up that ominous word. After all, as Vivian (2010) notes, our memories "subsist in a state of dispersion [rather than] in the form of a unified or stable presence" (p. 126). On the other hand, I vividly remember consulting a dictionary after my last confession in the Catholic Church a few years later, at the age of 13, when the priest asked me if I had offended God and I didn't know how to respond. Peeved at my ignorance, the priest told me to go home and not return to church until I had an answer.

In a moment that I still recall vividly and viscerally, I ran home and, after lying on my bed in tears and saying "*pendejo, pendejo, pendejo*"[3] to myself under my breath, I got a dictionary and looked up the word. Offend: "To arouse anger, resentment, or indignation in." Now whether I did or did not consult a dictionary at age 9 is in many ways secondary; the fact that I remember having done so suggests the extent to which our memories are not foundational but continuously revised on the basis of our later experiences. While the internal modalities of memory influence the shape and the ways in which we use the external modalities of sense we learn in school, they are in turn shaped by the external modalities as we work to develop a cohesive sense of the world.

Eight years later, in 1966, when an older sister invited me to spend the summer with her in Chicago, my godfather drove my mother and me to the bus station for the beginning of my 48-hour, 1,500-mile journey. After my bag was stored in the bus's lower compartment, I stood in the early evening drizzle and said goodbye to my godfather and mother. When my godfather stepped away to give us a moment of privacy, my mother took out a white envelope from her purse and said to me in Spanish, "Take this with you, *mi'jo*. It's your birth certificate. Just in case anyone asks you to prove you were born in this country." "*Gracias, mami,*" I said. Before I had a chance to take a step to board the bus, my mother asked me if I had a pencil. "*Si, aqui,*" I said as I pulled one out of my pocket. "Write this down, *mi'jito*. Capital S-a-l-o-m-e. Capital C-r-u-z. That's your father's name." I nodded my head, gave her a final hug, and boarded the bus.

Once I took my seat on the bus, I glanced out the window and saw my mother and godfather waving goodbye to me through the rain-stained window, and I waved back as the bus pulled out of the station. Within minutes of getting on the road, I pulled out the white envelope with my birth father's name on it, took out my pencil, and, with tears blurring my vision, erased it in a futile effort to regain a past that had provided the parameters of the life I'd come to know. What I realized some time later, of course, is that once something is written down, once something is entered into the modalities of memory, it can no longer be erased, can no longer be extinguished. From the moment it is brought into consciousness, it becomes an integral element of our navigational equipment and informs our emerging identities.

Over the next 48 hours, I sat on that bus as it travelled from my hometown in rural South Texas to Chicago, at the time the second largest city in the United States. At each stop, I found myself—as I had in that moment when I had opened the envelope on my way home from the baseball park 8 years earlier—in a rhizome between my past and my future, coming and going, increasingly conscious of my place in the world. During that journey, I also literally became part of a larger phenomenon: the diaspora of black and brown people migrating from the south to the north, a migration that had begun in earnest for Latinos the year before with the passage of the Immigration and Nationality Act of 1965.[4]

So what lessons do these autobiographical passages from my syncretic *testimonio* bring to mind for me about how we navigate and negotiate the challenges of Life in the Neither/Nor? On the one hand, I see myself in both cases caught at the outset in the certitude of Life in the Either/Or. As I travelled on my bike from the housing project where so many of us lived seemingly futile lives and crossed the railroad track to the White part of town where children were being prepared for very different lives, I had no reason to question my place in the carefully laid-out racist matrix or to imagine that my life would ever be any different from the way it was at that very moment. But when I opened that white envelope and saw, for the very first time, my life documented so boldly by the very state that governed our every move, I skipped over Life in the Both/And and momentarily entered Life in the Neither/Nor.

For the first time in my remembered life, cracks begin to form in the cage that contained me—if only because I finally knew that I was recognized as illegitimate, illegal, momentarily beyond the reach of the two worlds I had traversed. As I travelled on that bus to Chicago 8 years later, carrying that very document in my possession, I again found myself in a state of heightened consciousness—witnessing my world in transition as a wide spectrum of poor and working-class people from Texas, Louisiana, Mississippi, Tennessee, Missouri, and Illinois momentarily crossed paths with me.

My mother, who had arrived in what would become our hometown in the mid-1940s as an undocumented immigrant with a third-grade education and two daughters in tow, found a way to survive and nurture the three of us: her two Mexican-born girls and me, her first born in the United States. I suspect that is why she felt compelled to have me write my birth father's name down on that white envelope; she was concerned that the border patrol stationed some 80 miles up the road on the way to Chicago would decide my incomplete birth certificate was inadequate evidence of my citizenship and would deport me right then and there.

Years later, my mother filled in the gaps and told me how, when I had been born in a labor camp where she had been living with my two sisters, she had gotten into an argument with the midwife who when she brought me into the world insisted that my mother had no right to include my birth father's name on my birth certificate because they had never married. Somehow, though, my mother persuaded the midwife to sneak my birth father's surname into mine as a middle name. The modalities of memory have continued to shape and reshape all of these historical moments in ways that have come to constitute and reconstitute the provisional identities that I have embraced, especially when it comes to my relationship with literacy. It is, I suspect, not much different for the increasing number of historically underrepresented students who are enrolling in our colleges and universities. How we can use what we know about Life in the Neither/Nor and the modalities of memory to help our students navigate and negotiate their way through their educational experiences is what I want to turn to now.

Navigating and Negotiating a Multiplicity of Curricular and Pedagogical Spaces

The autobiographical passages from the syncretic *testimonio* that I just shared are meant to remind us and our students that, when it comes to pedagogical spaces, the trees we sit under and the buses we ride on are as important and as critical to our lives as the classrooms we share. At the same time, it's not enough for historically underrepresented students to come to terms with their historical pasts, especially those deeply hidden and shameful moments that raise the pain threshold in ways that, if we're lucky, heighten our consciousness. What I want to suggest instead is that students need to call on their internal modalities of memory any time they employ the external modalities of sense we repeatedly ask them to use in the classroom.

While we want to encourage our students to invoke their personal histories, to bring their lived experience into the classroom and to use it as a tool to navigate and negotiate the terrain of their unfolding lives, we also want them to think of these autobiographical moments not as opportunities for confession in the Foucauldian sense but as opportunities to constitute and reconstitute themselves in the process of becoming (Hogan, 2005, p. 151). When we represent aspects of our lived experience in the context of confession as a genre, we are constrained by the need to frame them as familiar narratives that display an internal coherence designed to strip them of their multiple contradictions. Students need to learn to use the modalities of memory to highlight the rhizomatic nature of their lived experience, to wrestle with the multiple contradictions that Life in the Neither/Nor brings to light. When we constitute or reconstitute ourselves, we purposefully disrupt the need we feel to make sense of the world in coherent and highly prescribed terms.

In her work, Gutiérrez (2008) provides a well-travelled and thought-out map for how we can help nondominant students acquire repertoires of practice, that is, "both vertical and horizontal forms of expertise . . . [that include] not only what students learn in formal learning environments such as schools, but also what they learn by participating in a range of practices outside of school" (p. 149). At the same time that it focuses on the sociohistorical influences on its students' language, literacy, and learning practices, the UCLA Migrant Student Leadership Institute (MSLI)—the subject of her research—addresses their social, economic, and educational realities. The curriculum and its pedagogy, Gutiérrez notes, "are grounded in the historical and current particulars of students' everyday lives, while at the same time oriented toward an imagined but possible future" (p. 154).

In Gutiérrez's carefully construed ecological approach, learning is organized in such ways that conversation, dialogue, and contradiction are privileged across learning activities with varied participation structures: tutorials, comprehension circles, writing conferences, *teatro,* minilectures, and whole-class discussions (2008, p. 154). In describing this terrain, Gutiérrez reminds us not to think of the collective Third Space as a utopian narrative because "work in these spaces is difficult and filled with contradictions, setbacks, and struggle" (p. 160). Instead, she wants us to think of it as "an example of what is possible when educators and educational researchers arrange educational environments in ways that incite, support, and extend students' repertoires of practice by organizing the frequency, co-occurrence, and difficulty of cultural practices and forms of mediation" (p. 160).

What I want to respectfully add to Gutiérrez's highly nuanced description of the tools nondominant (in her words) or historically underrepresented students (in mine) need to navigate and negotiate the provisional pedagogical spaces they inhabit in our schools, universities, and communities, is another set of tools that I believe these students must also acquire and use nimbly, tactically, and self-reflexively rather than only intuitively, to move *from* one physical space to another and *within* varied social spaces as well. What I hope my discussion adds is a different take, a different figural representation of the spaces that all students inhabit as they move from one social, cultural, discursive, material, and imagined space to another in their everyday lives. I want us to remind students that the spaces they occupy have been framed in different ways by the different ideological forces that shape and influence the institutions responsible for their education. And I want to argue that it's important for them to know that the tools they learn to use in the Third Space, in Life in the Neither/Nor, can also be used to navigate life in a range of other spaces, most of which tend to sedate them into automatically enacting the habitual patterns of our preformulated lives.

Finally, as educators, we need to think of our students, and we need to encourage them to think of themselves, as *nomadic subjects* who are continuously in the process of becoming (Braidotti, 1994, p. 25). They need to know that, while they will spend a good part of their lives in the Either/Or and the Both/And, they will also—particularly if they're disenfranchised—continue to live a good portion of their lives in the Neither/Nor. Ave, a 16-year-old migrant student whose syncretic *testimonio* Gutiérrez (2008) shares with us in her essay, writes:

> I grew up believing I was invisible and I learned that my vocation was that of an outside observer. . . . I learned to simply observe everything and everyone, but even that bothered people. I was never taught to fight, so instead I did what I was best at, stay quiet and take it all in. The silence somehow sent them the message that I was dumb and stupid. (p. 151)

In our syncretic *testimonios,* Ave and I both called on our modalities of memory to draw forth experiences that I suspect neither one of us had ever shared with anyone before. We engaged in what Hogan (2005) has described as "a kind of identity formation that is not coerced, but is a freely chosen subjective exploration of experience" (p. 121). We also learned to successfully navigate Life in the Neither/Nor by becoming assemblers of our own lived experience, which in turn alerted us to the new possibilities available to us in Life in the Either/Or and Life in the Both/And as well.

It took me more than 50 years to take command of and share painful moments of heightened consciousness with you in this essay. Fortunately for all of us who support the kind of work the Migrant Institute staff and students in their program have done, Ave shared similar moments in the context of a collective Third Space at the age of 15. My hope is that Ave is well on her way to learning how to use the tools she acquired at the Migrant Institute to navigate and negotiate the multiplicity of pedagogical spaces she will inhabit in the course of her life. Our task as educators is to make sure we continue to create conditions in our classrooms that provide students like Ave with endless opportunities to share and shape their lives as they come and go.

Notes

1 According to Bourdieu, a social space is a "system of relations." In his view, "we can compare social space to a geographic space within which regions are divided up. But this space is constructed in such a way that the closer the agents, groups, or institutions which are situated within this space, the more common properties they have; and the more distant, the fewer. Spatial distances—on paper—coincide with social distances. Such is not the case in real space. It is true that one can observe almost everywhere a tendency toward spatial segregation, people who are close together in social space tending to find themselves, by choice or by necessity, close to one another in geographic space; nevertheless, people who are very distant from each other in social space can encounter one another and interact, if only briefly and intermittently, in physical space" (1989, p. 16).

2 According to Braidotti, nomadic consciousness is akin to what Foucault called countermemory. It "combines features that are usually perceived as opposing, namely the possession of a sense of identity that rests not on fixity but on contingency. The nomadic consciousness combines coherence with mobility. It aims to rethink the unity of the subject, without reference to humanistic beliefs, without dualistic oppositions, linking instead body and mind in a new set of intensive and often intransitive transitions" (1994, p. 31).

3 This literally translates as "idiot, idiot, idiot."

4 According to the Center for Immigration Studies, the Immigration and Nationality Act of 1965 "phased out the national origins quota system first instituted in 1921" and replaced it "with a system based primarily on family reunification and needed skills" (2013, n.p.). The legislation unexpectedly led to "one of the greatest waves of immigration in the nation's history—more than 18 million legal immigrants since the law's passage," most of whom came from Asia and Latin America.

References

Bhabha, H.K. (1994). *The location of culture*. New York: Routledge.

Bourdieu, P. (1977). *Outline of a theory of practice*. New York: Cambridge University Press.

Bourdieu, P. (1989). Social Space and symbolic power. *Sociological Theory, 7*(1), 14–25.

Braidotti, R. (1994). *Nomadic subjects*. New York: Cambridge University Press.

Brandt, D., & Clinton, K. (2002). Limits of the local: Expanding perspectives on literacy as a social practice. *Journal of Literacy Research, 34*(3), 337–356.

Camus, A. (1955). *The myth of Sisyphus and other essays* (J. O'Brien, Trans.). New York: Vintage Books.

Center for Immigration Studies. (2013). Three decades of mass immigration: The legacy of the 1965 Immigration Act. Retrieved on February 15, 2014, from www.cis.org/1965ImmigrationAct-MassImmigration

Deleuze, G., & Guattari, F. (1987). *A thousand plateaus* (B. Massumi, Trans.). Minneapolis: University of Minnesota Press.

Giddens, A. (1991). *Modernity and self-identity: Self and society in the late modern age*. Stanford: Stanford University Press.

Guerra, J.C. (2004). Putting literacy in its place: Nomadic consciousness and the practice of transcultural repositioning. In C. Gutiérrez-Jones (Ed.), *Rebellious readings: The dynamics of Chicana/o literacy* (pp. 19–37). Santa Barbara: Center for Chicana/o Studies, University of California–Santa Barbara.

Gutiérrez, K. (2008). Developing a sociocritical literacy in the third space. *Reading Research Quarterly, 43*(2), 148–164.

Hall, S. (1996). Introduction: Who needs "identity"? In S. Hall & P. du Gay (Eds.), *Questions of cultural identity* (1–16). Thousand Oaks, CA: Sage.

Heath, S.B. (1983). *Ways with words: Language, life and work in communities and classrooms.* Cambridge: Cambridge University Press.

Hogan, K.J. (2005). Student subjectivity and the teaching of literature: The possibility of free space. Unpublished doctoral dissertation, University of Washington, Seattle.

Kostogriz, A. (2004). Rethinking the spatiality of literacy practices in multicultural conditions. Annual conference of the Australian Association for Research in Education, Melbourne. Retrieved on February 15, 2014, from www.aare.edu.au/04pap/kos04610.pdf

Kotre, J. (1995). *White gloves: How we create ourselves through memory.* New York: Free Press.

Moje, E., Ciechanowski, K., Kramer, K., Ellis, L., Carrillo, R., & Callazo, T. (2004). Working toward a third space in content areas literacy. *Reading Research Quarterly, 39*(1), 38–70.

Pahl, K. (2002). Habitus and the home: Texts and practices in families. *Ways of Knowing Journal, 2*(1), 45–53.

Soja, E. (1996). *Thirdspace: Journeys to Los Angeles and other real-and-imagined spaces.* Malden, MA: Blackwell.

Street, B.V. (1984). *Literacy in theory and practice.* Cambridge: Cambridge University Press.

Sulzen, J. (2001). Modality based working memory. School of Education, Stanford University. Retrieved on February 15, 2014, from http://ldt.stanford.edu/~jsulzen/james-sulzen-portfolio/classes/PSY205/modality-project/paper/modality-expt-paper.PDF

Vivian, B. (2010). *Public forgetting: The rhetoric and politics of beginning again.* University Park: Pennsylvania State University Press.

Wallach, H., & Averbach, E. (1955). On memory modalities. *American Journal of Psychology, 68*(2), 249–257.

Williams, B. (2003). Speak for yourself? Power and hybridity in the cross-cultural classroom. *College, Composition, and Communication, 54*(4), 586–609.

3

"IT'S ABOUT LIVING YOUR LIFE": FAMILY TIME AND SCHOOL TIME AS A RESOURCE FOR MEANING MAKING IN HOMES, SCHOOLS, AND COMMUNITIES

Kate Pahl

In this chapter I intend to focus on meaning making. By meaning making I am referring to acts of text making in homes and schools, including talk, oral storytelling, gesture, film, and photography as well as writing and making meaning from text, including reading. I want to explore the relationship between individual and shared subjectivities, people's identities-in-practice, and meaning making. Who you are does shape the way you make texts. Text making, however, is not static. As Jennifer Rowsell and I argued in our article on sedimented identities in texts (2007), meaning unfolds over time. In homes, particularly, routine practices are built up day after day, and over time these practices can be found "sedimented" in multimodal texts.

The processes by which these sedimentations occur, is, I would argue, something that requires further exploration and discussion. By focusing on time and space it is possible to isolate and describe the singularity of the moments of meaning making. Rather than see time as "uniformly flowing without regard for individuals or the actions they take" (Springgay, Irwin, & Kind, 2008, p. 88) we can understand time as shaped by memories and subjectivities, and then we can challenge the epistemologies that dominate and contain these subjectivities (Dillabough, 2009; Ricoeur, 1980).

In my discussion, I will also take in an engagement with theories of modernism, which I identify with a "grand narrative" that supersedes and rolls on regardless of people, things, and places and then with theories of postmodernism, in which these settled ways of being are fragmented and dissolved. I want to propose a space of meaning making which is,

> a baroque space, characterized by oscillations of scale and confusions of time, where stable hierarchies of subject and object, play and reality, text

and world, specific and general, are brought into productive disarray, and uncertainty becomes a resource for releasing difficult questions that recognize the complexity and the opacity of culture. (Jones, Holmes, Macrae, & Maclure, 2010, p. 89)

This quotation from Maggie Maclure, Christina Macrae, Rachel Holmes, and Helen Jones contributes to a wider discussion in their paper about the totalizing powers of descriptions in ethnographic fieldwork. Here, I argue that this destabilizing process can be particularly productive for literacy educators. I propose a "collage" of meaning making that takes account of memory, singularity, and identity and also allows for a fluid and intuitive mode of inquiry that takes its impetus from the epistemologies of collaborative arts practice as much as from the social sciences (Eisner, 2008; Springgay et al., 2008). In my recent work with artists (see Pahl, Comerford-Boyes, Genever, & Pool, 2010; Pahl & Pool, 2011), I have explored the way in which the collaborative space of inquiry that crosses the boundaries of arts practice, ethnography, and education can open up new epistemological spaces that, in turn, listen to meaning makers.

In this chapter I intend to try to disrupt the "grand narrative" of modernism with some interruptions from families and schools that I have been involved with over the past several years. By making my research focus on homes rather than schools, I have created a disruptive space that opens up. When asked about the age groups that I study, I say simply "all" age groups, including young children, babies, grandparents, siblings and parents and children in their own leisure spaces. This in itself is a disruptive activity. To visit a home involves engaging with new patterns of behavior and structuring structures. It requires attention to ways of being and behaving. This means that teachers who rely on set dispositions and ways of being that in school contexts are mediated by structural concerns, a preexisting "embodied habitus" (Christ & Wang, 2008), have to adjust their schemas in home settings.

Let me start with definitions. Modernism could be described as a *metadiscourse* that legitimates itself by reference to some "grand narrative" and could be described as "totalizing and controlling" (Cooper & Burrell, 1988). Postmodernist perspectives, by contrast, rely on a kind of disintegrative epistemological stance, a "search for instabilities" that focuses on difference, the other, and the unfixed (Cooper & Burrell, 1988). However, concerns from feminists and those engaged with contemporary struggles of class have continued to assert a need to engage with modernist perspectives, if only to account for narratives of oppression and the need to engage in a struggle that itself implies a modernist project, in contexts where contemporary neoliberal policies have destroyed communities' livelihoods through postindustrialization (Capper, 1998). Capper argues instead for a kind of "dialectical stance" between the modernist and postmodernist project (1998, p. 365), as exemplified by the work of Maggie Maclure and others who continue to argue for a sustained "entanglement with objects" and who, while arguing for a postqualitative epistemology, also allow that there is something "out there" to entangle with (Maclure, 2006).

Throughout this chapter, I will be engaging with these two conceptual frameworks (modernist and postmodernist), but, in the end, I might end up using neither. Instead, I want to explore, through my data, particular moments in time and space that open up meaning making. These might be shared moments, where dialogic inquiry with artists, children, and researchers takes us into new spaces. From these explorations, I will offer a series of propositions that might lead to new projects. I will ask where meaning can be found and how we, as educators, can make sense of meanings across times and spaces that are not bound by taken-for-granted structural spaces, the unfolding taken-for-granted nature of "clock time," but come from the ethnographic, the disruptive spaces of home, the epistemological challenges of the contested, the dialogic, and the critical. I will propose the importance of creating a collaborative space with artists and young people that can then take seriously the epistemologies of young people and suggest that, in that process, taken-for-granted concepts of time and space can be disrupted.

Why are concepts of time and space so important as critical concepts in education? It is the subject of this book, and I want to spend a few moments thinking about time and, indeed, space as heuristics for considering the question of identities and meaning making in homes, communities, and schools. Time, says Ricoeur (1980), is commonly understood as historical and sequential, "a linear time, defined by a succession of instants," that maps onto our initial definition of modernist thought as itself connected to a linear, marching present. Narrative time, argues Ricoeur, is public time and in some cases can be mapped onto chronological time. The problem is with individual memories that, in turn, disrupt this "grand narrative." Ricoeur argues that memory does not follow a linear trajectory but instead loops back on itself, disrupting time.

> Memory, therefore, is no longer the narrative of external adventures stretching along episodic time. It is itself the spiral movement that, through anecdotes and episodes, brings us back to the almost motionless constellation of potentialities that the narrative retrieves. (1980, p. 186)

In this chapter, I examine the spiral movements of memory as disruptive meaning generators within homes and within collaborative discussions with children and artists in schools. Time, I argue, is a tracer for disruptions and disturbances. As a heuristic for studying meaning making within families and across generations, time is itself a tracer for the postmodern moment. By disrupting taken-for-granted conceptions of time and space, I argue, from Scheurich and Young (1997), that it is possible to mount an epistemological challenge against Western, often racist constructions of identity and selfhood.

I also want to address space as a similar, related tracer within family narratives. Space has been understood from Lefebvre (1991) as socially constructed. Lefebvre describes different kinds of space:

- *Perceived space* includes people's everyday spatial practices.
- *Conceived space* can be understood as the framing of space through people's ideologies.
- *Lived space,* from Leander and Sheehy (2004), is space that the "imagination seeks to change." It can be found in spaces where meanings are generated that draw on both perceived and conceived space but are wrought anew from these spaces.

By seeing space as something not given but made, it is possible to interrogate space as bifurcated with discourses of power (Scollon & Scollon, 2003). Space is semiotically constructed through discourses and practices. Scholars working with space as a category tend to question, for example, the way in which adults define space for children (Lawn & Grosvenor, 2005) and how space is constructed often not with children in mind but around the needs of adults. New methodological tools such as visual and participatory methodologies to listen to children's spatial and embodied experiences are helpful as a way of disrupting taken-for-granted concepts of space in institutional settings (Clark, 2010). Likewise, methodological and theoretical tools that look at time differently account for ways in which children, for example, are simultaneously "in the moment" and also in the process of "becoming" as their "being status" is aligned to particular temporalities (Dillabough, 2009; Uprichard, 2008).

Drawing on some data from recent ethnographic projects, I will explore everyday conceptions of space and time in home and school settings. Methodologically, ethnography is a good way of identifying moments, where, as Agar (1996) says, a "rich point" opens up in the data, a "gap" between two worlds that exposes new ways of understanding. Agar's perspective enables an understanding of the "emic" concepts that emerge from the field, informing the researcher's perspective so that, rather than bring a full theoretical perspective to the table, we can develop, as Barbara Rogoff has identified, an "etic" approach that is derived from the "emic" (Rogoff, 2003). It is this "derived etic" approach I am trying to present here.

The first set of examples is from two ethnographic studies of home narratives, both funded by the Arts and Humanities Research Council, UK. With an artist, Zahir Rafiq, and a museum curator, Andy Pollard, I conducted a participatory research project between 2006 and 2007 that was an ethnographic study of five families in Rotherham, UK, resulting in a community exhibition of objects and stories (see Pahl & Pollard, 2010; Pahl, Pollard, & Rafiq, 2009). In order to build up an understanding of these objects and stories, the research team conducted a series of ethnographic interviews in homes with informants. The later study I describe, "Writing in the Home and in the Street," was a collaborative project with the department of English at Sheffield University and the Department of History at Leeds University, together with three creative artists, Steve Pool, Zahir Rafiq, and Irna Qureshi. It ran from October 2010 to the end of November 2011. Both projects were funded by the Arts and Humanities Research Council, (AHRC) UK—one through the Diasporas Migration Identities research project and the other through the AHRC's Connected Communities research project. These examples principally look at space.

The second set of examples comes from a two-year ethnographic study of the impact of three artists on children in a school in a former mining village called Thurscoe, in South Yorkshire. The project, "A Reason to Write," focused on the children's reasons to write in relation to different interventions by the artists. The project was funded by Cape, UK. The project involved an intervention in which three artists were invited to spend two years working across the school, along with the author and Steve Pool, the Creative Agent, that is, a person who is asked to support the work of the artists in the school and to encourage teachers and artists to work together collaboratively. (For more on this project see Pahl & Pool, 2011). The artists included a photographer, a musician, and a visual artist. In the second year, the children conducted a participatory research project with me, which had as its focus what the children thought was important in terms of school and creativity. These examples principally look at time.

'I Have Served My Jail Sentence': Space as Subjectively Constructed

Living Your Life in an Area

> he [her grandfather] lived in Pakistan and moved to Karachi and I was born in Ferham and I lived in Ferham all my life up till now, and my grandma you reminded me she had been there all my life, but, we have been there, my granddad was in the army and then they moved to Karachi and then they moved somewhere else and different parts of England, and my grandma because it is such a close community and she gets on with everyone around here she talked about moving but she would never do that now, you would think she would want to move back to Pakistan where she was born, they have got houses there, you know everyone wants to make a fresh start but she doesn't like the idea now, although she was born there, I think the area, Ferham in itself, she wouldn't like to move out of there now, I feel I am part of this area now.
> (interview with Mariam, a British Asian woman, December 13, 2006)

Knocking Down, Family and Identity

> When he came over my dad, because obviously my mum was over there . . . when he ended up bringing my mum my brother came and my cousin, we were around the same age, his brother's son, he brought him over as his own son as it were and he sort

of stayed with him and he raised him accordingly and they've got great memories of how they were living even right down to . . . you know where—Park is now they have knocked all the houses down as you go down the dual carriageway, that's where we used to live just over there, as you go down you take a right K——Road and go down there and the houses back off and toilets would be at the rear. (interview with Jaan Khan, August 16, 2006)

Moving House and Moving Home

AMINA: *It's taken me back to my family, I have lived here 15 years I have served my jail sentence. I shouldn't . . . I don't leave the house, you lose your parking space if you know what I mean, it's affecting the girls, I am afraid for them to get off the bus and walk on their own they walk up this way, past the shop.*

KATE: *Where is the new house?*

AMINA: *J——Street.*

TANYA: *(daughter age 8):You can see on the computer!*

KATE: *Street View.*

AMINA: *J——Street.*

TANYA: *We can go and see it mummy! I want to go! We could go on Street View.*

AMINA: *You can have a drive round.*

KATE: *Is it the other side of the motorway?*

  . . .

AMINA: *My dad was just exactly the same—it's shocking I was her age, all eight of us, we had the bathroom outside, my dad used to bath us, me mum and dad used to bath us, all eight of us, in a steel bath and then my dad bought a house in James Street when I was her age.*

TANYA: *(She stands up and faces the settee. She stretches out her right arm, and as she says this she points, her finger moving from left to right. At each point she describes a relative/neighbor.) I am going to see my grandad's house, my grandma's there, and then there is next-door neighbor and next-door neighbor and next-door neighbor and then it's our house, it's a blue one, and it's all ruined.* (Audio recording with Amina, a British Asian woman, and her daughter Tanya, 8 years old, November 22, 2010)

All of the people telling me about their experience of space and place were talking about one area of Rotherham, called Ferham, an area of Victorian terraced housing in the center of the town, which has a settled population of Pakistani heritage families. While two of the interviews took place in 2006 and one in 2010, the theme was the same, family stories and narratives in the context of the migration of Pakistani heritage families to the area from Pakistan in the 1950s and 1960s. The issues in each of these excerpts was where was "home" and the role of memory in constructing "home" (Tolia-Kelly, 2004).

In these episodes, space and time are conceptualized in relation to the subjective identities of the people telling me their stories. In the first example, the idea of "home" and "place" is redefined through the experience of migration, making "home" a complex but at the same time settled space (Tolia-Kelly, 2004). In the second example, the son remembers the houses that are no longer there; however, the memory and description are mixed up with a memory of his cousin being raised as his father's son. In the third example, "home" is a moment of return to an earlier self. Amina, who is British Asian but with a heritage from Pakistan, starts by telling me her house is a "jail sentence." Her daughter, Tanya, tells me we can see the house on Street View via Google Earth. Amina then loops back, in Ricoeur's terms, to a description of herself at the same age as her daughter, buying a house at the same time. In these accounts we can see the "loop" of memory disrupting the "grand narrative" of migration (Ricoeur, 1980). Epistemologically, we have to pay attention to the moving and dialogic space that is "belonging" for Amina. Amina challenges her conception of the space she then inhabited; talking of the racism she experienced in her neighborhood, she says, "I have served my jail sentence."

Scheurich and Young (1997) argue that "Modernism is an epistemological, ontological and axiological network or grid that 'makes' the world as the dominant western culture knows and sees it" (p. 7). They argue that it is a racist epistemology. An epistemological challenge to a modernist view of time would account for and recognize the oppression that these families experienced as migrants when they came to Rotherham; while only Amina names it, the families all allude to the "here" and the "there" and the displacements they experienced when moving from Pakistan to Rotherham. Scheurich and Young suggest that these epistemologies, both modernist and postmodernist, fail to take account of the lived realities of people of color. By interrogating these epistemologies, we begin to challenge the "logics of inquiry" that are themselves "the social products and practices of the social, historical experiences of Whites, and, therefore, these products and practices carry forward the social history of that group and exclude the epistemologies of other social groups" (Scheurich & Young, 1997, p. 8).

What these episodes tell us is that the experience of moving continents, of moving house, of growing up in a new space is episodic and circular and that, as Ricoeur (1980) observes, it "loops back." As Mariam circles around her grandmother's desire to stay put and Jaan describes his father's house that no longer exists, and Amina returns to her childhood home at the point when her daughter is the same age, there is a sense of returning, as well as loss. Intergenerational experience is evoked powerfully in each of these bits of talk.

What are the implications of these realizations?

- Family time is spatially and temporally located but is subjectively constructed.
- Meanings are linked to emotions ("I have served my jail sentence").
- Space is mediated both in real space (knocking down) and in virtual space (Street View on Google Earth).
- Grandparents, parents, cousins, and neighbors are all embedded within these times and spaces.

In my recent work I have used Tim Ingold's (2007) work *Lines* to look at the lines across and between different experiences. Just as Tanya moved from the talk about the new house to asking to look at the house on Street View, the spatial connections across these oral narratives need to be unpacked and considered more carefully. I argue that a subjective understanding of what is "known," drawing on these accounts, needs a new, more shared epistemology to make sense of the spaces of postcolonialism and diaspora.

Living Your Life because It's the Only Life You've Got: Deconstructing Time in a School Context

I am now going to move to a school and to an "out of time" experience in school time. These bits of talk were recorded at the end of a two-year research project. Steve Pool, who was at that time working as the Creative Agent in the school, and I had worked with a small group of young people in order to find out what was important to them. I used ethnographic, visual, and participatory methods to find out what the children were interested in. The five young people spent a year collecting data and then sifted through it to select key episodes. Steve Pool and I recorded the discussion the young people had about the images (Pahl & Pool, 2011). The episode they were most keen on was an image of Declan, dancing (see Figure 3.1).

FIGURE 3.1 Declan Dancing

Photograph by Kate Pahl. Used with permission.

KATE: *What is important about the picture of Declan dancing?*
COURTNEY: *It is children learning to not fight, put all the stuff together and make one nice picture.*
KATE: *Thank you.*
COURTNEY: *It's not about being good all the time at school it's about spending your life in school because it is the only chance you've got.*
KATE: *You said something else about drama and in between. . . .*
COURTNEY: *When you are in drama you can act out but you can also act out in school it's about spending your life, and it's is not just about drama you can just live your life.*
KATE: *Across the school day.*
COURTNEY: *Yeah.*

In this episode, Courtney identifies the way in which "spending your life" involves school. Courtney realizes, in a space such as Thurnscoe, with limited educational and job opportunities, that school is "the only chance you've got." However, she also identifies that while you can (legitimately) act out in drama, you can (less legitimately) act out in school. This acting out can be constructed as "naughty," or it can be a way of expressing an art form, a drama. In this she neatly sums up the dilemmas she is presented with; she can identify the image of Declan dancing as being about "acting out" (naughty) or about "acting," which is legitimate creative expression. School allows for only a part of what Courtney is wanting to do—outside school she is "living her life." Courtney's chronotope, her timescales, are longer, more serious, and more expressive than those held within the school (Adam, 1990).

Out of school time is constructed through the landscapes and timescales of childhood. The subjective immediacy of Robbie's response reveals the enduring friendship that Robbie has with Declan:

KATE: *Robbie, say why it is an important photograph for you, because this is me and Steve's article—they are going to co-write it with us, by the way.*
ROBBIE: *It's just, it's just, it's weird, it's funny, he's me best mate.*
STEVE: *Come on, tell us then.*
ROBBIE: *He's like Alvin off er, off er Chipmunks.*
STEVE: *(laughs) Right.*
                                    (Transcription Gooseacre, Wednesday, May 19, 2010)

When we explored why Declan was so important later in the discussion, Robbie said this:

ROBBIE: *Do you know when I met Declan?*
STEVE: *When did you meet him?*
ROBBIE: *I think it were in his old house he used to have dummies [stuffed animals], he used to always have his dummy until he was seven.*

Steve Pool and I then asked the children to come to the university to help us write an article about this process (Pahl & Pool, 2011). While the young people were not especially keen on writing an academic article, they discussed further the process of selecting the key piece of data for discussion.

ROBBIE: *Before it, Declan he said, let me video you, he said no, I went to take picture,*
Declan danced like that, I took a picture, it went all blurring so we deleted
that one, we were going to do loads so we could like just place finger and make
it into a video/
Steve Pool animation
A: *We were all like messing about Declan started dancing.*
R: *It's a good picture though I like the picture.*

(Transcription Gooseacre, July 13, 2010)

Reflecting on Declan dancing here are some key thoughts, based on analysis of the conversation:

- Declan dancing is about the interpretations put on activity—is it acting up or acting out?
- Declan dancing is a moment outside the school day, an in-between space where nothing was scheduled.
- The interpretation came out of a epistemological space shared with the artist, Steve, myself as researcher, and the children, and was recorded.
- Declan dancing taps into the longer lives of the children; Robbie and Declan have been friends for years, and their friendship is outside school.
- Declan dancing is also about drama, music, and meaning making.

In this episode, there were different versions of time and space jostling each other. There was "living your life" and "living the life you lead in school," which offered two different accounts of lived time. There were also two different spatial understandings: "acting up" (being naughty) and acting as a professional spatial practice.

The children collected more than 100 short clips, using FLIP videos and still cameras, and out of this plethora of data only two episodes, the one of Declan dancing and the episode in the playground, were selected. In a video captured as a still, Robbie captured the intensity of playground time, and this was also one of his favorite episodes (see Figure 3.2).

The video shows a rush of noise and children running away from the camera, with Robbie shouting, "You're being videoed! You're on Tele!" It lasts less than 30 seconds.

This episode again catapults us into a different rhythm, a different tempo, as Adam (1990) puts it, whereby pace and speed are much faster than classroom pace and speed. This provides a window into the epistemological "knowing" of the children and their own internal rhythms. Steve Pool and I, with the children,

FIGURE 3.2 Still of Video

Video still by Kate Pahl. Used with permission.

realized that the process of doing the project opened up the epistemological spaces the children inhabited as well as offered us a shared epistemological space we could explore further (Pahl & Pool, 2011). Time and space are artifacts of our epistemologies. This is something that we need to understand when working in communities where there are diverse students, who may have migrated from a number of different countries. Our own interpretations of time and space, whether structured by school time, our own home time, or historical time, need to be challenged if we are to take these epistemologies seriously.

What Are the Implications of Deconstructing Time and Space for Literacy Education?

We need to understand the process of learning in terms of multiple timescales (Burgess & Ivanic, 2010). The strongest version of time, according to Adam (1990), is "clock time," but in the episodes we have described, the complexity of the children's experience becomes more visible. School time, as shown, contrasts with "living your life." Also, spatial dimensions need interrogating. The spaces that the informants, who provide an "emic" perspective (Heath & Street, 2008), allude to in the interviews cross continents but come close up when describing neighbors, relatives, and friends.

How Can We Listen to "Emic" Notions of Time and Space?

I think we need to construct a *listening methodology* that enables us to hear the "out of time," "living your life" talk that takes place in the in-between spaces of home and school. Janet Maybin (2007) talks of children's talk "under and over the desk." Les Back talks of the "art of listening" (2007). Clark (2005) talks about "beyond listening" and the ways in which it is possible to listen constructively to young children to create change (Clark, 2010). Our ways of listening also need to rest on nonlinguistic conceptions of the world, including *sensory and embodied understandings* of what is going on (Mason & Davies, 2009; Pink, 2009) These entanglements can go beyond a notion of what is "real" and "known" under the terms of realist social science. I have found it useful to work with artists (Pahl et al., 2009) as a way of creating ways of "knowing" (Eisner, 2008) that go beyond the empirically grounded. We also need to connect objects found in the world to the stories our informants tell us about them. In our book (Pahl & Rowsell, 2010), Jennifer Rowsell and I argue that an *artifactual-literacies approach* opens up a way of listening to everyday experience that reverses notions of value that are taken for granted. Just as time is often seen just as chronological, we rely too often on a kind of materialist, consumer-driven notion of objects. By listening to objects as a way of unsettling conventional concepts of value and importance, we also disturb time and space. Place, likewise, is a local and storied resource for learning (Comber, 2010; Pink, 2009). By understanding place and space to be experientially constructed, we can shift our understandings of narrative.

Once we have done this, we can create some interrogations. In our book, *Artifactual Literacies* (2010), Roswell and I asked educators to think about the following in relation to objects:

- What is an object's value, and how can we engage students in disputing consumer notions of value in the marketplace?
- What is an object's timescale, and how is it related to value and historical events, as well as to personal events?
- Where is the object located within space, including both local and global spaces, cultural spaces, and public and private spaces?
- What is the history of the object's production, and how was the artifact produced?
- What mode is the object contained within, and how can we engage students in a discussion of its feel, shape, color, and aural dimensions and of which mode is most dominant in the artifactual experience?
- What is the relation of the object to institutions of power, and which discourses materialize in the artifact? How do particular ideologies surface in the artifact? (Pahl & Rowsell, 2010)

This retheorizing of hierarchies of value that we explored in *Artifactual Literacies* can also be extended to a retheorizing of time and space in educational settings. I would argue that we need an epistemological frame that fits the social history of those we teach (Scheurich & Young, 1997, p.10). If we are teaching those who have migrated from somewhere else, those who inhabit spaces where the jobs have gone, and the postindustrial landscape is bleak, as it is in South Yorkshire, UK, we need to take account of their conceptions of time and space. This might involve a dissolving of settled spaces whereby "Ideas, images, discourse itself, are now to be viewed as a material force that dissolves the conception of a human world as a series of divisions" (Cooper & Burrell, 1988, p. 105). We might have to draw on a much embodied, moving conceptualization of time and space; as Ingold (2011) articulates, "lives are led not inside places but through, around, to and from them, from and to places elsewhere" (p. 148). This process, which he calls "waymarking," dissolves the settled materiality of time and space to focus instead on the *experience* of moving through time and space.

What Are the Implications for Literacy Education?

In all of this, I have not really talked about writing or reading, although there are literacy practices embedded within the examples I gave you. Tanya wanted to go on the computer and look up her house on Street View and provided for me an example of a home literacy practice that involved a digital literacy experience. "Declan Dancing" was an example of the creative expressive arts that could be called "Drama." Must of the research I did with the young people was about their reasons to do things, including their reasons to write. But, in both cases, the primary experience of text was oral discourse.

But what I am describing is foundational to literacy education. It is about the meanings we ask our students to create in the classroom. We need to listen to our students' internal maps, as Tanya describes:

> I am going to see my grandad's house, my grandma's there, and then there is next-door neighbor and next-door neighbor and next-door neighbor and then it's our house it's a blue one and it's all ruined.

What kind of writing should Tanya be doing in school? Map making, or telling the story of each of her neighbors or relatives in each house? Perhaps her narrative could be spatially located?

Robbie's engagement with his friend Declan could emerge in a life narrative of Declan, where by his friendship is entangled with the "messing about" that they both engage in, perhaps in a dramatic form.

ROBBIE: *It's just, it's just, it's weird, it's funny, he's me best mate.*
STEVE: *Come on, tell us then.*
ROBBIE: *He's like Alvin off er, off er Chipmunks.*

The image of Declan dancing could become the starting point for a dramatic encounter.

Final Thoughts

In the work I have been doing, both for the AHRC "Writing in the Home and in the Street" project and for the "Reason to Write" project in the school, I have been working collaboratively with artists. This has meant that I have developed these ideas in collaborative ways and that these are shared thoughts that I present in this chapter. Eisner (2008) has argued that this kind of collaborative inquiry is intellectually exciting; however, he also writes:

> To encourage such activity will require a modification of promotion criteria that are typically employed in most American Universities, particularly in research Universities. We typically expect pre-tenure productions to be solo, yet in the hardest of the sciences, physics, work is very often collaborative. . . . What this suggests is a new conception of who does research with whom and what kind of research they do. The vision I am describing is considerably more collaborative, cooperative, multi disciplinary and multimodal in character. (Eisner, 2008, p. 10)

Likewise, spaces that take the epistemologies of young people seriously might need to rethink the grand narratives that I have been discussing and unsettle the taken-for-granted theoretical edifices, residing more directly in the in-between moments of shared understanding that move in and out of the institutional and hegemonic spaces of school.

A model of inquiry that is collaborative and that links with socially engaged arts practice (Kestor, 2004) can create a space of improvisation where modes of being and doing, the customary, the "habitus," can become a space for improvisation. This space of practice can be genuinely collaborative; young people, artists, teachers, and researchers can work to exchange meaning making using a variety of modes, including film, oral language, gesture, photography, and writing. This means that normative constructs, such as time and space, can be interrogated anew to enable us to recognize more clearly the epistemologies of the people we engage with in educational settings.

References

Adam, B. (1990). *Time and social theory*. Cambridge: Polity Press.

Agar, M. (1996). *The professional stranger: An informal introduction to ethnography* (2nd ed.). New York: Academic Press.

Back, L. (2007). *The art of listening*. Oxford: Berg.

Burgess, A., & Ivanic R. (2010). Writing and being written: Issues of identity across timescales. *Written Communication, 27*(2), 228–255.

Capper, C. (1998). Critically orientated and post-modern perspectives: Sorting out the differences and applications for practice. *Educational Administration Quarterly, 34*(3), 354–379.

Christ, T., & Wang, X.C. (2008). Negotiation of "how to" at the cross-section of cultural capital and habitus: Young children's procedural practices in a student-led literacy group. *Journal of Early Childhood Literacy 8*(2), 177–211.

Clark, A. (2005). Ways of seeing: Using the Mosaic approach to listen to young children's perspectives. In A. Clark, P. Moss, & A. Kjørholt (Eds.), *Beyond listening: Children's perspectives on early childhood services* (pp. 29–49). Los Angeles, CA: Sage.

Clark, A. (2010). *Transforming children's spaces.* London: Routledge.

Comber, B. (2010). Critical literacies in place: Teachers who work for just and sustainable communities. In J. Lavia & M. Moore (Eds.), *Cross-cultural perspectives in policy and practice: Decolonizing community contexts* (pp. 46–57). London: Routledge.

Cooper, R., & Burrell. G. (1988). Modernism, postmodernism and organisational analysis: An introduction. *Organization Studies, 9*(12), 91–112.

Dillabough, J. (2009). History and the making of young people and the late modern youth researcher: Time, narrative and change. In *Discourse: Studies in the Cultural Politics of Education, 30*(2), 213–229.

Eisner, E. (2008). Art and knowledge. In J. G. Knowles & A. L. Cole (Eds.), *Handbook of the arts in qualitative research* (pp. 3–12). Los Angeles, CA: Sage.

Heath, S.B., & Street, B.V. (with Molly Mills). (2008). *On ethnography: Approaches to language and literacy research.* New York: Teachers College Press.

Ingold, T. (2007). *Lines: A brief history.* London: Routledge.

Ingold, T. (2011). *Being alive: Essays on movement, knowledge and description.* London: Routledge.

Jones, L., Holmes, R., Macrae, C., & Maclure, M. (2010). Documenting classroom life: How can I write about what I am seeing? *Qualitative Research, 10*(4), 479–491.

Kestor, G. (2004). *Conversation pieces: Community and communication in modern art.* Berkeley and Los Angeles: University of California Press.

Lawn, M., & Grosvenor, I. (Eds). (2005). *Materialities of schooling. Design-technology-objects-routines. Comparative Histories of Education.* Oxford: Symposium Books.

Leander, K., & Sheehy, M. (Eds). (2004). *Spatializing literacy research and practice.* New York: Berg.

Lefebvre, H. (1991). *The production of space* (D. Nicholson-Smith, Trans.). Oxford: Blackwell.

Maclure, M. (2006). The bone in the throat: Some uncertain thoughts on Baroque method. *International Journal of Qualitative Studies in Education, 19*(6), 729–745.

Mason, J., & Davies, K. (2009). Coming to our senses? A critical approach to sensory methodology. *Qualitative Research, 9*(5), 587–603.

Maybin, J. (2007). Literacy under and over the desk: Oppositions and heterogeneity. *Language and Education, 21*(6), 515–530.

Pahl, K., Comerford-Boyes, L., Genever, K., & Pool, S. (2010). Artists, art and artefacts: Boundary crossings, art and anthropology. *Creative Approaches to Research, 3*(1), 82–101.

Pahl, K., & Pollard, A. (2010). The case of the disappearing object: Narratives and artefacts in homes and a museum exhibition from Pakistani heritage families in South Yorkshire. *Museum and Society, 8*(1), 1–17.

Pahl, K., with Pollard, A., & Rafiq, Z. (2009). Changing identities, changing spaces: The Ferham families exhibition in Rotherham. *Moving Worlds, 9*(2), 80–103.

Pahl, K., & Pool, S. (2011), "Living your life because its the only life you've got": Participatory research as a site for discovery in a creative project in a primary school in Thurnscoe, UK. *Qualitative Research Journal, 11*(2), 17–37.

Pahl, K., & Rowsell, J. (2010). *Artifactual literacies: Every object tells a story*. New York: Teachers College Press.

Pink, S. (2009). *Doing sensory ethnography*. London: Sage.

Ricoeur, P. (1980). Narrative time. *Critical Inquiry, 7*(1), 169–190.

Rogoff, B. (2003). *The cultural nature of human development*. Cambridge: Cambridge University Press.

Rowsell, J., & Pahl, K. (2007). Sedimented identities in texts: Instances of practice. *Reading Research Quarterly, 42*(3), 388–401.

Scheurich, J. J., & Young, M. D. (1997). Coloring epistemologies: Are our research epistemologies racially biased? *Educational Researcher, 26*(4), 4–16.

Scollon, R., & Scollon, S. (2003). *Discourses in place*. London: Routledge.

Springgay, S., Irwin, R. L., & Kind, S. (2008). A/R/topographers and living inquiry. In J. G. Knowles & A. L. Cole (Eds.), *Handbook of the arts in qualitative research* (pp. 83–92). Los Angeles, CA: Sage.

Tolia-Kelly, D. (2004). Landscape, race and memory: Biographical mapping of the routes of British Asian landscape values. *Landscape Research, 29*(3), 277–292.

Uprichard, E. (2008). Children as "being and becoming": Children, childhood and temporality. *Children and Society, 22,* 303–313.

4

USES OF COLLECTIVE MEMORIES IN CLASSROOMS FOR CONSTRUCTING AND TAKING UP LEARNING OPPORTUNITIES

Margaret Grigorenko, Marlene Beierle, and David Bloome

One way that students and teachers think about themselves and others as situated in time and space is through the process of collective remembering. Within any group and as part of the process of acting as a group, past events are brought to bear in a present context through public narrativization. These conceptions of the past and their application to a present or future context provide an interpretive frame from which students and teachers engage in classroom interactions. We contend that such rememberings are an inherent part of the social construction of learning opportunities in classrooms. The social construction of collective memories in classrooms requires that collective memories be publicly declared, publicly acknowledged, and acted upon and that they have consequences for defining students' learning opportunities.

In this chapter we report findings about collective memories from one language arts classroom that was part of a larger study (Bloome, Beierle, Goldman, & Grigorenko, 2009). The findings here illustrate the following three constructs:

Students and teachers utilize collective memories to hold each other accountable to procedural expectations and to past events or texts that relate to current topics of study;

Students and teachers use collective memories as part of the process of socially positioning each other; and,

Students and teachers use collective memories to construct situated epistemologies that direct the academic content and practice within the context of the school and classroom.

How We Are Defining Collective Memory

Conceptions of time are social constructions that inform the way that people view the world as well as how they view their positions and roles in society.

The ways that people metaphorically divide their lives into time periods or the ways that people consider themselves moving through time influence the ways that they conceive of the world and thereby impact how they interact with time, space, and others within time and space (Bakhtin, 1981).

Wertsch (2002) discusses how groups of people develop ways of thinking about themselves and others as situated in time and space through the process of collective remembering. This kind of remembering is often considered to be history, but Wertsch problematizes that idea by noting that history is considered to be a comprehensive record of past events, while collective remembering is the act of narrativing events that happened in the past and that are being remembered in the present for a particular purpose. In discussing what historians do, Lotman (1990) points out that representing past events is not a transparent recording process but is mediated by the ways that the events are narrativized and made public:

> The historian cannot observe events, but acquires narratives of them from the written sources. And even when the historian is an observer of the events described (examples of this rare occurrence are Herodotus and Julius Caesar) the observations still have to be mentally transformed into a verbal text, since the historian writes not of what was seen but a digest of what was seen in narrative form. . . . The transformation of an event into a text involves, first, narrating it in the system of a particular language, i.e., subjecting it to a previously given structural organization. The event itself may seem to the viewer (or participant) to be disorganized (chaotic) or to have an organization which is beyond the field of interpretation, or indeed to be an accumulation of several discrete structures. But when an event is retold by means of language then it inevitably acquires a structural unity. This unity, which in fact belongs on to the expression level, inevitably becomes transferred to the level of content too. So the very fact of transforming an event into a text raises the degree of its organization. (Lotman, 2002, p. 14)

Zerubavel (2003) elaborates on the ways that collective memories intersect with what he terms "timescapes" or "sociomental topographies" of the past. Zerubavel explains how the collective memories of groups impact the present:

> A *socio*mental topography of the past helps highlight this pronouncedly social dimension of human memory by revealing how entire communities, and not just individuals, remember the past. . . . In transcending strictly personal recollections, the sociology of memory effectively foregrounds what we come to remember as *social beings*. While there are many memories that we share with no one else, there are specific recollections that are commonly shared by entire groups. . . . Indeed acquiring a group's memories and thereby identifying with its collective past is part of the process of acquiring any social identity. (Zerubavel, 2003, pp. 2–3)

Acknowledging a collective memory is one way that people signal their membership within a particular collective. People use collective memories to contextualize actions, to claim and assign social identities, to construct knowledge and establish epistemological claims, to structure social relationships among individuals, groups, and institutions, and to enact and respond to a broad range of social and cultural agendas.

Following these conceptions, we define collective memory as a narrative that is publicly declared and for which there is public accountability. Collective memories are narratives about past events that are acknowledged by the members of a collective (in this case the teacher and students within a classroom), and to which the group members respond. These narrativized past events may have happened or may be imagined; nonetheless, members of the collective hold one another accountable for acting in ways that acknowledge these collective memories as representing events that have occurred and that matter in the present and future. In this chapter, we are interested in how collective memories are used in classrooms and, in particular, in the construction of learning opportunities.

We are using the term "learning opportunity" to refer to a social event in which a person or people are positioned to adopt and take up a set of social and cultural practices associated with academic domains (cf. Rex, 2006). Following Bakhtin's (1981) discussion of appropriation, we define a learning opportunity as an event that provides the space for participants to take up the narratives and discourse of others. Although a learning opportunity may implicate participants in learning, it is not the same thing as learning.

Methodology

The research study in which we have been engaged is oriented toward the use of thick descriptions and microethnographic discourse analysis to generate theoretical constructs about the use of time (time as process) in classrooms (cf. Bloome, Carter, Christian, Otto, & Shuart-Faris, 2005). The corpus of data consists of daily audio- and video-recorded language arts events that captured one complete unit in three language arts classrooms: a ninth-grade urban classroom, a sixth-grade suburban classroom, and a third-grade rural classroom.

Normally occurring classroom activities were audio- and video-recorded, then transcribed with the talk being parsed into message units. Each message unit was analyzed for time references, including verb tenses, deictic references, lexical references to time, memories, time-scale references, and intertextual and inter-contextual references. We then looked for connections (both explicit and implicit) that teachers and students constructed across the lessons. In addition, field notes and samples of student work were collected.

Analysis showed that references to time and conceptions of time were multiple and ubiquitous. The teacher and students constructed particular conceptions about the way that they, as well as characters or persons within texts, were moving through time and space. The conceptions of time were made visible when the classroom participants constructed and utilized a set of collective memories to which they referred and for which they were held accountable. Some of these references included previous classroom events, historical events (that were collectively known or that had been collectively experienced by members of the class), popular culture (e.g., movies, music), and previously read texts. By constructing and employing collective memories, students and teachers used certain conceptions of time within particular sets of events to frame how they proposed and interpreted meaning, creating opportunities for students to learn.

While references are made to the grade 3 and 6 classrooms, the transcripts presented as illustrations in this chapter are all from an urban ninth-grade Language Arts classroom. In the class there were 22 students: 9 males and 13 females, 14 White students and 8 African American students. The teacher was Latina, in her third year of teaching, and had participated the previous summer in a seminar on how theories of intertextuality could be integrated into classroom teaching. The unit that we analyzed was the first unit of the year, which had been designed around Sandra Cisneros's book, *The House on Mango Street* (1984). As part of the unit, students read chapters of Cisneros's book as well as other related short stories and poems. In addition, they wrote compositions on teacher-assigned topics related to the text and read their compositions aloud in class. All names used in transcripts are pseudonyms.

Collective Memory, Accountability, and Learning Opportunities

One way that collective memory was used by teachers and students was to hold each other accountable to procedural expectations and to past events, discussions or texts that related to current topics of study. Both teachers and students referred to prior texts or prior instruction, expecting the others in the classroom to remember what they had read, seen, or discussed. Students were expected to make connections between what happened in the past and the current activity and to participate in particular academic activities, such as reading, writing, and discussion based upon their memories. These intertextual or intercontextual connections were a particular subset of what educators refer to as "prior knowledge" since they represented memories that had been brought into the public arena and that were assumed to be shared by all participants. The assumption that members of the class shared certain memories was then used to hold students accountable to procedural knowledge and/or content knowledge. Utilizing these kind of memories, students were given opportunities to connect prior knowledge, practices, and events to new texts or topics, providing opportunities for them to expand their understandings and gain new insights.

An example of how one teacher utilized collective memories in multiple ways to make connections with previously taught content and procedures and to thereby hold students accountable is presented in Transcript 1 (Figure 4.1). In this

Line Number	Speaker	Utterance	Notes
1	Teacher	Well, we've been talking about names and I've been telling you	
2		"Oh we'll write a short story, write a short story"	
3		so here it is	
4		so anywhere you write down your assignments	
5		I need you to write this out.	
6		So everyone get our your planners	
7		and write this on the board right here.	Points to board
8		This is the assignment.	
9		This is the short story.	
10		You're going to be following the mode of "My Name" from *House on Mango Street* as a model.	
11		Write a story on your name.	
12		In this story you will need to include the meaning of your name.	
13		umm	
14		You need to use a simile to compare it as a number.	
15		Esperanza said, "My name is like the number 9," so use a simile.	
16		And here's the, here's the definition of a simile.	Pointing to the board
17		It's a comparison of two things using the work like.	
18		Life is like a box of chocolates.	Line taken from the movie *Forrest Gump*
19	Student	You never know xxxxx.	
20	Teacher	So it's comparing two things.	

FIGURE 4.1 Transcript 1 (8/26)

case, the students had previously read a series of texts connected to the theme of "names," and the teacher had conducted instruction related to language arts content, including simile and short story. Students had been asked to investigate the origin, meaning, and family connections of their names and had written a series of essays. Many of the students had read their essays aloud in class.

In line 1, the teacher temporally frames the discussion by using the past progressive tense to signal that this event is part of an ongoing series of connected classroom events. She refers to a past event and quotes herself, claiming that she has told the students that they will be writing a short story in the future. This dramatization implies students' memories of this past event. This is a faux quote since the teacher never actually made the statement in a previous class, and at best it was a paraphrase of what she had said. But, regardless of the accuracy of her claim, she creates a collective memory by narrativizing the past in the present for the purpose of having students complete a writing assignment. The statement is not a factual description of what occurred in the past, but instead it is an iteration of the past events, presented in a particular way that created a collective recognition of past interactions among the participants and promoted the teacher's educational agenda. Students acknowledged the proposed collective memory by not questioning the correctness of the statement and by meeting the teacher's expectations for their writing.

As part of constructing and elaborating on this collective memory, the teacher makes a series of connections to past events that serve as indexicals. In line 6 she refers to the students' planners which are a tool for remembering information from one time and accessing it in a future time. In lines 7 and 16, the teacher points to the whiteboard, another connector of events over time and a link to prior instruction. In line 7, she refers to the assignment that she had written on the board earlier in the same day in which the lesson was taught. In line 16, she refers to the place on the whiteboard where the definition of "simile" had been written two days earlier and erased after an instructional sequence in which she had taught about the term "simile." The reference assumes that the students collectively remember what had been written there. Further, the teacher evokes collective memories of the previously read portion of *The House on Mango Street* when she reminds students of what the character Esperanza says about her own name. She additionally refers to students' memories of a line from the movie *Forrest Gump* in her example of a simile, connecting not only to their assumed knowledge of the line from the movie but also to the connection to the previous lesson in which she had used the line as a teaching sample.

The function of this constructed collective memory is to create a warrant for holding the students accountable for both content and procedures in being able to complete the assigned short story. In order to meet the teacher's expectations, the students need to know and connect the multiple components (both content and procedural) of the assignment that the teacher assumes to be part of their collective memories. In addition, they need to share the teacher's interpretations of each component. On the one hand, utilizing collective memories becomes a teaching resource by which the teacher can help students make intertextual and intercontextual connections and demonstrate their new understandings. On the other hand, the construction of the collective memory by the teacher assumes that each student has a working understanding of the previously presented issues and shares the teacher's interpretations to the degree that they can be held accountable and given an assignment for which they will be graded. If any student does not or cannot access all components of the assumed collective memory (for example, if the student had been absent from a class or had not viewed the film *Forrest Gump*), that student would be at a disadvantage in being able to perform the requested academic work.

Thus, collective memories are constructed over time in classrooms and utilized by teachers and students to form a shared frame to which new insights or information can be connected. This framework may create an expanding set of resources to provide learning opportunities for students. Collective memories take on moral obligations since they are used to hold participants accountable to certain events, knowledge, and procedures that are assumed to be commonly understood and accepted. The use of collective memories may become problematic if some members of the group do not have access to, do not remember, or choose not to accept or adopt components of the constructed memories to which they are held accountable.

Collective Memory, Social Positioning, and Learning Opportunities

In addition to the purpose just described, collective memories were used as part of the process of social positioning, evident both in discussions of literary characters and in the interactions among members of the classes. A component of the act of collective remembering is the process of coming to think about self and others as situated in particular ways in relation to one another. As part of the process, members of the class used collective memories to define and negotiate social positions of themselves and others on the basis of collective historical memories combined with ongoing interactions.

In the ninth-grade classroom, during one of the class discussions around the topic of names, students engaged in an extended discussion about how historical perspectives can impact one's current social interactions. As part of an extended conversation about names and why someone might choose to change his or her name, Ron expressed the class consensus that certain social markers such as a name can come to take on social value that positions a person.

In Transcript 2 (Figure 4.2), Ron uses a series of contrasting verb tenses and pronoun shifts to express a disconnect between how a person desires to be perceived and how that person is positioned based upon an historical connection. In this case Ron makes an intertextual connection to the movie *The Young Frankenstein* to illustrate his point related to social positioning that may occur on the basis of a collective memory that a group has adopted that assigns negative connotations to certain stereotyped characteristics, practices, or markers. Though this concept was developed and made public as part of the discussion of literary characters in the ninth-grade classroom, the principle was observed as part of the social interactions in both the third-grade and the sixth-grade classrooms as well.

For example, in the sixth-grade classroom, a new student, Kalynn, had entered the class. She was placed in an existing book group. Initially, the members of the group socially collaborated to limit her interactions within the group and did not acknowledge or take up on her contributions during discussion time. At one point, the teacher engaged with the group members and acknowledged an important insight that Kalynn contributed. From that point forward, she was allowed more participation and respect in the group.

Line Number	Speaker	Utterance	Notes
241	Teacher	Ron, what was your comment?	
242	Ron	It was xxxxxxx	
243		maybe some	
244		like your name maybe have like	
245		like someone else might have had this name	
246		and you kinda have a reputation of being what this other person had	
247		cause everyone kind of sees you as that	
248		and what your name actually means doesn't count	
249		cause like this other	
250		like your father	
251		may have been someone like	
252		and you don't want to take his name	
253		like there is a movie for example	
254		*like Franken— the Young Franken*	
255	Student	*/Stene*	
256	Lesley		laughs
257	Teacher	*Steene*	
258		The *Young Frankensteene*	
259	Ron	/like you know	
260		he was like trying to change like xxxxx	
261		the way the name sounded because	
262		xxxxxxx	
263		Frankenstein whatever	
264		You know his father was…	
265	Teacher	So so	
266		there could possibly be that to separate	
267		separate yourself er from some some bad.	

FIGURE 4.2 Transcript 2 (8/25)

In a follow-up interview with the group members, the students expressed that they had collaboratively limited Kalynn's interactions initially because they had associated her with a former student (Deon) whom they perceived to be unknowledgeable and unwilling to participate. By bringing their collective memories of Deon into the interaction and by interactionally categorizing Kalynn as a Deon-type person, they had socially positioned her and limited her learning opportunities. Only when the teacher's comments interrupted their assumptions about Kalynn did the students reevaluate the perceptions that were part of their collective memory and reconstruct the social relations within the group.

Similarly, in the third-grade classroom that was observed by researchers, certain students had come to be labeled as "struggling readers" and as such received differential treatment from their peers. As we observed and interviewed the students, it became apparent that students were using memories from past years, categorizing and positioning one another on the basis of certain social markers including how quickly a student had learned to read, how well the student could perform perfectly rendered word-by-word oral reading, and what books the student read outside class. Though certain students had developed all the reading skills that would allow them to meet grade-level expectations, they were considered and treated as inferior readers by their peers. The classroom teacher worked hard to create collaborative lessons and to monitor student interactions, but it was clear that the form of the activity as conceived by the teacher did not define the substance of the interactions among the students. The classroom participation structures that were selected by the teachers could not account for or control the social dynamics that were part of the peer-to-peer exchanges. In this case, the collective memories that had developed over the course of three school years about some of the students' reading abilities impacted the social relations of the class-room and students' consequent perceptions of themselves as capable and accepted.

In one essay, a ninth-grade student expresses the emotional impact of negative social connotations that were collectively applied to him because of perceptions related to his name. In this essay, which he wrote and then read aloud to the class, Horace makes public the negative social positioning that he perceives to be related to his name and to the socially constructed perceptions that are associated with his name. In Transcript 3 (Figure 4.3), lines 129–130, he states his perception that his name diminishes his significance, giving his name the number 0. In lines 131 and 141, he explains how he is negatively socially positioned and laughed at by his peers, seemingly not related to his performance or character but simply because of social connotations related to his name. He also makes an allusion to the connections that the name Horace made to his father, who shares the name. Horace states that the name's meaning and social implications suited his father but inappropriately label him. This can be assumed to be an intercontextual connection to the discussion about *The Young Frankenstein,* since the essay was assigned shortly following the class discussion in which Ron had discussed the need for some people to distance themselves from a name that had negative connotations. Horace then uses a series of five metaphors and similes to vividly portray the negative and distasteful images that he associated with his name. Horace's declarations in lines 139–141 and 150–152 reveal his awareness of the social weight of the negative perceptions of himself on the basis of a social marker, his name. Horace reveals that he cares about how others respond to his name but that he doesn't show it. He finishes the essay with a rhetorical question that emphasizes the emotional distress that he connects to being differentially treated because of his name. In this essay, Horace gives insights into the social relations that have been established over time within the class and into his perceptions of the social positioning that results from the collectively constructed memories about him as an individual and a student.

Collective memories are constructed over time as part of how a group adopts sets of values in regard to social relations and markers. These values become visible in the ways that certain characteristics, practices, or preferences take on social weight within a group and are viewed as inherently positive or negative. Opportunities for learning may open when naturalized categories implicit in the collective

Line Number	Speaker	Utterance	Notes
125	Horace	My name is Horace.	Reading his composition
126		My name means out of time,	
127		But I have none whatsoever.	
128		My name should be something that means busy or confused.	
129		My name is like the number zero,	
130		no significance.	
131		It just sits there for every other number to laugh at.	
132	Students		Laughing
133	Horace	Xxxxx why I'm really proud to be at the center of everything.	Overlapping with laughter from class
134		My name is like my dad.	
135		Every time I see him he has time to spare	
136		which makes Horace perfect for him,	
137		but not for me.	
138		I should have a name like Terrance, Tim, or Karey.	
139		I care but don't show it.	
140		Why should I?	
141		Whenever my name is called, all the other names laugh at it.	
142		Why where is their xxxx? Where is their xxxx?	
143		Mine tastes like sour milk.	
144		It leaves an aftertaste.	
145		My name, my name is like a ringing in the ear.	
146		It never goes away.	
147		It's like the smell of something that's been dead for three days.	
148		My name is like a scab that runs all the way down your arm and will never go away.	
149		My name looks like a bundle of letters that have no significance whatsoever.	
150		Horace is a name like any other—	
151		like Lisa, like Sam, like John, like Bobby, like everyone else's.	
152		So why should my name be treated any different from anyone else's?	

FIGURE 4.3 Transcript 3 (8/26)

memories with which a group is being conducted are recognized and evaluated. Alternatively, unexamined collective memories may create social positions within a classroom that limit some students' learning opportunities.

Collective Memory, Situated Epistemology, and Learning Opportunities

Finally, collective memories were used to construct knowledge and establish situated epistemological claims that directed the academic content and practice within the context of the school and classroom. The way that participants defined knowledge and evaluated what counted or didn't count as knowledge affected both the content and the practices that defined learning in the classroom.

In all three of the classrooms we observed, teachers and students interacted within the constraints and demands of educational policy and curriculum to construct a particular epistemology that defined how classroom participants approached the study of literary text. Students were expected, in differing degrees, to accept the information expressed by the teacher and the curricular materials and to present their understanding of that material in particular ways in order for it to be counted as knowledge. In all three classrooms, teachers emphasized the need for students to make claims about what they read on the basis of textual content and to defend those claims by citing evidence from the text.

However, in two of the classrooms, teachers exposed students to multiple texts related to their selected topic. They allowed and encouraged students to publicly express personal ideas and experiential accounts that related to the texts, expanding the range of what and whose knowledge was valued. In the cases where those contributions were acknowledged and later incorporated or adapted by the teacher or classmates, the collective memories were utilized as a knowledge resource, thereby creating learning opportunities.

Transcript 4 (Figure 4.4) is an example of the way that the ninth-grade teacher approached textual interpretation with her students.

Line Number	Speaker	Utterance	Notes
133	Student	Is this, is the narrator?	
134		I mean, whose point of view is this from?	
135		Is this the girl's sister or what?	
136	Stephanie	xxxxxxxxxxx	
137	Teacher	How do you know?	
138	Stephanie	Cause she xxxxxx.	
139	Teacher	Find that.	
140	Students		Talking to each other
141	Teacher	Yeah it says,	
142		Umm, well, look on page 81.	
143		It's on the back of the first page.	
144		Do you see where it's the,	
145		it's the paragraph after the break xxxxx?	
146		Do you see that?	
147		Okay, *reading from the text.*	
148		Well, she's asking her a question, and she says xxxx.	
149		Maggie is the sister, and the narrator is the mom.	
150	Student	Okay.	

FIGURE 4.4 Transcript 4 (8/26)

In Transcript 4, the teacher uses a question-and-answer approach to direct students' comprehension of a literary text that the class is collaboratively reading. The teacher asks students to answer factual and/or inferential questions related to the characters, setting, or action in the text *and* to defend those answers by citing or quoting the text. In line 36 Stephanie answers the question of another student, and the teacher responds immediately by asking, "How do you know that?" Even though Stephanie is able to answer the teacher's question (line 138), the teacher requires the student to find evidence for her response in the text. In lines 141–149, the teacher models her expectation for responding to comprehension questions about the text by finding the passage in the text, referring to the page number, and directly quoting the text as defense for her response. This model of asking questions and requiring the students to defend their answers with citations from the text was a pattern that was observed not only in the ninth-grade classroom but in every grade-level class that was observed. However, in some of the classrooms, teachers expanded the written and/or oral texts that were allowed to be included in meaning-making discussions around texts.

Transcript 2 was taken from a segment in which the ninth-grade teacher was using the commonly observed approach to textual comprehension by having students discuss the text ("Everyday Use," by Alice Walker [1973]) by answering questions and finding textual references. In that segment of Transcript 2, however, an opportunity is opened for Ron to bring his knowledge of popular culture (in the form of the movie *The Young Frankenstein*) to bear in the discussion of why a person would change his name. Thus, the teacher creates an expanded opportunity for meaning making by allowing students to make cultural and personal connections to the literary text. In doing so, the teacher creates a space for the students to construct collective memories and to develop a situated epistemology that broadens learning opportunities.

Collective memories, then, serve as part of the way teachers and students establish and maintain epistemologies that expand or constrain the learning opportunities that are made available in classrooms. The organization and demands of the state and institution promote particular understandings of what counts as knowledge and what practices are acknowledged as demonstrations of that knowledge. Though all the teachers we observed were constrained by institutional demands, some of the teachers made choices when structuring the class curriculum to broaden the official epistemological stance by including a wider range of texts and by allowing and encouraging students to contribute to the knowledge set that was valued and acknowledged in the classroom. Thus, the ways that students and teachers constructed and used their collective memories to broaden or restrict what was presented to students for consideration either created or limited students' learning opportunities.

Summary

A number of researchers have examined how conceptions of time are connected to social interactions. Adam (2000) summarized the importance of examining conceptions of time when she stated, "a timescape analysis is not concerned to establish what time is, but what we do with it and how time enters our system of values" (p. 137). This study has presented a set of theoretical constructs related to how teachers and students constructed and utilized one temporal feature, collective memory, to create or constrain learning opportunities. Educational researchers have previously recognized that accountability to school culture, social positioning, and situated epistemology have resulted in differentiated possibilities for students to be successful in school. However, this study gives evidence for *how* teachers and students use conceptions of time more generally and collective memories more specifically to construct learning opportunities in the day-to-day, face-to-face world of language arts classrooms. Microethnographic discourse analysis has made visible the ways that students use language to construct timescapes within classrooms, which in turn establish value systems that extend or limit learning opportunities for students. By examining and recognizing these processes, educators may envision new possibilities for using conceptions of time to expand learning opportunities for all students.

References

Adam, B. (1990). *Time and social theory*. Philadelphia: Temple University Press.

Bakhtin, M. M. (1981). *The dialogic imagination: Four essays*. Austin: University of Texas Press.

Bloome, D., Beierle, M., Grigorenko, M. & Goldman, S. (2009). Learning over time: Uses of intertextuality, collective memories and classroom chronotopes in the construction of learning opportunities in a ninth-grade language arts classroom. *Language and Education, 23*(4), 313–334.

Bloome, D., Carter, S. P., Christian, B. M., Otto, S., and Shuart-Faris, N. (2005). *Discourse analysis and the study of classroom language and literacy events*. Mahwah, NJ: Lawrence Erlbaum.

Cisneros, S. (1984). *The house on Mango Street*. New York: Vintage Books.

Lotman, Y. (1990). *Universe of the mind: A semiotic theory of culture* (A. Shukman, Trans.). Bloomington: Indiana University Press.

Rex, L. A. (Ed.). (2006). *Discourse of opportunity: How talk in learning situations creates and constrains*. Cresskill, NJ: Hampton.

Wertsch, J. (2002). *Voices of collective remembering*. Cambridge: Cambridge University Press.

Walker, A. (1973). Everyday use. In Walker, *In love and trouble: Stories of black women*. New York: Harcourt, Brace, Jovanovich.

Zerubavel, E. (2003). *Time maps: Collective memory and the social shape of the past*. Chicago: University of Chicago Press.

SECTION 2

Timespaces and the Present in Literacy Research

"Flashsideway"

In chapter 1, Saldaña used the term "flashsideway" to refer to times when he stepped out of ongoing action to theorize and contemplate. As we introduce Section 2, we humbly borrow the term *"flashsideway,"* but we use it to reference the present—the experience of being situated within ongoing action that we are forced to contemplate even as it unfolds. In Section 2, we invite readers to consider the timespaces of the present. While the present is continuously fleeting—defying our ability to reflect on the present without it passing before our eyes even as we reflect—we do occupy spaces and times. We act, interact, make decisions, and learn in lived time. While we can never operate outside vectors that draw on the past and the future, this section highlights timespaces of learning in lived time. Everyday experiences constantly occur in classrooms, schools, and in a range of other learning spaces. We cannot help being involved, engaged, and interact with what is around us. Timespaces of the present provide opportunities to be engaged—to act, interact, learn, and live.

5

WRITE ON TIME! THE ROLE OF TIMESCALES IN DEFINING AND DISCIPLINING YOUNG WRITERS

Lorraine Falchi and Marjorie Siegel

Questions about Schooltime

"Why do we have school for 6 hours and 20 minutes?"
"Why do we go to school during the day and not at night?"
"Why do we not have school on the weekends instead of the weekdays?"

From the first day of his first-grade year, Lori's young son, Marcello, has bombarded her daily with questions about "schooltime," a term we use to signify the distinctive temporal organization of schooling. Far from naïve, Marcello's questions point to his awareness of time as a significant dimension of schooling that works in ways he finds puzzling. Schools run on a linear time schedule that is thought to reflect universal norms about children's learning and development, but Marcello has balked at the arbitrary nature of this institutional structure and is learning there are consequences for not living in time with this rhythm.

Across the United States, children are under pressure to produce more in less time and are increasingly held accountable for that work although many children need different pacing. While the "cultural flows" increasingly present in small towns as well as major metropolitan areas across the country affect "the scope of time and space" (Lam, 2006), schools often operate as if literacy development occurred in a lockstep manner with predictable stages (Dyson, 2001). This is especially true for children who are written into policies as the "all" children (Dyson, 2003), a label that carries deficit assumptions about children from nondominant groups. With the passage of the No Child Left Behind Act (U.S. Department of Education, 2002), the rhythm of schooltime has intensified as school districts turn to scripted and paced curricula in an effort to meet literacy standards that reduce literacy to five "core" skills (National Reading Panel Report, 2000) and subtract the multiple languages and literacies children bring to school (see, for example, Dyson & Smitherman, 2009; Zacher Pandya, 2011).

Where are children located within these fast-paced times of contemporary schooling? How do they experience these tight-timed spaces? How are their cultural resources, literate performances, and semiotic artifacts read by their teachers, and what are the consequences of not "writing on time," even in the earliest years? These were some of the questions we grappled with in the course of our yearlong ethnographic case studies of young children's experiences with school literacy, which we undertook at the same New York City public elementary school at different points in time (Falchi, 2011; Kontovourki & Siegel, 2009; Siegel, Kontovourki, Schmier, & Enriquez, 2008). During both studies, we became aware of the daily writer's workshop as a space where the regulatory role of time was especially noticeable and "writing on time" was critical to school literacy success. Like Marcello, some children seemed to be "out of sync" with the expected rhythm of the writing curriculum, which was organized as units of study lasting from 3–8 weeks, each focusing on a distinct genre (e.g., personal narrative, memoir, how-to, nonfiction, fiction). The writer's workshop always began with a brief minilesson, followed by independent writing and then a short sharing time. Children were explicitly taught an aspect of the genre or of writer's craft during the minilesson, with the expectation that they would try out the teaching point when working on their own writing. Yet, we noticed that some children did not always produce the genre that was the focus of the designated unit of study, either in the context of independent writing or in timed writing assessments known as "on demand" writing.

In this chapter, we trace the histories of two young children's texts in order to explore the role of time in defining and disciplining young writers in the social spaces of school literacy during "NCLB time" (Genishi & Dyson, 2009). Doing so offers a way to examine the multiple timescales (Lemke, 2009) at work in the classroom writing curricula, specifically, the yearlong curriculum writing curriculum, individual units of study, and the organization of the daily writer's workshop, as well as the interactions among peers and between the teacher and students. Our analysis addresses questions of how children navigated these timescales, how these timescales framed teachers' readings of the children's textual artifacts and learning, and how these readings contributed to the labeling of some children as "struggling" or "at risk" for school literacy success.

Researching Children's Literacies at School

Literacy and children's literacy learning are changing everywhere except in schools, and it was this tension that led us to study children's lived experiences with a balanced literacy curriculum. As we have noted, school literacy curricula are increasingly framed by a narrow definition of literacy, especially for the "all" children, whose language, social class, race and ethnicity, and nationality are too often read as predictors for school failure (e.g., Snow, Burns, & Griffin, 1998). Yet, researchers argue that these children come to school with a full backpack of knowledge and resources, including multiple languages and literacies that reflect their participation in a new communication landscape, characterized by the global reach of digital technologies; a participatory ethos; multimodality, remixing and hybridity; and the warping of temporal and spatial boundaries (Knobel & Lankshear, 2007; New London Group, 1996).

Each of our studies explored children's lived experiences and social meanings of school literacy in a school with a workshop model of "balanced literacy," but each framed the problem differently to reflect the issues we considered most compelling. During the 2003–2004 school year, Marjorie studied a kindergarten classroom in which children composed with a mouse as well as a pencil to understand how children negotiated the intersection of multiliteracies and the balanced literacy curriculum. Lori's study was undertaken as part of a longitudinal study of children whose families had emigrated from Mexico and spoke Mixteco, an indigenous Indian language. This study was conducted in the fourth year (2009–2010) of the larger study and examined children's participation in a dual-immersion bilingual (English/Spanish) second-grade classroom with a balanced literacy curriculum. The site for both studies was a PreK-5 public elementary school in a predominantly bilingual community in a large metropolitan area. The primary method of generating data in both studies was participant observation of literacy events and practices in the literacy block, supplemented by artifact collection and semistructured interviews with teachers and families. Data were documented in field notes, audio- and videotape, and reflective journals. Data analysis was a multistage process that began with indexing and coding field notes and identification of literacy events as the unit of analysis. Selected events in which focal children participated were transcribed in full and analyzed to identify the cultural and symbolic resources children brought to the writing curriculum, their preferred modes of engagement, and their positioning as students.

Both studies were grounded in multiple theoretical perspectives on literacy and literacy learning, each of which provided a distinct lens through which to frame the problem of study and construct readings of the data. Sociocultural theory foregrounds what human beings *do* as organized in *activities* that are *practiced* by *social* groups. The italicized words suggest that human action is the primary focus of sociocultural theory and, moreover, that these actions are culturally mediated social practices enacted over time within particular cultural, historical, and institutional settings. This suggests a dynamic, reflexive relationship between text and context in which the spotlight is on the actors and their actions with texts (Siegel & Panofsky, 2009). This lens led us to design our studies as ethnographic case studies of children's participation with school literacy that focused on the children's literacies and texts as produced through actions, interactions, and the cultural-historical arrangement of the balanced literacy curriculum. With the shifts in the communicative landscape noted earlier, literacy studies have taken a semiotic turn. Across both studies, we took up a semiotic perspective on literacy that foregrounds sign-making as a generative process involving more than words and recasts texts as multimodal, an "assemblage of signs" (Chandler, 2002, p. 2) of all kinds (e.g., linguistic, visual, gestural, musical). We thus read the balanced literacy curriculum as largely verbocentric in that language was privileged above other modes for making meaning, and treated as the sole access to literacy, an assumption that remains the dominant understanding of early literacy development despite evidence that children take multiple pathways to literacy (Dyson, 2001, 2003).

Until recently, research on literacy education has treated literacy teaching and learning as a neutral practice, reflecting the field's disciplinary roots in psychology. Even with the emphasis given to social practice in sociocultural and semiotic theories, research has been largely silent on questions of power and social injustice. Yet, researching literacy in the starkly inequitable schools of New York City made it abundantly clear that the dominant liberatory narrative about literacy is a fiction. Like other literacy researchers concerned with the ways schools severely restrict what counts as literacy and who can be literate, we read the classroom actions and interactions we documented through a critical sociocultural lens (Lewis, Enciso, & Moje, 2007) that situates literacy learning within sociohistorical and geopolitical contexts and calls attention to the play of power, identity, and agency in literacy curricula. Our interest in time as a disciplinary technique that narrowed children's literacies and identities emerged from this perspective.

Disciplining Classroom Literacy

Discipline has multiple meanings for literacy educators, but the meaning we take up in our analysis of time and school literacy draws on social theorist Michel Foucault's (1995) historical investigations of the rise of disciplines in the 19th century and their role in producing "docile bodies" (p. 135). Foucault argues that disciplinary knowledge produced techniques for regulating human activity, and this control over the body was exercised through constant attention to procedures governing time, space, and movement. Walkerdine (1984) extends this analysis to the development of psychology as a discipline and shows how psychology produced ideas about "normal" child development that came to govern children's bodies. As the emerging fields of mental measurement and child development fused, the idea that children's development proceeds in an unfolding of linear stages was treated as knowledge. Observing and classifying children according to these stages thus became essential early childhood practices. The checklists, classification schemes, and other practices we recognize today as part of informal as well as formal assessments are the very means for exercising control. Walkerdine (1984) thus concludes that school is "an apparatus of regulation and classification . . . founded in *science*" (p. 164). Her point is that the school disciplines the social body not through the imposition of power from above (e.g., the chancellor, the principal, the "state") but through administrative practices that regulate the details of life at school.

Numerous administrative practices were evident in the classrooms we studied. For example, when the kindergarten class gathered in the meeting area for morning meeting, shared reading, minilessons, and sharing sessions, children were expected to sit on their assigned rug square in a "perfect magic 5" (legs in a pretzel, hands in lap, mouths closed, eyes forward, ears ready to listen). The main bulletin board was covered with schedules and charts indicating the daily schedule as well as job charts, calendars, and other artifacts the teacher used in the routines that kept order. Time and space disciplined children's bodies throughout the day. Children knew where they could and could not go and at what times of the day. They sat on the rug for morning meeting and moved to their table groups only during independent writing; there were assigned reading spots, and if children had been assigned to an early invention program, they were sent out in the hall to work with the paraprofessional. Centers for science, block building, dramatic play, and art making were available only during the afternoon choice time.

The writing curriculum was also organized by time, and teachers often referred to the unit plan for each genre study as the "calendar" that set the pace for children's writing. The 40-minute writer's workshop was further divided into a 10-minute minilesson at the rug, 20–25 minutes of independent writing at tables, and a brief sharing session back at the rug. Children were expected to try out the strategy introduced in the minilesson in their own writing, while also keeping track of the various texts they had produced or were working on across the timeframe of the unit. Across both classrooms, formal (e.g., writing "on demand") and informal (e.g., running records) assessments as well as individual reading and writing conferences provided the teacher with knowledge of the children's literacy development that informed decisions about what to teach as well as how to classify children (e.g., as "struggling" or "successful"). In these ways, children were disciplined and learned to discipline themselves without the force of explicit coercion.

Timescales and School Literacy

Understanding how schooltime disciplined children's engagement with school literacy requires more than noting the division of time in the writer's workshop or the pacing calendars for units of study. Conceptualization of time depends on how it is framed and by whom. Lemke (2000b) notes that all phenomena can be conceived as dynamic processes interacting within disparate timescales, and therefore a single timescale of human activity cannot offer a satisfactory or complete explanation of the processes. The central problem, he argues, is how humans make meaning across multiple timescales:

> A process or experience that takes minutes is very different from one that takes hours, or from one that takes weeks, or years, etc. This concept of

> relatively independent timescales in turn problematizes the ways in which
> humans do in fact integrate or cumulate meaning, experience, or identity
> across vastly different timescales. (Lemke, 2009, p. 143)

In highlighting the integration of meaning across different timescales, Lemke
offers a way to examine children's experience of time in the classrooms we studied. Within the writer's workshop, what appears to be a single timescale—the
accumulation of brief amounts of time devoted to a minilesson, independent writing, and sharing—consists of timescales of briefer, faster activities (e.g., uttering
a word, participating in a dialogue, following along while a teacher demonstrates a strategy). Yet, Lemke argues, these brief activities in a short timescale
do not simply add up to produce the meaning of a process on a long timescale.
Rather, the "events more remote in time [on a long timescale] may be more relevant to a present here-and-now than are events more recent in time," a process he
calls "heterochrony" (Lemke, 2000a, "Multi-scale Analysis of Ecosocial Systems,"
para. 15). This suggests that children must navigate different timescales in the context of school literacy, as do teachers as they read children's artifacts, development,
and literacy learning. However, the image of a longer timescale folding back on
a shorter timescale means that long timescales, such as the yearlong writing curriculum or a child's history of participation in school, may be more consequential
than those of a single interaction in the writer's workshop.

Semiotic artifacts, such as the texts children produce during the writer's
workshop, serve to mediate multiple timescales by circulating through the network of timescales. These "artifacts (i.e., books, buildings, bodies) . . . enable
coordination between processes on radically different timescales" (Lemke, 2000b,
p. 275). How children design these texts and how teachers read them thus
become critical dimensions of understanding the way timescales of school literacy discipline children's writing. What happens when children design texts
that represent meanings through images but few words or when they remix
family memories and personal reflections with retellings of classic fairy tales? In
what follows, we explore the space of the writer's workshop by examining how
children's semiotic artifacts coordinated multiple timescales, and what meanings
these coordinations had for the children and their teachers.

Tracings of Children's Writing across Timescales

In this section, we trace the writing of Jewel and Rebeca, young girls whose families had immigrated from Bangladesh (Jewel) and Mexico (Rebeca), respectively.
Starting with their textual artifacts, we examine show how these texts mediated different timescales and how time acted as a disciplining force in the writing curriculum where "good habits" were employed as a "disciplinary technology"
along with "time tables" and specific "rules of document use" (Chouliaraki, 1996,
p. 106). Both textual tracings also point to the subtractive ways these children were

positioned in school literacy assessments, due to their preferred resources (modes, languages) and writing practices but also their social location as children whose families were recent immigrants to the United States, speak a language other than English, have incomes below the poverty line, and do not possess the social and cultural capital that White middle class families generally bring to schooling.

Jewel Navigates Fiction Writing (Marjorie)

At the end of the year I spent in Jewel's monolingual kindergarten classroom, Jewel's teacher described her as a "real kindergartner" who needed time with tools and manipulatives rather than pen and paper. Jewel had entered kindergarten with an identity as a "silent" child, so it was notable that her teacher pointed to her oral-language growth (in English) as her primary achievement at the end of the year. During the writer's workshop, Jewel could often be observed leaning over, her head close to her paper, pen in hand, silently drawing images in the unlined upper half of her paper but writing few letters and words aside from her name, unless prompted. In the computer lab, however, Jewel seemed like a different child. She sat up straight, adjusted the screen to her liking, and made full use of the features of the KidPix program to create diagrams, maps, and pictures, sometimes even offering advice to a child in need of help. From a multimodal lens, Jewel used the available tools (paper, screen) to tell stories through pictures and to show understanding through diagrams, but without enough words, her texts did not meet the expectations for school literacy.

As noted earlier, the writing curriculum was organized in genre studies. Children began the year writing personal narratives, before moving on to how-tos, poems, and nonfiction. In May children were finally allowed to write fictional stories, a genre that was initially discouraged in favor of personal narratives on the assumption that children would be better able to revise if they had firsthand knowledge of the narrative events. On the first day of the fiction genre unit, the teacher announced that starting today, they could make up their own stories. She asked for examples of characters, emphasizing that the character needed to do something that wasn't real. The first example offered was "the cat in the hat," a favorite with the class. When the children were sent to their tables to begin independent writing, Jewel began drawing a figure she called "the cat in the hat" and then added butterflies. When I asked her about her character, she told me she was "doing the cat in the hat." Her teacher then came to confer with Jewel and asked about her character. After thinking a while, Jewel answered "the cat in the hat." The teacher asked if she was making her own story of the cat in the hat (they could use a familiar character but were expected to create an original fictional storyline). Jewel did not respond, and, when the teacher left, she continued drawing. The following day, when I asked Jewel about her "cat in the hat" story, she told me it was a picture of her letting the butterflies go, a transformation that may have been inspired by the events of the morning, when the children noticed that the butterflies they'd been observing had emerged from their chrysalises.

When Jewel finished her picture on the front of her page, she turned to the back and drew a figure. The character wore a crown on her head, and Jewel added more details and talked about her drawing in a very quiet voice. I asked if she has drawn herself and her sister, and Jewel eventually turned to the camera to say that she had drawn her brother and that they were all in the park because it was his birthday. Then, before independent writing ended, she chose a new sheet of paper, drew an image, and told me that the cat in the hat came to her house. Here we begin to see the way her text becomes a material object that links longer-term and shorter-term processes. Lemke (2000b) continues:

> The material characteristics of the object also function as *signs* for an inter-preting system of meanings that belong to processes on a very different timescales than that of the event in which the interpreting process is taking place. (p. 281)

The shorter-term and longer-term timescales that seem to operate in this example are the short-term processes of the fiction unit and the longer-term processes of the yearlong writing curriculum. Jewel's texts link these two differ-ent timescales by serving as a sign of her identity as a writer in this classroom. On the shorter-term timescales of the fiction unit, she must demonstrate that she can write an original fictional story using characters from an existing fiction story. But her overall identity as a writer is linked to her performance as a writer across the longer-term scale of the entire writing curriculum. We could move to an even shorter-term timescale and consider the way the three texts she produced on the first day of the fiction unit link the 10-minute minilesson with the 20-minute independent writing period and, further, how the brief exchange between Jewel and her teacher (an act of conferring) is linked to the longer-term timescales of independent writing and the mini-lesson. Yet, as Lemke (2000b) points out:

> Rather than a short timescale even having long-term consequences ... we can have the case of heterochrony, in which a long timescale process pro-duces an effect in a much shorter timescale activity. This is a very common phenomenon is human social activity. I believe it is the basis for human social organization across timescales. (p. 280)

What he seems to be describing here is the way time produces meanings within a cultural, historical, and political system such as a school writing curricu-lum. As he notes, the semiotic meaning of the material text is an effect not simply of accumulating shorter timescales into a longer one but of the longer timescale giving meaning to a shorter timescale activity. This is why the historical tracing of Jewel's texts begins with her positioning as a "silent" child. Before she enters the kindergarten, she is read as "not ready," and, as the following episode demonstrates, her ability to make connections across the genre units is read as a sign of a struggling writer. Yet, this misreading not only serves to discipline her literate practice and limit who she can be as a writer but ignores her efforts to link different timescales across the arbitrary boundaries of the curriculum.

The next day, Jewel designed a detailed drawing the she described as a narrative about her family life. When her teacher asked her if the story was "made up or real," Jewel admitted it was real. She was told she needed to add a fictional character to her story since they were now writing "made up" stories. A week later, Jewel created another drawing in which her fictional character was a butterfly. When her teacher asked what kind of trouble the butterfly would get into, Jewel narrated the life cycle of the butterfly, a link back to the nonfiction writing about frogs she and her partner, Terrance, had done two months earlier. Jewel's texts can thus be read as an "intertwining of ongoing trajectories" (Comber, 2011), a phrase that captures the complexities of Jewel's lived experience in the classroom and suggests the way different timescales were intertwined within a single text to define her as not yet literate in the present and at risk for literacy success in the future.

Rebeca Remixes a Fairy Tale (Lori)

Rebeca and her friends usually spoke Spanish to one another, although her home language was Mixteco, an indigenous language in areas of Mexico. She participated in literacy activities in both English and Spanish in her dual-language classrooms, where they also used a balanced literacy program that adheres to a reading and writing workshop model. The program uses a system of leveled books, and Rebeca was not considered to be decoding or comprehending books at her second-grade level. Rebeca's writing was often considered less than satisfactory and assigned a 1 on a rubric of 1–4, which led teachers to feel anxious about her reading and writing. Despite the dominant view of her reading and writing work, Rebeca happily participated in the activities, especially when she was able to collaborate with friends.

One fall morning, Rebeca sat at her table of four people, reading a mixed-genre story, *Wolves* (Ramsey, 1999), which references the fairy tale *Little Red Riding Hood*. After quite a few pages of her reading, I asked if she knew the story of *Little Red Riding Hood*, and, because she did not, we found and read it. Nearly a month later, she engaged me in reading the same text by asking, "Do you remember this?"

Several months later, in her other classroom, where she learned in Spanish, Rebeca was asked to write a story on demand as a final assessment of what she had learned in a unit on fairy tales. She created a piece called "Caperosita Roja y el Lobo" [Little Red Riding Hood and the Wolf] in response to a read-aloud. The teacher had read *Caperucita Roja, Verde, Amarilla, Azul y Blanca* [*Little Red Riding Hood, Green, Yellow, Blue, and White*], and other alternate versions of Little Red

---

Caperosita Roja y el Lobo
(in correct order of pagination)* Por Rebeca
[Little Red Riding Hood and the Wolf by Rebeca]

Page 1: un dia una caperosita estaba caminando por el bosque y derepente vino el
tiegre dijo y dijo te voy comerte niña dijo tigre. Y yo me gusta eso cuento del mi
historia y lo coji eso historias del mio
Page 2: despues se corrio a disir que paso con ella porque estar gritando dijo la
abuela y el tigre rombio la la casa con su piern
Page 3: y coji mos el telefono y dijimos que lleva a la carse para todos los dia y nuea
no sale cuando cuando ella estaba jugando.

Page 1: one day a little riding hood was walking in the forest and suddenly a tiger
came the tiger said and said I am going to eat you girl said the tiger. I like this story
of my story and I picked this story of mine
Page 2: after she ran to tell what happened to her screaming she said to the
grandmother that the tiger broke the house with his leg
Page 3: and we picked up the telephone and we said that they should come to take
him to jail for the rest of his days and then he did not get out when she was playing.]

* In Rebeca's original story, pages 2 and 3 were stapled out of order.

Note from the teacher, Ms. F.: Muy bien Rebeca, escribistes mucho y tu historia
tiene elementos de los cuentos de Caperucita pero tienes que leer lo que escribes
para que tenga sentido.
[Very good, Rebeca, you wrote a lot and your story has elements of the little riding
hood story but you have to read what you write so that it makes sense.]

FIGURE 5.1 Rebeca's Version of "Caperosita Roja y el Lobo" with Feedback from
Her Teacher

Riding Hood stories where several story elements were different from those in
the popular versions of the tale. Figure 5.1 presents the version of the story that
Rebeca generated.

Rebeca and her classmates were introduced to the genre in their unit of study
within the constraints of a curricular calendar. For example, during a minilesson
in their unit of study on fairy tales, they were told they would have 15 minutes
to make up their villain and protagonist (fieldnotes, January 19, 2010). Children
were to include a story mountain, wherein the protagonist meets a villain, there
is a problem, and a solution is found. They were prepared to be "good readers"
or "good writers" during minilessons, which meant they would need to read or
write within specific norms.

Rebeca was often described as a less-than-successful writer. Here I examine
her aforementioned writing, an artifact she created about a girl and her grandmother battling a wolf. In tracing that artifactual history, I analyze the artifact
and its hybrid nature, identifying sources across timescales for various aspects of
the piece.

Three weeks to the day before writing her on demand piece about a girl and her grandmother, Rebeca had told me a story about her own grandmother, a vivid moment of personal history:

> Rebeca wrote, "Yo voy a ser un coracon de para mi abuela del mi mama." [I am going to make a heart of for my mother's mom, my grandmother.] She said that she had died. I asked her when it was, and she said, "Hace tiempo." [A while ago.] And she told me she had blood on her forehead. She asked me if I wanted to know how she died, and, when I said yes, she told me that she had been dancing when she was pregnant and then died in childbirth. (fieldnotes, February 9, 2010)

As she had never met her grandmother, she told me what she had heard through family stories. Whereas the genre of fairy tales for this unit of study was based in an oral tradition, it was converted into a written genre using unilinear time within the narratives. Rebeca shared her story orally and, after their time to share had concluded and her teacher received her work, she stapled the two final pages out of order.

Rebeca created a remix in her narrative; however, according to the criteria of the "on demand" writing (an assessment practice), there were details and elements that were missing, as well as certain elements that were not appropriate. Her voice in her writing was not deemed to be coherent because of her interjection of asides such as "I like this story of my story and I picked this story of mine." Her hybrid text—a product of her thinking in the fairy tale genre—constructed a modern-day heroine with a cell phone that she used to call while on the road. While Rebeca, an emergent bilingual, and her peers may require scaffolding to achieve the expected academic results, attention was not given to her purposeful literacy practices of book language and her hybridized version of the fairy tale where the young girl initiates an arrest. Rebeca's measurable outcome indicated that she was not a "good writer"; that is, she had not met the curricular benchmark. This definition of Rebeca as a less-than-adequate writer in that specific genre (fairy tales) repeated the often-perceived narrative of her as an unsuccessful writer across the curriculum.

What is missing in this assessment of Rebeca as a writer is the ways her story exists within the timescales of her life. Her story of her own grandmother never surfaces, while the mythical grandmother of Riding Hood overcomes the tiger and saves her granddaughter with her cell phone. The relative strengths of Rebeca's writing, including her story language (e.g., "for the rest of his days") and the challenges Rebeca faces to convey the idea that the tiger kicked the house ("the tiger broke the house with his leg"), deny the timescales in which the story was created. The familial timescales of a child whose grandmother had died in child-birth, the timeline of being a second-language learner who is working to acquire the language she needs to convey the ideas that are in her head, and the timeline of the on-demand task and its rubric that will prove her inadequacies limit the possibility that Rebeca can be described as anything but a struggling writer.

Discussion

In studying children's participation in literacy activities and practices in a local community, we began to see how children negotiated schooltime. Children's participation, practices, and resources over and across longer timescales illuminated their navigation across timescales; semiotic artifacts such as the children's writing were part of complex, dynamic processes in systems where signs and meanings were read and interpreted and played a part in the social life of children in schools. Tracing children's writing across timescales makes visible the expectation that the focal children were to write "on time" as well as the disciplinary techniques for doing so. Here we discuss a tension that existed around schooltime as it served as a disciplinary technique through adherence to rigid schedules. These rigid schedules within fast-paced units ignored the complex navigation across timescales that writing in the space of a writer's workshop required. We begin by noting that the children's writing was disciplined by the way teachers read the texts in relation to a short timescale rather than the longer one. Although the children (and we as ethnographic researchers) had the long view and treated all the genres studied as a resource, they were disciplined by the teachers' focus on the shorter timescale of the particular genre unit. The teachers' readings thus appear to contradict Lemke's argument about heterochrony, that is, the impact of longer timescales on here-and-now events. In the case of Jewel, her texts were read as a case of the wrong genre at the wrong time, when they could have been read as mediating across multiple timescales. Similarly, Rebeca's text was not only misstapled but misread as lacking coherence. The teacher did not necessarily see the nuances of Rebeca's writing, such as the fact that she did not seem to know the word for "kick" in Spanish, her second language, nor did the teacher note the powerful book language at the end of the narrative. Instead, the teacher focused on the nonlinear quality of this narrative, as it did not conform to the expected structure (story mountain, cohesive ties) of the genre. Successful performance in the writer's workshop meant treating each genre unit as a distinct timespace that, while invisible, set the pace, sanctioning certain writing as acceptable and exerting authority on teachers and children.

As the girls moved across multiple timescales, they navigated them in relation to their multiple identities and symbolic resources (languages, modes, genres), as well as the longer timescale of the entire year's writing curriculum. Thus, we take up critical sociocultural perspectives to complement a focus on timespace in theorizing the processes in which production of social space takes place during diverse timescales. In analyzing data on focal children like Rebeca and Jewel, we used timescales to examine how each had been framed and produced by an "at-risk" narrative since her entry into school. While the children exercised agency within their school settings, their own sense of time collided with the linear time of scope, sequence, and the calendar year. The pacing calendars did not match up to the ways in which these children, both emergent bilinguals, were developing and changing as multilinguals. Disciplinary techniques such as school assessments and records classified them as not literate or as "at risk" for literacy success in the future. Increasingly, children are framed not just as "at risk" to themselves; in "NCLB time," they are positioned as liabilities to the school's own track record and trajectory as a "good" or successful school, producing students who are recognized as successful writers. Both personal and institutional identities are then linked by the social interactions and processes that are constructed in complex ways, integrated across timescales, as authoritative and sanctioned or in need of remediation.

References

Chandler, D. (2002). *Semiotics: The basics*. London: Routledge.

Chouliaraki, L. (1996). Regulative practices in a "progressivist" classroom: "Good habits" as a "disciplinary technology." *Language and Education, 10*(2&3), 103–118.

Comber, B. (2011, February). Assembling literacy repertoires: Placing teachers' work in time and space. Workshop presented at the annual meeting of the National Council of Teachers of English Assembly for Research, Madison, WI.

Dyson, A.H. (2001). Writing and children's symbolic repertoires: Development unhinged. In S.B. Neuman & D. Dickinson (Eds.), *Handbook of early literacy research* (pp. 126–141). New York: Guilford Press.

Dyson, A.H. (2003). Popular literacies and the "all" children: Rethinking literacy development for contemporary childhoods. *Language Arts, 81*(2), 100–109.

Dyson, A.H., & Smitherman, G. (2009). The right (write) start: African American language and the discourse of sounding right. *Teachers College Record, 111*(4), 973–998.

Falchi, L. (2011). Emergent bilinguals: Multiple literacies in changing contexts. Unpublished doctoral dissertation, Teachers College, Columbia University, New York.

Foucault, M. (1995). *Discipline and punish: The birth of the prison* (2nd ed.). New York: Vintage.

Genishi, C., & Dyson, A.H. (2009). *Children, language, and literacy: Diverse learners in diverse times*. New York: Teachers College Press.

Knobel, M., & Lankshear, C. (Eds.). (2007). *The new literacy sampler*. New York: Peter Lang.

Kontovourki, S., & Siegel, M. (2009). Discipline and play with/in a mandated literacy curriculum. *Language Arts, 87*(1), 30–38.

Lam, W.S.E. (2006). Culture and learning in the context of globalization: Research directions. *Review of Research in Education, 30*, 213–237.

Lemke, J. (2000a). Multiple timescales and semiotics in complex ecosocial systems. Paper presented at the International Conference on Complex Systems (ICCS 2000), New England Complex Systems Institute, Nashua, NH. Retrieved on February 15, 2014, http://academic.brooklyn.cuny.edu/education/jlemke/papers/NECSI-2000.htm

Lemke, J. (2000b). Across the scales of time: Artifacts, activities, and meanings in ecosocial systems. *Mind, Culture, and Activity, 74*(4), 273–290.

Lemke, J. (2009). Multimodality, identity, and time. In C. Jewitt (Ed.), *The Routledge handbook of multimodal analysis* (pp. 140–150). New York: Routledge.

Lewis, C., Enciso, P., & Moje, E. (Eds.). (2007). *Reframing sociocultural research on literacy: Identity, agency, and power*. Mahwah, NJ: Lawrence Erlbaum.

National Reading Panel (2000). *Teaching children to read: An evidenced–based assessment of the scientific research literature on reading and its implications for reading instruction: Reports of the subgroups.* Washington, DC: National Institute for Child Health and Development.

New London Group. (1996). A pedagogy of multiliteracies: Designing social futures. *Harvard Educational Review, 66*(1), 60–92.

Ramsey, J. (1999). *Wolves.* New York: The Wright Group.

Siegel, M., Kontovourki, S., Schmier, S., & Enriquez, G. (2008). Literacy in motion: A case study of a shape-shifting kindergartener. *Language Arts, 86*(2), 9–18.

Siegel, M., & Panofsky, C.P. (2009). Designs for multimodality in literacy studies: Explorations in analysis. In K. Leander, D.W. Rowe, D. Dickinson, R. Jimenez, M. Hundley, & V. Risko (Eds.), *58th National Reading Conference Yearbook* (pp. 99–111). Oak Creek, WI: National Reading Conference.

Snow, C., Burns, M.S., & Griffin, P. (1998). *Preventing reading difficulties in young children.* Washington, DC: National Academy Press.

U.S. Department of Education. (2002). *No Child Left Behind Act of 2001.* Retrieved on February 15, 2014, www2.ed.gov/policy/elsec/leg/esea02/index.html

Walkerdine, V. (1984). Developmental psychology and the child-centered pedagogy: The insertion of Piaget into early education. In J. Henriquez, W. Hollway, C. Urwin, C. Venn, & V. Walkerdine (Eds.), *Changing the subject: Psychology, social regulation, and subjectivity* (pp. 153–202). London and New York: Methuen.

Zacher Pandya, J. (2011). *Overtested: How high-stakes accountability fails English language learners.* New York: Teachers College Press.

6

HOW MOMENTS (AND SPACES) ADD UP TO LIVES: QUEER AND ALLY YOUTH TALKING TOGETHER ABOUT LGBTQ-THEMED BOOKS

Mollie V. Blackburn and Caroline T. Clark

The relationships among times, spaces, and lives are integral to what Lewis and del Valle (2009) identify as the third wave of literacy and identity research. This third wave is distinct from the first two, the first of which is grounded in a notion of identity as stable and unified and the second of conceptualizes identity as negotiated and performative. The third wave, however, offers an understanding of identity as "hybrid, metadiscursive, and spatial" (p. 316). Although this third wave resonates with our ideas of and experiences with identities, we grapple with what it means, both conceptually and empirically, for identities to be hybrid, metadiscursive, and spatial. We understand this exploration as one with longevity, so even though we understand the three characteristics—hybridity, metadiscursivity, and spatiality—to be intricately intertwined, for the sake of understanding them better, we have pulled them apart and will address only one in this chapter. We imagine that we will eventually pull them together again, but this pulling together is beyond the parameters of this essay. Here we focus on what it means for identities to be spatial.

When Lewis and del Valle (2009) talk about identity as spatial, they describe it as both "enacted (in time) and placed (in space)" (p. 318). Following their lead, then, we, too, take up the concepts of both space and time. We draw on de Certeau (1984) to understand space as a "practiced place" (p. 117). He exemplifies the distinction between place and space in these ways: "the street geometrically defined by urban planning is [a place] transformed into space by walkers" (p. 117), and, more abstract but also more related to our focus, "an act of reading is the space produced by the practice of a particular place: a written text, i.e., a place constituted by a system of signs" (p. 117). Talburt (2000) expands on de Certeau's distinction between place and space by describing *place* as "an order of distributed relationships, location, and fixity, such as a given culture to be transmitted, an interpretation to be learned, or defined skills and methods of reasoning to be acquired" and space as "emergent, incomplete, and unpredictable" (p. 19). *Places* exist in and of themselves, but *spaces* are places brought to life.

Lemke (2000), however, asserts that the "'spatial' view is incomplete, and indeed is not . . . the fundamental view needed to understand complex systems, especially human ecosocial systems" (p. 274). It's worth pausing for a moment to consider what he means by ecosocial systems, to see if it fits what Lewis and del Valle (2009) are talking about. He defines ecosocial systems as people and things that one makes meaning about and with over time. Integral to ecosocial systems are "socially meaningful interactions" (p. 283). Moreover, he conceptualizes a "self-conscious personal identity" (p. 283) as a system, since a person cannot be understood apart from his or her context or in any single moment in time. So, Lemke's critique of the limits of the spatial apply as we grapple with understanding identity. He proposes that attention be paid to time, which we do here. We return, however, to space at the close of this chapter.

To pay attention to time, Lemke argues that the "fundamental unit of analysis is a process" (p. 275). To focus on a process means attending less to who someone is and more to who that person is becoming. According to Lemke, focusing on process requires attention to timescales by asking: What is happening within a particular timescale? and "How are processes integrated across different timescales?" (p. 275). By timescales, Lemke means the number of seconds a particular process takes, so, for example, the timescale associated with the process of an exchange between people might be anywhere from 1 to 10 seconds, but the timescale for, say a semester or school year might be 10^8, or, even more dramatic, that for evolutionary change might be 10^{14}. In the other direction, the timescale associated with a vocal articulation is 10^{-1}, or less than a second. (I am drawing on Lemke's calculations here.) The importance of recognizing various timescales is, in part, to acknowledge the simultaneous occurrence of and dialogic relationship between both small and large timescale processes, such as, say, a single utterance and social change, but also to facilitate thinking about how material objects link short-term and long-term processes, which he calls "heterochrony." Heterochrony, as he uses it, is the "intersection of processes and practices which have radically different inherent timescales" (Lemke, 2008, pp. 25–26). So, for example, a book written in or about an era different from that lived in by those reading it can mediate heterochrony. Or, an older person talking with a younger person and reflecting on his or her experiences as a youth can also mediate heterochrony. Understanding the connections across timescales allows us to understand how "moments add up to lives" (Lemke, 2000, p. 273).

That is Lemke's (2000) question: "How do *moments* add up to *lives?*" (p. 273). We are particularly interested in how moments mediated by LGBTQ-themed texts add up to the lives of queer and ally youth together.

Seeking Answers

Our current project focuses on a long-term book discussion group that emerged from an ongoing teacher inquiry group. The inquiry group, the Pink TIGers (Blackburn, Clark, Kenney, & Smith, 2010), began meeting in August 2004 and has met monthly ever since. The focus is combating homophobia and heterosexism in classrooms and schools through literature and film. National Council of Teachers of English's Research Foundation was generous enough to support the work of this group for several years. Pink TIGers read together LGBTQ-themed texts and imagined reading them with their students in their schools. Some Pink TIGers read such texts with their students, but many insisted that they simply couldn't do it because of experienced or anticipated homophobia, particularly from their students' parents and administrators. As an alternative, we started a book discussion group.

The group was proposed in the spring of 2006 and began in the autumn of that same year. Pink TIGers brought queer and ally students, typically from their Gay Straight Alliances, to the local center for LGBTQ youth to select, read, and discuss LGBTQ-themed books that we were able to purchase for the students. The group met 20 times over the course of 3 years to talk about 24 texts. During that time, 32 people participated, 22 youths and 10 adults. Of these participants, 22 were female, 8 were male, and 2 were transgender (female to male). Six participants identified as lesbian, 8 identified as gay, 16 identified as straight, and the 2 transgender participants both identified as female attracted. Of the participants, 26 were White, three were African American, and three were biracial.

These identity markers, however, are just a sort of shorthand to provide a sense of group members rather than definitive statements about them. We recognize that they fail to capture the complexity and fluidity we witnessed and experienced with the members of the group and are incompatible with Lewis and del Valle's (2009) third wave of literacy and identity research. Still, we use them because we know the identities those markers represent matter in the material lives of group members and therefore provide significant information in coming to understand the students. Such material consequences are apparent in many group members' experiences with the heterosexual matrix, which Butler (1990/1999) conceptualizes as the omnipresent and invisible rules and regulations that rely on and reify dichotomous notions of males and females, men and women, and masculinity and femininity and demand that desire be experienced across these dichotomies, that is, between men and women.

During the book discussion group sessions, though, we worked together to create a space in which the heterosexual matrix existed but was actively critiqued through the selection, reading, and discussion of LGBTQ-themed literature. The meetings were audiotaped and those audiotapes were transcribed. These transcripts are the basis for the study we discuss here. For this study, we focused on youth in particular. Therefore, we immediately narrowed the data by focusing only on youth participants. In an effort to study time, or people talking over time, we then identified those who participated in the largest number of meetings over the longest periods of time. We were committed to studying both a queer and an ally participant, so we then categorized the most active youth participants accordingly. We call the most active queer participant Liz, who self-identified as gay and lesbian, and the most active ally participant Melissa. Liz attended 12 meetings over 1 year and 3 months. Melissa attended 18 meetings over 2 years and 9 months, which was the entire duration of the book discussion group. This data set allowed for a focus on what Lewis and del Valle describe (2009) as youth's processes for discursively bringing identities into being.

We turned to Lemke and his idea of timescales to inform our analysis. Lemke (2000) asserts, "It is useful to analyze scale hierarchies in groups of three levels at once" (p. 276) because processes at any given level are interdependent on those above and below. With that in mind, we focused on exchanges (which he calculates as lasting anywhere from 2 to 10^2 seconds), discussions (lasting $10^{3 \text{ or } 4}$ seconds), and the periods of the participants' involvement in the group (ranging from 10^7 or 10^8 seconds). Lemke advises that researchers, when studying dynamical systems, such as these two participants, across timescales, ask:

- "What processes, what kinds of change or doing, are characteristic of each relevant timescale of organization of the system/network? And
- How are processes integrated across different timescales?" (Lemke, 2000, p. 275)

To address the first question, we analyzed transcripts looking for *processes* in exchanges, discussions, and the collection of discussions across the periods of involvement by the two focal participants. Because of our particular interests, we focused on processes related to queer and ally identities. In an effort to explore the second question, we went back to particular moments that allowed for heterochrony. That is, we looked for places in the transcripts where short timescale processes produced effects in much longer timescale activities and vice versa (Lemke, 2000, p. 280). Thus, we worked to understand how these two youth, across these three timescales, were be(com)ing gay, lesbian, and ally together through reading and discussing LGBTQ-themed literature in queer-friendly spaces over time.

Be(com)ing Gay and Lesbian: Liz's Processes

Liz came to the group as a high school junior, and the group ended just after she was graduated from high school. Focusing on the 15 months of Liz's participation in the book discussion group reveals Liz's processes of be(com)ing gay and lesbian. Within those processes were processes at the discussion level and, in turn, at the exchange level. Of course there were processes at both larger and smaller timescales, but these three are the focal timescales for this chapter. Within these timescales, we observed Liz be(com)ing gay and lesbian overtly, which we discuss first, but then also more subtly as she explored her relationships with homophobia, with allies, and with the heterosexual matrix.

Liz explicitly constructed herself as gay and/or lesbian in almost every meeting she attended. She constructed herself as gay, more generally, by being distinctively interested in gay-themed stories; connecting with gay characters, particularly gay narrators; and reading from the point of view of a gay person. For example, Liz, who was often a very discriminating reader, sometimes loved books that others in the group considered to be of lesser quality. These books shared the quality not only of being LGBTQ themed but also of having a lesbian or gay narrator. This came up in our discussion of *The Geography Club*. At first we, as a group, were carefully critiquing it, quite aware of the fact that it had been recommended by one of the group members. Then one group member said sarcastically, "I thought it was great," and then seriously, "No, I didn't like it." This prompted group members to characterize it as juvenile, generic, bland, and stereotypical. At this point in the conversation, Liz walked into the meeting. There were brief introductions before a return to the book discussion, which Caroline prompted by asking whether Liz had read the book. Liz said she had and was "so sucked in by it." Caroline expressed surprise, and Liz explained, "I'm a sucker for these kinds of books." She recognized it as "crappy" but continued with how she much she liked it. When pushed to explain why, she talked about connecting to the gay narrator. She said:

> Because that's how I felt in middle school, like, I was like, "I'm like totally alone in this. There's no one here," um, so it's kind of like that. . . . And the sneaky like, "let's form a club, like, let's get together" kind of thing. Yeah. And our high school reality, I know.

By connecting so intensely with this book and this narrator and by drawing on her own experiences to do so, Liz constructed herself as gay.

Liz explicitly constructed herself as lesbian, as distinct from gay, most often in our discussions about lesbian-themed books. She did so by imagining herself as lesbian characters, becoming invested in characters in lesbian relationships, and becoming decidedly interested in lesbian authors and actors but also by wondering about and thus distinguishing herself from gay men. For example, in our discussion of *Fried Green Tomatoes at the Whistle Stop Café,* a young gay man in the group said he had less interest in female protagonists and would be more interested in the book "if it was two guys in a relationship." The relationship he referenced was between the characters Idgie and Ruth, two women who met, fell in love, raised a son, and ran a restaurant together in the 1920s and '30s in a small rural community in Alabama. The couple enjoyed relative acceptance, and the group was discussing whether their acceptance hinged on their assuming heterosexual-like roles; that is, Idgie was in many ways masculine and Ruth feminine. Caroline wondered aloud whether the story could have happened with two guys as the central couple, and the same young man stated plainly that it "would not work." Liz began imagining what it would look like for two men to mimic a heterosexual relationship and considering that the assumption of a more feminine role by one of the men would only draw more homophobia. Thus, Liz's curiosity about gay men and the homophobia they experience, at least as we discussed them, helped her to distinguish herself as lesbian.

Liz also constructed herself as gay and lesbian by exploring her own relationship to homophobia. Her processes included both knowing homophobia and learning about homophobia. She conveyed her knowledge of homophobia when she acknowledged the challenge of starting a Gay Straight Alliance at a local school, anticipated trouble as a homophobic storyline unfolded, and adored a righteous character who lives in fear. She also, though, strove to understand homophobia. For example, in our discussion of *The God Box,* Liz talked about being excited to learn about Christianity-based homophobia, something that has always baffled her, as both Jewish and lesbian. She said the book

> clarified things that people have said to me like, yeah. People, like, just spit out these bible verses like they do in this book, and I don't know how they do it, but I've always wondered, but I mean, I had them, directed toward me and some of them I recognized in here, and I'm like, "oh, well, that's why you think this kind of thing."

She even empathized with a homophobic character, explaining that the character "had a lot of fear in general" and that she was afraid of anything unfamiliar to her, including LGBTQ people. Thus, even though Liz knew homophobia, she worked to understand it better.

Another way that Liz constructed herself as gay and lesbian was in relationship to allies, although she did this only in her first meeting, when we discussed *The God Box.* Immediately Liz expressed an intense reaction to an ally in the book: the main character's father. Although the father had struggled to come to terms with his son Paul being gay, when Paul was insulted by their church, his father defended him publicly. Liz said, "There was a part that, like really just moved me . . . it was the dad . . . the church . . .that made me cry, yes . . . I don't know what, it was just, like, so sweet and just right." Later, in that same discussion, she wished aloud that she had an ally in her family like Paul's Abuelita, who acknowledged and accepted Paul's relationship with another boy. In other words, Liz valued the role of the allies in the literature we read and discussed and wanted such allies in her life.

Probably the most complex processes in which Liz engaged were about her positionings relative to the heterosexual matrix, which she interrogated while recognizing its material significance. She interrogated it, for example, when she asked, in the context of discussing *The Color Purple,* what makes a lesbian book lesbian. She described Shug, a character who has sex with both men and women, as just sexual, rather than heterosexual, homosexual, or bisexual. Just because she problematizes it, though, does not mean she does not function within the heterosexual matrix; she does. This was particularly evident in our discussion of *Written on the Body,* a novel in which the narrator's sex and gender are artfully concealed, something with which Liz actively struggled. She said,

> then they [characters in the book] go and talk about like the narrator had past relationship with a woman, and then they're talking about a past relation- ship with a man, and then the man went and had a relationship with another man. So I wasn't sure like how to take that and like was that, were you a woman with that man? I don't know.

This provoked discussion about when readers interpreted the narrator how and why. Ultimately, in this exchange, Liz said, "The entire book like I was going back and forth. It was like there is no way I cannot think about this." In other words, whether the narrator was in same-sex or opposite-sex relationships mattered very much to Liz. Just because the heterosexual matrix effectively dismissed Liz as a lesbian did not mean that she could live her life outside it. Instead, she had to work within and against it, as she did in the book discussion group.

To be clear, we are not suggesting that everyone who was interested in gay- themed stories and connected with gay characters was or was becoming gay. Nor are we saying that everyone who imagined herself as a lesbian character, became invested in characters in lesbian relationships, and was interested in lesbian authors and actors was or was becoming lesbian. And it was not only gay and lesbian participants who expressed interest in learning more about homophobia or in having allies. And certainly functioning within and against the heterosexual matrix is not limited to gay and lesbian people. This study is not an attempt to nail down the intricacies of gaydar. Rather, here, we are arguing that Liz's processes, as we describe them here, at the levels of exchange and discussion, discursively brought her into being as gay and lesbian. That is, this collection of moments led up to her life, at least this portion of her life, be(com)ing gay and lesbian.

Be(com)ing an Ally: Melissa's Processes

Melissa had just started high school when the group first started meeting, and she had just concluded her junior year when the group ended. Focusing on the 33 months of Melissa's participation in the book discussion group reveals Melissa's processes of be(com)ing an ally. Within those processes were processes at the discussion level and, in turn, at the exchange level. Within these timescales, we observed Melissa be(com)ing an ally in relationship with LGBTQQ people and characters and in relationship with allies in her life and in literature. She also constructed herself as an ally by positioning herself as not-homophobic and not-heterosexist and ultimately, as a continuous learner.

Melissa constructed herself as an ally by associating and empathizing with LGBTQQ people. She associated with LGBTQQ people by participating in her school's Gay Straight Alliance and sharing close friendships with LGBTQQ people. That she empathized with LGBTQQ people was evident in our discussion of Bo, a flamboyant young man in the novel *Finding H.F.*, when she said that she underlined a section of the text that described Bo's angry and homophobic father because, in her words, "I was thinking of how hard it must be for Bo." Her associations with and empathy for LGBTQQ people and characters fostered her identity as an ally.

Melissa also constructed herself as an ally by recognizing other allies and identifying with them, again, in both her life and in literature. She described ways that her mother and sister were supportive of her commitment to LGBTQQ communities, for example, but she also identified with allies in the books we read and discussed. In our discussion of *The God Box,* Melissa, like Liz, applauded Paul's father for not "freak[ing] out" and supporting his son in their church. Much earlier, in our discussion of *Perks of Being a Wallflower,* the group was talking about a scene in which Patrick, a gay character, kisses Charlie, the straight narrator. Melissa explained, "I think Charlie was just kind of letting Patrick. It's his friend, so he was just kind of . . . trying to help him feel better, so he just let him." In these ways, Melissa constructed herself as an ally by connecting to and identifying with other allies.

Melissa also constructed herself as an ally by positioning herself as not-homophobic, a position she asserted at almost every discussion she attended. She did this by rejecting homophobia and affirming others who did the same. For example, she liked *Boy Meets Boy* because it focused less on homophobic reactions to a same-sex couple and more on the boys' feelings. She also conveyed that she was decidedly not-homophobic by repeatedly conveying her interest in LGBTQ-themed stories, her comfort with same-sex relationships and sex scenes, her interest in issues pertinent to LGBTQQ people, and her belief that LGBTQ-themed content is appropriate for school. For example, in our first meeting, she said that *Boy Meets Boy* was the first LGBTQ-themed book she had read but that she wanted to read more. In our next meeting, she said she liked to talk about issues pertinent to LGBTQQ people. This became more explicit over time when she started to name specific stories and specific scenes or relationships within novels that captured her attention. Ultimately, she argued on behalf of reading particular LGBTQ-themed texts in schools.

Just as Melissa constructed herself as not-homophobic, she also constructed herself as not-heterosexist. Heterosexism, as distinct from homophobia, is the assumption that all people are straight or that, if they are not, straight people are superior to LGBTQQ people. That Melissa constructed herself as not-heterosexist is evident in her comfort with sexual ambiguity. For example, when Melissa described her sister, she explained that she's currently romantically involved with another woman for the first time after having shared several relationships with men. She stated, "I don't really know my sister's sexual orientation," and she seemed fine with that. Melissa's comfort with sexual ambiguity also applied to herself. She self-identified in terms of sexuality only two times: once in our second meeting and then even only implicitly by referencing her boyfriend, and then again, almost a year later, by answering affirmatively when asked whether she had a boyfriend. Moreover, she described being misunderstood as lesbian because one of her female friends "grabs" her. Again, she seemed not at all bothered by either the misinterpretation or the physical affection. Thus, Melissa conveyed her awareness of a variety of valid and valuable sexual orientations and in this way constructed herself as not-heterosexist.

In the last four discussions in which Melissa participated, she began to construct herself as ally in a distinctive and important way, that is, as a continuous learner. In these final discussions, Melissa showed evidence of really struggling to understand more about homophobia, heterosexism, and being an ally. For example, she shared with the group a conversation she was part of at her lunch table in which a friend of hers expressed disapproval of same-sex marriages. Melissa reported:

> Today at lunch, actually, we got on the topic of gay marriage, and how [another member of the book discussion group] and I were talking about how we really wanted to see it come about like everywhere while we were still alive because our sisters, and, one girl at our lunch table said, she's like, "I have no problem with gay people, but I just can't see a man and a man or a woman and a woman because marriage is between a man and a woman," and she has no problems with gays or anything, but she's got that like embedded in her mind because it's what she's been taught and she can't let go of it. She wasn't trying to be mean or defensive or anything, she was just being honest, like that she couldn't see it, she couldn't grasp it, and understand it.

This account provoked a discussion about how other people interpreted, experienced, and might respond to such a stance. Liz asked whether the stance was one grounded in religion, and Melissa said it was. Mollie then said,

> people who say that, like want to distinguish civil unions and marriage feel just as warm and welcoming to me as the love the sinner, hate the sin, you know? Like what it feels to me is, like, I appreciate the honesty. I hear, like your comment on being honest and, like, not trying to be mean or defensive or anything like that. It just feels to me, ignorant. Like, you don't know you're hurting me, so you feel better about it, but I feel worse about it.

Melissa continued to articulate her friend's argument, to which Mollie offered an embarrassingly flawed metaphor: "I can sit in the back of the bus. Thanks." And Liz said, "That's really what it is." In this exchange, we see Melissa genuinely exploring the issues on same-sex marriages and deliberating provoking discussions that will inform her own stance in the debate. In this way, Melissa was constructing herself as an ally by continuously learning about topics pertinent to LGBTQQ people.

This continuous learning is important because innate to the larger processes of be(com)ing an ally is making mistakes. Consider, for example, a time when Melissa tried to connect with a young gay man in the group. The group was discussing a scene in *Finding H.F.* where several gay and lesbian characters were watching two men holding hands, walking through a park. Bo, whom we mention earlier, felt sad as the couple walked away, and a young gay man in the group said, in reference to the scene, "It made you so sad." And another young gay man in the group responded: "Because you're like, 'I'm alone, so when am I going to find someone.'" This led to an interaction in which several allies, including Melissa, connected with this feeling on the basis of being single. Mollie raised the question to the two young men who initiated the exchange whether this is what they meant. She told this story:

> One of the things I remember when I first came out, first coming out, when I saw same-sex couples, particularly women, I would want to stare at them ... I just need to see that this is real, that I'm not misinterpreting their actions, that they, we really exist.

One of the young men responded, "And the same way that they describe in the book, it gave them hope knowing that," to which Mollie responded, "Yeah and some of the sadness of them walking away is like, 'are you real,' or 'don't go away, don't go away, I need to believe you're real.'" Here, Melissa, along with other allies, misunderstood the significance of this particular scene to several of the LGBTQQ people in the group, but, in conversation with them, she continued to learn about be(com)ing an ally.

In her time in the book discussion group, Melissa discursively brought herself into being as an ally by talking about her connections with LGBTQQ people and their allies, her active work against homophobia and heterosexism, and her continuous learning. All of these processes were important for *her* construction of herself as an ally, but they are by no means prescriptive. These processes, as well as Liz's processes, are characteristic of exchanges, discussions, and the collection of discussions that led up to gay, lesbian, and ally lives, at least as Liz and Melissa embodied them in the periods of time that they participated in the book discussion group. How these processes are integrated across the three focal timescales seem to me implicit. Next, we make them more explicit by closely examining moments that allowed for heterochrony.

Heterochrony

Heterochrony, as we mentioned, is the intersection of processes that have radically different timescales and can be mediated by people and texts. Here, we point to two examples: one in which a short timescale process affected a much longer timescale process and another in which a long timescale process produced effects in much shorter timescale processes. The former focuses on a person as mediator and the latter on a text as mediator. In an effort to understand better the integration across timescales of Liz's and Melissa's processes, in particular, we focus on examples in which they are central.

For our first example, we look at a short process affecting a long process where the intersection is mediated by a person. In a single exchange, Melissa, as a biracial person, both African American and Middle Eastern, be(com)ing an ally, interrupted the very long process of developing and perpetuating the stereotype that African American people are more homophobic than White people. The group was talking about a young effeminate man whom several of the group members knew from school. They were wondering aloud why this young man was more frequently the target of homophobic abuse than one of the participants in the group. Both were young effeminate men, but the one in the group was White and the other one was Black. The White gay young man suggested that the Black students at their school were "ghetto and hood and all of that." He went on to say that being gay is "not really spoken about in those communities or it's frowned upon, so he doesn't really fit in with that group of people, that are in the same race group as he is." Melissa immediately responded with, "I was watching *The Real World* one day, and I thought it was weird because the guy was like, 'the whole Black community has gone homophobic.' 'What?' I'm like, 'No, that is not always true.'" Thus, in this single exchange Melissa served as a mediator who effectively disrupted the long process of Black people being stereotyped as homophobic by problematizing the assumptions articulated by one of her peers. We are not arguing that the shorter process of this exchange undid the longer process of imposing homophobic values on Black communities. Certainly it did not. But, the intersection served as an interruption in that process, at least as it was embodied by her White gay peer if not by all the participants in the discussion. Studying intersections where small timescale processes affect long timescale processes makes visible the ways that what people say and do in a moment matters in terms of social change.

Alternatively, studying intersections where long timescale processes affect short timescale processes makes visible the potential weight of any moment in time in terms of constructing identities. Consider, for instance, our second example and the intersection between one of our book discussion groups, which met for 90 minutes on a single day in January 2009, and our talk within that meeting about *Fried Green Tomatoes,* which was published in the 1980s and spans more than 60 years, from the 1920s to the 1980s. The intersection of the relatively small timescale, that is, the book discussion group meeting, and the relatively long timescale, that is, the time encompassed by the novel, was mediated by the book. We should note that Lemke uses nonfiction texts in his examples of textual mediators of heterochrony, but we assert that fictional texts can accomplish the same sort of mediation, as we discuss next.

Liz "loved" the book but was curious about the apparent acceptance of the same-sex couple central to the 1920s storyline. She was initially distrustful of it, saying, "Yeah, I kept waiting for something to happen." She pointed, though, to places in the text that "made [her] believe that [the same-sex relationship was] not a big deal." This belief was complicated in our discussion by the recognition that one of the two women, Ruth, seemed to be more aware of and even afraid of the possible consequences for being coupled with another woman. As we mentioned earlier, group members tried to figure out why the same-sex couple was so accepted, and Liz, in particular, considered what this might look like in contemporary society. Caroline characterized Whistle Stop, where the story takes place, as idyllic, initiating this exchange:

CAROLINE: It makes me wonder how much of it reflects something that is true for Fannie Flagg [the author] about the south that we don't—
LIZ: Yeah, I was also wondering that too. Like, what, just, I would want to hear from somebody who lives in, you know, a community similar. . . . And like, is it sort of just, is it just the way things are, we're not going to touch it kind of?

Liz's question prompted another lesbian in the group to tell this story:

Actually, I lived in a really small town too, and it was almost the same. We actually had, they were really close friends of the family, um, it was a lesbian couple, one of whom had gone into [providing] foster care so they had really at risk children living in their house and they got, they were named an award for it, like mom of the year or something like that and it was really, really, I have the actual newspaper clipping on my wall because they went through the entire story, and they never mentioned, like, they'd always say, and her friend, and her, they didn't say roommate, they said housing partner, I don't know. . . . It was so really, almost like, very transparent and they had the picture and of course they were sitting there, they were kind of laying there together and it was just, like, they put it on the great big section of the lifestyle section of the paper, but they never said lesbian, ever.

Liz then asked, almost disbelievingly, "But no one bothered them?" She then connected this account to a 2006 documentary entitled *Small Town Gay Bar,* in which a variety of people in two rural communities in Mississippi were interviewed. She reported that some of those people were,

like, "don't come near me, I can't believe we have this bar." But then they have where a lot of people who kind of have that, like, just like, the "live-and-let-live" sort of "just don't, you know, I don't have a problem with you, don't get in a fight with me. . . . Let's just not talk about this and just live in peace," um, so I just thought about that too, sort of similar.

Thus, Liz explored what it might look like to live in a time and space in which same-sex couples are permitted to "just live" by reading, reflecting on, and discussing a book set in such a time, even if an historical and fictional one, and connecting it to her present. In these ways, *Fried Green Tomatoes* mediated heterochrony.

The idea of heterochrony is one we find compelling. We appreciate how it provides a concrete way of examining time that is not confined by the linear, that challenges us to think beyond the linear, that provokes complex analyses. So, instead of thinking of a book group that spanned 3 years or a discussion that lasted 90 minutes or an exchange that lasted a minute or two, we are challenged to think about what happens when a 1-minute exchange, for example, intersects with a decades-long process or when a single discussion intersects with 60 years represented in a novel. We value the depth this offers to our understanding of how moments add up to lives.

Exploring Space through Geographical Scales and Heterochory

We return here to the question of how spaces add up to lives. Space matters. That these young people came from schools with GSAs to a book discussion group among LGBTQQ and ally youth and adults in a youth center for LGBTQ youth to read and talk about LGBTQ-themed literature that they felt they could not read in their schools is significant. Clearly spaces matter. De Certeau's notion of space (1984) is theoretically compelling but empirically a bit frustrating. Valentine's (2001) geographical scales, however, offer the spatial equivalent of Lemke's time scales. He organizes his thinking about "how social identities and relations are constituted in and through different spaces" (p. 2) in relative scales, ranging from the body and the home to community, institutions, the street, the city, the rural, the nation, and the globe. We can imagine applying Lemke's (2000) idea that the unit of analysis should be not any one scale, such as a person, but a process across "scale hierarchies in groups of three levels at once" (p. 276), that is, say, a body in a community in an institution or, more specifically, Liz in the book discussion group in the youth center. Such an analysis might bring us to the spatial equivalent of Liz's processes of be(com)ing gay and lesbian or Melissa's processes of be(com)ing an ally in the book discussion group in the youth center.

Further, to consider how processes are integrated across different geographical scales, as Lemke challenges us to do with timescales, we need the spatial equivalent of heterochrony, something that captures what happens when one space intersects with another mediated by, perhaps, a person or a text. So, for example, when Melissa talks at the book discussion group in the youth center about her conversation about same-sex marriages with her friend in the lunchroom in her school, she mediates a spatial intersection. Or, when a text represents a church in a small Texas town, as *God Box* does, or an apartment in a rural community in Kentucky, as *Finding H.F.* does, that text mediates a spatial intersection. The person or text effectively brings one space, which is a layered space, into another layered space. To talk about this, we suggest the term "heterochory."

"Heterochory" is a derivation of Lemke's heterochrony. As a reminder, heterochrony references the intersection of processes and practices which have radically different *timescales* mediated by people and/or texts. We replace "chrono," which comes from the Greek prefix for words that are in relation to time, with "chora," which, in Greek means "the space lying between two places or limits" (Thayer & Smith, accessed October 18, 2011), to arrive at "heterochrony," which we define, by bringing Valentine's idea (2001) of geographical scales to Lemke's definition of heterochrony, as the intersection of processes and practices that have radically different *geographical scales* mediated by people and/or texts. In doing so, we offer a concrete and complex way of analyzing intersections of space. In other words, relying on and modifying Lemke's insights, heterochory might be one way to explore how spaces, like moments, add up to lives.

Further, it seems to us that the two might pair up well together: heterochrony as a way of analyzing intersections of time and heterochory as a way of analyzing space, allowing us to get at the spatial aspect of Lewis and del Valle's (2009) third wave of literacy and identity research, that is, analyses that take seriously both time and space.

References

Blackburn, M.V., Clark, C.T., Kenney, L.M., & Smith, J.M. (Eds.). (2010). *Acting out: Combating homophobia through teacher activism*. New York: Teachers College Press.

Butler, J. (1990/1999). *Gender trouble: Feminism and the subversion of identity*. New York: Routledge.

De Certeau, M. (1984). *The practice of everyday life*. Berkeley: University of California Press.

Lemke, J.L. (2000). Across the scales of time: Artifacts, activities, and meanings in ecosocial systems. *Mind, Culture, and Activity, 7*(4), 273–290.

Lemke, J.L. (2008). Identity, development and desire: Critical questions. In C.R. Caldas-Coulthard & R. Idema (Eds.), *Identity trouble: Critical discourse and contested identities* (pp. 17–42). New York: Palgrave Macmillan.

Lewis, C., & del Valle, A. (2009). Literacy and identity: Implication for research and practice. In L. Christenbury, R. Bomer, & P. Smagorinsky (Eds.), *Handbook of adolescent literacy research* (pp. 307–371). New York: Guilford Press.

Talburt, S. (2000). *Subject to identity: Knowledge, sexuality, and academic practices in higher education*. Albany: State University of New York Press.

Thayer, J. The New Testament Greek Lexicon. Retrieved October 18, 2011, from www.studylight.org/lex/grk/view.cgi?number=5561

Valentine, G. (2001). *Social geographies: Space and society*. Harlow, England: Prentice Hall.

7

LOST VOICES IN AN AMERICAN HIGH SCHOOL: SUDANESE MALE ENGLISH-LANGUAGE LEARNERS' PERSPECTIVES ON WRITING

Bryan Ripley Crandall

> The Dinka believe the secret gift went to the people of the West. It helped them invent and explore and build and become strong. Meanwhile the Dinka never built factories or highways or cars or planes. They were content to be farmers and cattle raisers. They lived happily for centuries.
>
> —John Dau, *Lost Boy, Lost Girl: Escaping Civil War in Sudan*

According to the United Nations High Commissioner for Refugees (2009), approximately 42 million people are currently uprooted as a result of civil unrest and conflict. They are individuals who meet the criteria set by the U.S. Immigration and Nationality Act (INA): "a person who is unable or unwilling to return to his or her country of nationality because of persecution or a well-founded fear of persecution on account of race, religion, nationality, membership in a particular social group, or political opinion" (Martin & Hoefer, 2009, p. 2). Almost half of the world's refugee populations reside in African nations where rhizomes of 19th-century imperialism and 20th-century globalization have sprouted civil wars and human atrocities. In 2001, approximately 3,000 Sudanese male refugees were provided political refuge in the United States, and since then family members have relocated to be with them. The "Lost Boy" narrative has been captured in film (e.g., *The Lost Boys of Sudan*), memoir (Dau, 2007; Dau, 2010), fiction (Eggers, 2006), biography (Bixler, 2005), and research (e.g., McMahon, 2007; Perry, 2008, 2009), yet little has been written about the challenges Sudanese youth face with regard to English literacy in secondary schools. These are young people who must reconcile their complex histories with their new environments upon relocation and, if ignored by educational facilities, may remain *lost voices* in our schools.

English-language learners, including students relocated under a refugee status, are the largest growing demographic in U.S. secondary schools. It is likely the United States will continue to support relocation of refugee populations in the future, including school-age youth with limited and interrupted formal education (DeCapua & Marshall, 2010). Teachers and researchers might better understand the complex spaces where youth reinvent literacies if young people are invited to share personal experiences and perspectives on their learning (Moje, 2002).

I began working with English-language-learning populations in 1998 when demographics in my classroom changed. I volunteered with the Kentucky Refugees Mission and mentored Sudanese adult males, who, in return, also shared their relocation experiences with my high school students. In addition, a history teacher and I collaborated on an interdisciplinary unit to study the impact of imperialism and colonization and to help students explore shifting populations in the 21st century. My classroom and volunteer work led me to research the perspectives of eight African-born Black male youth who relocated to the United States between 2003 and 2006 (Crandall, 2012). Three of the eight participants in the study were young Sudanese Dinka men immersed in mainstream classrooms who were held accountable to the same curriculum and assessments as American-born peers.

Influenced by the National Writing Project and portfolio-based writing assessment in Kentucky, I wanted to hear from the young men about becoming writers in a new nation. I asked: *For what purposes do these young men write in the United States? What are the contexts for their writing? What tools do they use to compose?* The three participants noted that they had multiple purposes for writing, yet were frustrated by the lack of writing instruction received in school. They wished U.S. teachers were more knowledgeable about Sudanese history, the realities of refugee populations worldwide, and the societal pressures placed on them as youth who navigate among their relocation experiences, their family responsibilities, and the complexities of learning as English-language learners in mainstream classrooms.

Research on Writing in Secondary Schools

Research has demonstrated that adolescents in secondary schools are not writing enough (Applebee & Langer, 2009) or performing proficiently on national writing assessments (Salahu-Din, Persky, & Miller, 2008). These results are often framed within on-demand writing assessments, though, that report a deficit view of what youth can write. Instruction in many schools is limited to test-taking strategies for helping a school meet Annual Yearly Progress (AYP) requirements. Research on out-of-school literacies (e.g., Kinloch, 2010), in contrast, has highlighted that adolescents bring competence to writing when they are given opportunities to compose on their own terms. It is not that youth do not write; it is that current writing assessments lack a way for capturing the multiplicity of what youth write outside high-stakes testing. The emphasis is placed on preparation for state examinations instead of development of writing skills and processes for a variety of genres.

Immigrant youth inhabit spaces between old and new-world expectations (Ibrahim, 2008) and between home and school cultures (Sarroub, 2002). Campano (2007) refers to such spaces as the second classroom, a location that,

> runs parallel to, and is sometimes in the shadow of, the official, first classroom. It is an alternative pedagogical space. It develops organically by following the students' leads, interests, desires, forms of cultural expression, and especially stories. (p. 40)

Awareness of second-classroom spaces suggests that teachers can improve writing instruction when out-of-school lives of youth are acknowledged and opportunities for sharing stories and language practices are incorporated within the curriculum. Migration histories of refugees can be used to explain school achievement and to provide context for educational needs (Awokoya & Clark, 2008).

Recent research with adult Sudanese refugee experiences acknowledges the importance of storytelling and language brokering (Perry, 2008, 2009), but few studies have looked at literacy practices of school-age refugee youth. The voices of Sudanese adolescents—a small sample of students with limited and interrupted formal education enrolled in U.S. classrooms—deserve to be heard by teachers, scholars, and policymakers. We can improve writing instruction in secondary schools by including youth perspectives within school spaces.

Theoretical Framework

Activity theory, new literacy studies, and postcolonial critiques provided the framework I used to promote participants' perspectives on writing. The three Sudanese participants remarked that writing for them was entwined within the realities of 21st-century urban classrooms and the digital worlds they inhabited out of school. They also reported the influence of Dinka history, Dinka traditions, and their relocation experiences from Sudan to the United States as important to their writing identities.

Writing-activity genre research (Russell, 2009) and activity theory (Engeström, 1998) provide a heuristic model, an activity system, to report how an individual (subject) writes through a set of established rules, available tools (including mental thoughts and physical artifacts), divisions of labor, and influences of communities to reach a written outcome. One's environment, experiences, histories, and individual purposes (objects) for communicating are socially, culturally, and historically created. Similarly, New Literacy Studies situates writing within the complex arenas of power relationships; as Gee (2000) wrote, "reading and writing only make sense when studied in the context of social and cultural (and we can add historical, political, and economic) practices of which they are but a part" (p. 180).

Postcolonial critiques (Gikandi, 2002/2006) also "provide new vistas for understanding cultural flows that can no longer be explained by homogeneous Eurocentric narrative of development and social change" (p. 473). To be critical of Western education and subjectivities, it was important for me to listen to participants' perspectives in context of global histories and the activity systems they reported both in the United States and Africa. Literacy has always been political and used to advantage and disadvantage particular groups, both locally and globally. The ability to read has historically been used to label one's ability to think and reason (Gates, 1986). A place as relocated refugee youth in 21st-century classrooms partially resulted from colonial and imperialist history.

Methodology

Ethnographic case studies (Dyson & Genishi, 2005) were implemented as a way to learn participants' perspectives on writing and to make suggestions for teaching. For six months I collected data in and out of participants' mainstream English classrooms at a high school located in the northeastern United States. I established three English classrooms as the epicenter of this study, yet the young men named additional spaces (activity systems) that influenced their writing. These included locations where they shared history, the classrooms they attended at school and in after-school programs, community centers, athletic fields, neighborhoods, online communities, public parks, and homes. An ESL teacher at the school estimated that approximately 160 African-born English-language learners were enrolled at the high school during the time of this study, and approximately 80 of them were male. The racial/ethnic population at the school was 25% White American, 3% Asian/Native Hawaiian/Other Pacific Islander, 8% Hispanic or Latino, 1% American Indian, and 63% Black or African American. The school did not differentiate between African American–born and African-born students in reports. The high school also did not meet Annual Yearly Progress standards for graduating students who were Black or African American and/or economically disadvantaged and reported that slightly more than 50% of students reached a passing score on the state English examination (compared to a 98% passing rate in nearby suburban schools and a 70% passing rate in urban schools in the state with similar demographics).

Panther, Samuel, and London—pseudonyms chosen by the three participants— were young men from Sudan with limited and interrupted formal education who were enrolled in mainstream classrooms after meeting minimal language requirements. Participants' teachers, Ms. Hartford and Ms. Hamilton, were White females who each had four years of teaching experience. The classes of participants observed averaged 28 students: 20 African American youth and 8 English-language learners. At the end of the data collection, however, approximately half of the American-born students still attended; many had dropped out or were expelled. Panther, Samuel, and London were the only Sudanese youth in their English classrooms, although they were not the only recently immigrated students. Classmates had also relocated from countries such as Iraq, Bhutan, Somalia, Liberia, Congo, and Sierra Leone.

I worked to maintain a critical awareness of my subjectivies so that I could better understand my biases and the way I understood colonial and racial histories (Eastmond, 2007). Although I have volunteered as a language and cultural broker with refugee families since 2001 and taught in an urban school, I did not learn about students with limited and interrupted formal education until I took a life history methodologies course and cowrote manuscripts with young men from Liberia, Sudan, and Bhutan. They introduced me to other refugee youth at Robinson High School, including Panther, Samuel, and London.

Data Collection and Analysis

Open conversation protocols were used to interview each participant twice. During the first interview, I asked participants to tell me about their childhood in Africa and their relocation experiences. During the second interview, I asked participants to elaborate on the classes and locations that had influenced their writing. Ms. Hamilton and Ms. Hartford were each interviewed once to provide context for the high school, the state English assessment, views of participants, training to teach English, and curriculum. Formal and informal interviews were also conducted with individuals named by participants as important to their education (e.g., brothers, ESL teachers, friends).

Open coding from the first interview introduced me to the importance history had for each young man, and, in recognition of this, I used biographical profiles to report participants' perspectives and histories. As young writers (subjects), the three participants inhabited several activity systems beyond school. For these reasons, 78 participant observations occurred in English classrooms and at locations they named (e.g., soccer fields, homes, neighborhoods). Materials were also collected that included event programs, school newspapers, district documents, sample state assessments, teacher handouts, lesson plans, articles sent from participants, e-mails, and websites.

Historical Spaces in the Relocation of Dinka Youth

According to Enciso (2007), the use of activity theory has the potential to allow researchers "to engage with the multiple, often divergent histories that glide across and whisper alongside every action and object we are able to see or hear" (p. 72). It was important to locate participants' perspectives in the context of global histories. As they discussed their experiences, I began to read about Sudan's civil wars and national conflicts. The more I learned, the more the young men were willing to discuss memories with me and share their thoughts about U.S. schooling.

Sudan, the largest nation in Africa, with a population of more than 42 million, has been divided for most of its history. Its name was shortened from the Arabic *Bilad al-Sudan*, a degrading reference used to describe individuals in southern Sudan as the "Land of the Burnt-Faced Ones" (Bixler, 2005, p. 39). Knowledge of slavery is important to understanding the two Sudanese civil wars that have occurred between northern and southern Sudan since World War II (Bixler, 2005) and, consequently, disrupted the childhood of the young men. Panther, Samuel, and London were members of the Dinka tribe, the largest ethnic group in southern Sudan. Arab populations in the north enslaved ethnic groups of southern Sudan, including the Dinka, during the 19th century. Before and after slavery, the Dinka fished, herded livestock, harvested grains, danced, and told stories. When British armies abolished slavery during imperial rule, a strong hatred for Arab northerners remained. John Dau (2010), whose quotation is used to begin this chapter, recalled that young Dinka boys were often told a creation story (cf. Eggers, 2006). In the story, God presented a choice between a cow and a secret gift called the *What*. The Dinka chose the cow, but the secret gift, the *What*, went to others. Weapons, wars, and destruction, the results of scientific and industrial revolutions, were used against Dinka populations throughout history, although the Dinka have always led a peaceful life of herding cattle.

The pastoral life in southern Sudan, however, was disrupted by two civil wars in the 20th and early 21st centuries. The conflicts culminated from the 18th- and 19th-century slave trade, the scramble for Africa during the Age of Imperialism, the collapse of African nations after World War II, the political chess match between the United States and the Soviet Union during the Cold War, and, most recently, the discovery of oil in the south (Johnson, 2003). According to McMahon (2007), "the Sudanese have suffered more war-related deaths during the past 15 years than any single population in the world" (p. 12). Conflicts resulted in 2 million deaths and the displacement of 4 million individuals (Bixler, 2005), including Sudanese Dinka youth.

Panther: Ninth-Grader from Khartoum, Sudan

Panther was born in Khartoum, Sudan's capital, in 1994. When he was 4, his art-teaching father died of a heart attack and his mother's ability to raise two sons in a nation of increasing conflict was put into question. Relatives advised his mother, "We see a lot of potential in your kids and believe you should take them to America so they will get a better education." His mother fled with the children to Cairo, Egypt, but continued to face hardship. Panther explained that his mother "would do anything to bring us food, but she wouldn't eat food herself. I saw my mom suffering. She tried to hide it, but I saw it."

Panther's mother instilled in him a respect for Dinka traditions and a pride in cultural history. She made Panther memorize the names he had inherited from past generations as a way to help her son maintain integrity and respect for family heritage.

> My mom said if you know your whole name, no matter where you go you'll never be lost. Cause the thing is, a lot of these kids who come [to America], they forget their language. They forget who they are.

Panther received no formal education in Sudan or Egypt, and, before he arrived in the United States as a 10-year-old, he recognized only basic Arabic. "We kind of went to school," he remembered, "but it wasn't really a school. It was like a church. They held classes. They didn't teach you how to read or write or anything."

Panther, his three brothers, his mother, and a stepfather relocated to the United States in the fall of 2003 through the assistance of a Catholic church. Panther enrolled in third-grade ESL and, 3 years later, transitioned to a middle school with American-born students. Panther reported, "Being Sudanese is basically my identity. It's who I am," but reflected that he got into "mad fights" with American-born classmates, most of who were African American youth. "It was the same way Egyptians treated Blacks in Cairo," Panther explained. He reported he was harassed in both locations for having dark skin. He had to learn to fight back and, in the United States, he quickly got a reputation as a troublemaker. He admitted, "I got to know the principal really well."

While in middle school Panther was taught John Dau's (2007) memoir, *God Grew Tired of Us,* and his teachers brought the author to school to speak about his book. The visit positioned Panther as a cultural expert in Sudanese heritage, and he felt confident and respected by his teachers. He enjoyed writing workshops and Socratic seminars that were implemented by his middle school teachers and reported, "The teachers would make us write. They would push me. I always do more writing if the subject is interesting."

Panther reported, though, that he wrote much less in high school. He wanted to achieve, however, because he "knew what it was like growing up without an education." He became close friends with an African American young man named J'Quon, and the two of them made a pact to achieve in school.

> I mean, if I grew up in America, I wouldn't care. If I grew up in America, I would be just like them other kids. I'd probably be in jail right now or selling drugs and I probably would drop out of high school.

Midway through our data collection, only three kids in Panther's English class had passing grades. His aunts and uncles pleaded with his mother to switch him to a private school, but Panther refused and remarked, "I learn more about life in this school than I would at those White schools." Despite Panther's desire to achieve and do well, he stopped putting forth effort and broke his pact with J'Quon. He skipped classes and, at times, returned to his middle school, where he felt more respected.

Most of the writing that occurred in Panther's ninth-grade English class was to practice on-demand writing prompts for the state English assessment. English teachers were monitored by the school district to ensure that their students demon-strated improved scores, and one strategy implemented was to give the 11th-grade assessment to 9th-graders. Ms. Hartford explained, "We give the state tests to every-one and their grandmother." Literary analysis on two of the state essays triggered the teachers to place an emphasis on reading literature. Students often filled out comprehension packets where they answered questions and applied literary terms. "I don't think we really had to write a lot this year," Panther lamented, although he liked several of the books he was assigned.

During one assignment, atypical of the normal English class routine, Panther was required to choose a photograph from those Ms. Hartford provided. Panther chose a picture of the Earth taken from outer space and wrote:

> The world is full of mysteries waiting to be discovered
> The world is full of histories waiting to be recovered
> As the world spins and turns, time passes out and burns
> What's in the past will never return,
> So I spend my time trying to learn

In and out of school Panther engaged friends with conversations about global inequities and loved to debate politics and history. He considered himself a thinker and observer who sought "mysteries waiting to be discovered" and "histories waiting to be recovered," yet reflected that there were few opportunities for him to express his own opinions at school. He became disconnected from classroom expectations and suggested, "Teachers need to understand more about where we come from. . . . They need to have people teach about the ways we lived and encourage them to know more about their world."

Panther failed Ms. Hartford's ninth-grade English class, yet said that he wrote two to three hours a day at home, especially on Facebook. During a day when one of his teachers ridiculed him for not having a pen in class, he posted, "Why don't I have a writing utensil? Let's see. It's 8 a.m. They're lucky I'm even dressed." Panther resisted assignments that did not connect with his individuality and preferred those that allowed him to share opinions, to argue, and to entertain. He wished teachers gave youth more opportunities in school to write for each other, instead of only for a grade.

Samuel: 10th-Grader from Bor, Sudan

Samuel, the youngest of 10 children, was born in 1992 outside Kakuma refugee camp in Kenya. His mother went into labor as they fled Sudan and were almost at their destination. His father, who raised cattle in Bor before joining the Sudanese People's Liberation Army (SPLA), died of an infection in the refugee camp. Samuel also lost three older siblings while there. He had few memories of schooling in Kakuma and remembered, "We only learned basic sentences in English because we might someday be able to come to America."

Samuel's older brother, Dominic, came to the United States as one of the "Lost Boys" in 2001 and earned a college degree in geology. Through part-time work and collaboration with an Episcopalian church, Dominic sent money to relocate his family closer to where he lived. Samuel entered a fifth-grade ESL class at an elementary school in 2003 and a year later moved to a middle school, where, like Panther, he encountered bullying. "I got in trouble a lot cuz I didn't know how to get along with others," he remembered. "They just make fun of me . . . the other Black kids." Unlike other schools in the district, his middle school had few English-language learners. Samuel, who entered his first mainstream English classroom in the eighth grade, found the work difficult. "Most of the time the kids were making too much noise," Samuel remembered. "They [students] are there just to be with their friends and not to learn. School was just a big social time."

Samuel's brothers reported that he maintained good grades in middle school; his grades slipped, however, when he entered high school. Samuel noted:

> I am an average student. I've failed a couple of classes a couple of times. I've failed English once, no twice. Global History two times. Math three times. I'm average. I'm a jock. I'm average.

Dominic and another brother, James, felt responsible for pushing Samuel to excel. James especially felt it was his duty to reprimand Samuel.

> The way my family works is, when you are little, the older guys force you want to be successful. When I was young, my older brothers pushed me and now I have to . . . all of us have to push Samuel, ya know?

When Samuel's report cards came home, the brothers enforced this: "Dude, you have to, like, pick it up." Their mother had no formal education and, concerned for Samuel's future, also struggled to get Samuel to take school seriously. One of Samuel's other brothers and an older sister had previously dropped out of Robinson High School; Samuel's mother was afraid he would do the same.

Samuel played varsity soccer for the school and participated in a club team at suburban athletic facility. He was admired by teammates and had great relationships with his coaches. He practiced seven days a week and spent most of his out-of-school time participating in the sport. Dominic used Samuel's love of soccer as a threat and declared, "If we're going to allow you to do soccer, you're going to have to do your school work, too. You can have both, but you can't only have soccer." His family worried he was acting "too American" and that he had lost touch with being Sudanese. For Samuel, though, he was typical of his peers. He wished his teachers, however, were like his coaches because "They push us and make us want to play better."

Samuel demonstrated a strong aptitude for reading that afforded him glimmers of school success. He passed the state English examination as a sophomore and received the highest score in his class. His English teacher, Ms. Hamilton, encouraged his reading appetite, as well, by providing silent sustained reading time in class and by recommending young-adult novels. He attended English class every day, although he ritually skipped his other classes to hang out in the library. There, he read about soccer, played cards with friends, and debated sports incessantly. He described himself as "lethargic," but his commitment to playing the sport and socializing was far from lazy.

Samuel was most excited about writing when Ms. Hamilton, via a student teacher, introduced a six-week unit on script writing. The teachers taught the language of screenplays as they read Walter Dean Myer's *Monster* (2001). Through drafting, writing conferences, and peer editing, Samuel wrote his most developed piece collected in our study. His teachers taught and modeled several screenplays and assigned the students to draft one of their own. The *stretch, skill, drill, practice, play,* and *reflect* instruction paralleled the coaching Samuel enjoyed on the soccer field. His screenplay began:

Fade In:
  Ext. B. Ajak High School, Morning
    It is the first day of school. Teenagers are walking around, showing off their gear [clothes] and checking schedules. Students faces look extremely annoyed to be back in school.

A mother and son are seen walking towards the school. The boy, dark skinned, is skinny, and the mom, dressed in African clothes, looks annoyed at all the students walking around. The population is diverse.

CT. Mother's face is panned with a focus on her eyes.

CT. Images of Sudan appear. Snapshots of departing. Snapshots of village. Snapshots of cattle. Snapshots of school. Snapshot of women crying.

The script depicts images of a U.S. school and of a refugee camp in Africa. Samuel included one flashback of a soccer game where youth uses a "surgical glove" as a ball. As the mother and son enter the school's main office, though, a security guard is depicted as restraining a cursing youth. The mother is told, "Once you get settled in, it'll just seem like a playground." The mother is not impressed by the chaos.

The script was submitted in a district-required writing portfolio at the end of the semester, but Samuel felt that a majority of the writing expected of him was for test practice alone. He struggled to have enough material to include in his portfolio because he chose to not write for the practice tests throughout the year. Unenthused by such writing, he put forth minimal effort. Instead, Samuel wished teachers would "let us pick something we like to do and see if it's, um, related to anything we like, instead of a teacher picking out something for us to do." He wanted to write about his passion for sports, especially soccer, and to argue his knowledge gained from reading a variety of texts. He barely passed his 10th-grade English class, and both he and his teacher admitted he was "given the benefit of the doubt."

London: 11th-Grader Born in Tonj, Sudan

London's uncle Martin arrived in 2001 with the first wave of Sudanese "Lost Boys." When Martin learned his nephew was still alive in Sudan, he made arrangements to bring him to the United States. "My uncle left when he was my age because of the war," London reflected. "He grew up alone. He understands my story." London was born in Tonj, Sudan, in 1992 and lived with a blind mother, two older sisters, and an older brother. His father, who was a member of the Sudanese People Liberation Army, disappeared the year London was born. London recalled:

> I was a good boy. I took care of my mother. I farmed corn. I had to bring water to people, plus some snacks. Or maybe throw some seed. We just have to work hard. That's what children are for.

London felt tremendous responsibility to succeed in the United States and had a goal of bringing his mother and sister to be with him. Two months before this study began, his older brother died from unknown causes. London suspected it was from "bad spirits."

London's relocation to the United States began when his uncle sent money for him to live with another uncle in Uganda. "I didn't go to school in Sudan," remarked London, yet he sometimes followed his older brother who did. He explained that education cost money that his family did not have. "We weren't a rich Dinka family. We didn't have cows," he reflected. Traditionally, the eldest boy was sent to school if it was affordable. At age 12, London experienced formal education for the first time. His schooling in Uganda lasted for one year, though, because he lacked funding to enter second grade. Then, in 2006, his uncle brought London and London's grandmother to the United States. London entered a 7th-grade ESL class the last month of the school year and continued to receive ESL services until the end of 10th grade. He maintained tremendous appreciation for ESL teachers, especially Mr. Cooper, who offered him lots of encouragement.

> Like, he used to say I'm a good writer. I didn't call myself a writer. Like I don't see me like this. But he called me a writer. That's what every teacher should do—encourage students to believe in what they do.

London felt that ESL teachers at Robinson had more respect for English-language learners than did the other teachers and that they took an interest in global histories because they were more "culturally aware." This, he felt, made the ESL teachers better teachers of writing.

London lived in an apartment with his grandmother until she chose to return to Sudan. "She felt she couldn't help me with school," London explained. "She would be more useful to other grandchildren in Sudan." As a result, London temporarily moved into his uncle's house outside the school district and relied on public transportation. His school day lasted 12 hours between the busing, classes, and his extracurricular activities. He hated the commute and also complained that his uncle's wife did not like having him in her home. Midway through data collection, London moved into Panther's apartment and slept on his floor. London explained, "They bought me a desk where I can study even if they [Panther and his brothers] make fun of me for being a nerd." London also received emotional and economic guidance from members at a church who mentored him and drove him to cultural programs, sporting events, and school activities.

London was enrolled in Ms. Hamilton's 11th-grade English class with four other English-language learners. He took the state English test as a sophomore and failed it. He pestered Ms. Hamilton to provide test-only instruction.

> I need to pass this English test. I need to pass this state exam. I am worried most about the English exam. English is my second language and the pressure comes to me. My time is running out.

Ms. Hamilton remarked, "That boy drove me nuts," but she proudly reflected, "I don't know, whatever I did must have worked." She taught students "cluster paragraphing"—a strategy for writing solid introductions, using topic sentences, and supporting an argument with details. In less than a year London increased his score by 30 points and switched his worries to the SATs. "I'm an African kid. I have nothing," London said. "I've been in the country a few years and the American kids cheat off of me. It's silly."

London was the captain of the JV soccer team and participated in a college preparatory program that provided academic support. At home he kept personal journals and hoped to write a book about his life one day, "one like Barack Obama or Sidney Poitier"—whose books he read on his own. London was conflicted about what he wrote in school, though, because his uncle told him it was unwise to write about his life in Sudan. London kept private journals at home but did not share what he wrote. He explained that he recorded memories, dates, and thoughts but that they were off limits to others.

London wished that teachers offered real-world writing in school so that students could have better preparation for college and/or careers. "I didn't grow up learning what jobs are like or where people know how languages work," he said.

> In America, people think that killing an animal is not a skill. The work that Africans do is not considered a skilled work. They think that if you're White, and read books, those are skills that one needs for work. Those jobs, to get them, you have to read and write.

London wanted to prove he came ready to succeed in the United States but was irritated when he was unable to connect with the curriculum. For example, when Ms. Hamilton assigned a college essay, London worried, "I can never write like those kids. I'm not White. They aren't from a kid like me." He took the assignment to tutors at the college preparatory program and was offered individualized attention, models for the genre, and coaching. The staff asked him many questions about his life and helped him frame his college essay for the writing task. He felt the college essay models shared in Ms. Hamilton's class did not articulate the history of a young man like him.

Listening to Voices in an American High School

Moje (2002) wrote, "To study youth literacy is to study the complexity of literacy's power" (p. 107). Youth, like the three Sudanese young men discussed in this chapter, may continue to be lost if schools fail to listen to them about their literacy practices. Locating the complex social and cultural histories across time and space that youth bring to school can help schools improve writing instruction. In order to accomplish this, however, teachers need to be encouraged to listen to students as experts on their worlds. Panther, Samuel, and London felt writing was empowering but explained that they rarely wrote in mainstream English classrooms for purposes that mattered to them. Their teachers, too, reported that the pressures for improving scores on the state English assessment tests limited the writing instruction they could offer. In this sense, writing (an outcome) was taught in anticipation of tests (rules) that were established in spaces beyond Robinson High School. As a result, understanding and analyzing literature for the tests constituted most of the activities (tools) in English classes. Both youth and teachers were subjected to instruction for examinations (divisions of labor) that was often disconnected from the writing they wanted to do. English class spaces seldom provided the tools to help youth develop their voice in writing. Writing, instead, was disconnected from who the three young men imagined themselves to be.

Panther wanted opportunities to entertain and debate with others. He accomplished this on Facebook, where he received quick feedback from real-world audiences that replied to what he wrote. In this sense, he composed for an audience that mattered to him. Samuel wanted chances to write about his passion for soccer and for teachers to promote inquiry-based writing. He spent a lot of time debating statistics, comparing scores, and arguing about sports (hence, showing proficiency in the ability to analyze and argue). He was interested in his world, read avidly, but was not a fan of writing about literature. Similarly, London wanted to learn how to write in ways that might benefit his future. He desired test-only instruction from Ms. Hamilton, though, because he saw it as a direct link to his success. The achievement in one space would provide access to the other spaces he valued. Still, he wished teachers helped kids like him to be better prepared for writing beyond school.

State assessments fail to recognize additional purposes youth have for writing and, concomitantly, encourage a bad practice of viewing students as numbers alone. Participants saw writing as a creative and personal endeavor but felt this was not encouraged in school. When they were given time and space to negotiate among lived experiences, interests, and curiosities—which was rare—they felt more invested in what they wrote. The three young men, however, arrived at a time in U.S. history when students (subjects) enter classrooms (activity systems) with limited writing instruction (Hillocks, 2002). Teachers spend less time helping English-language learners in the 2nd classroom (Campano, 2007) because high-stakes testing encourages test-only instruction rather than a celebration of the diverse voices and rich cultural experiences youth bring (including the purposes they see for writing).

The relocation of youth like Panther, Samuel, and London brings new challenges to secondary schools but also provides tremendous resources. The presence of students with interrupted educational histories in U.S. classrooms offers potential for teachers to locate local practices within the larger context of global realities. It is the responsibility of teachers, administrators, and policymakers to learn from such voices. Otherwise they will continue to be lost.

References

Applebee, A.N., & Langer, J.A. (2009). What is happening in the teaching of writing. *English Journal, 98*(5), 18–28.

Awokoya, J.T., & Clark, C. (2008). Demystifying cultural theories and practices: Locating black immigrant experience in teacher education research. *Multicultural Education 16*(2), 49–58.

Bixler, M. (2005). *The lost boys of Sudan: An American story of the refugee experience.* Athens: University of Georgia Press.

Campano, G. (2007). *Immigrant students and literacy: Reading, writing, and remembering.* New York: Teachers College Press.

Crandall, B.R. (2012). "A responsibility to speak out": Perspectives on writing from Black African-born male youth with limited and interrupted formal education. Unpublished doctoral dissertation, Syracuse University, Syracuse, NY.

Dau, J.B. (2007). *God grew tired of us: A memoir.* Washington, DC: National Geographic Society.

Dau, J.B. (2010). *Lost boy, lost girl; Escaping civil war in Sudan.* Washington, DC: National Geographic Society.

DeCapua, A., & Marshall, H.W. (2010). Students with limited or interrupted formal education in US classrooms. *The Urban Review, 42*(2), 159–173.

Dyson, A.H., & Genishi, C. (2005). *On the case: Approaches to language and literacy research.* New York: Teachers College Press.

Eastmond, M. (2007). Stories as lived experience: Narratives in forced migration research. *Journal of Refugee Studies, 20*(2), 248–264.

Eggers, D. (2006). *What is the what.* San Francisco: McSweeney's.

Enciso, P. (2007). Reframing history in sociocultural theories: Towards an expansive vision. In C. Lewis, P. Enciso, & E.B. Moje (Eds.), *Reframing sociocultural research on literacy* (pp. 49–74). Mahwah, NJ: Lawrence Erlbaum.

Engeström, Y. (1998). Activity theory and individual and social transformation. In Y. Engeström, R. Miettinen, & R.-L. Punamäki (Eds.), *Perspectives on activity theory* (pp. 1–38). Cambridge: Cambridge University Press.

Gates, H.L. (1986). *"Race," writing, and difference.* Chicago: University of Chicago Press.

Gee, J.P. (2000). The new literacy studies: From "socially situated" to the work of the social. In D. Barton, M. Hamilton, & R. Ivanic (Eds.), *Situated literacies: Reading and writing in context* (pp. 180–196). London: Routledge.

Gikandi, S. (2002/2006). Globalization and the claims of postcoloniality. In B. Ashcroft, G. Griffiths, & H. Tifflin (Eds.), *The post-colonial studies reader* (pp. 473–476). New York: Routledge.

Hillocks, G. (2002). *Testing trap: How state writing assessments control learning.* New York: Teachers College Press.

Ibrahim, A. (2008). The new flâneur. *Cultural Studies, 22*(2), 234–253.

Johnson, D.H. (2003). *The root causes of Sudan's civil wars.* Bloomington: Indiana University Press.

Kinloch, V. (2010). *Harlem on our minds: Place, race, and the literacies of urban youth.* New York: Teachers College Press.

Martin, D. C., & Hoefer, M. (2009). *Refugees and asylees 2008: Annual flow report.* Office of Immigration Statistics, U.S. Department of Homeland Security. Retrieved August 30, 2009, from www.dhs.gov/xlibrary/assets/statistics/publications/ois_rfa_fr_2008.pdf

McMahon, F.R. (2007). *Not just child's play: Emerging traditions and the lost boys of Sudan.* Jackson: University of Mississippi Press.

Moje, E. (2002). But where are the youth? On the value of integrating youth culture into literacy theory. *Educational Theory, 52*(1), 97–120.

Myers, W.D. (2001). *Monster.* New York: Amistad Press.

Perry, K. (2008). From storytelling to writing: Transforming literacy among Sudanese refugees. *Journal of Literacy Research, 40,* 317–388. doi: 10.1080/10862960802502196

Perry, K. (2009). Genres, contexts, and literacy practices: Literary brokering among Sudanese refugee families. *Reading Research Quarterly, 44*(3), 256–276. doi: 10.1598R RQ.44.3.2

Russell, D.R. (2009). Uses of activity theory in written communication research. In A. Sannino, H. Daniels, & K.D. Gutiérrez (Eds.), *Learning and expanding with activity theory* (pp. 40–52). New York: Cambridge University Press.

Salahu-Din, D., Persky, H., & Miller, J. (2008). *The nation's report card: Writing (NCES 2008–468).* Washington, DC: National Center for Educational Statistics, Institute of Education Sciences, U.S. Department of Education.

Sarroub, L.K. (2002). In-betweenness: Religion and conflicting visions of literacy. *Reading Research Quarterly, 37*(2), 130–148.

UN High Commissioner for Refugees (2009). *2008 global trends: Refugees, asylum-seekers, returnees, internally displaced and stateless persons.* Retrieved August 30, 2009, from www.unhcr.org/4a375c426.html

8

SPATIALIZING SOCIAL JUSTICE RESEARCH IN ENGLISH EDUCATION

sj Miller

The chapters in this book stem from a common genesis: the idea that injustice is socially produced as a by-product of power, reinforced through a geographic, temporal, economic, political, gendered, and heteronormative polis, and sustained by explicit and/or implicit complicity with tradition stemming from values derivative of the Enlightenment era, where scientific thought was privileged and education was an extension of the government. We have inherited from this polis unjust and uneven advantages and disadvantages and mythologized social norms, which, although they are historically situated, we never made. However, these chapters also highlight time as space and powerful tools that can be used to construct *Fourth Spaces* that invite teachers, students, and researchers to identify sites for agency and action.

Building onto Soja's (2010) observation that research is undergoing a "spatial turn," which suggests that geographies are informing our critical consciousness about how we read the world and that "a rebalancing is beginning to occur between social, historical, and spatial perspectives, with no one of the three ways looking at and interpreting the world inherently privileged over the others" (p. 3), the vision of the contributors to this volume bridges this spatial turn as they challenge how binary literacy signifiers have kept social norming in place. As demonstrated by the chapter authors, this collection shows how developing collaborative and co-constructed literacy spaces can generate and produce agency for students spatially and temporally. By agency, they recall Freire (1970), who said that students (the oppressed), when their oppression is unveiled to them and they acquire literacy tools, can act on and transform themselves individually as well as the spaces around them. Such spaces, in turn, have the potential to inform their identities as they eventually participate in a fragile democracy. Informed participation can help to rebalance what should be fair and equitable scales of social justice in society at large. Collectively, this volume pedagogically addresses how to dismantle wrongs that have perpetuated unjust consequences for students and their progeny. To this end, this volume draws upon transdisciplinary theories that pivot us toward healing injustice in all its forms and that are committed to developing a new spatialized consciousness that is not fixed or static but flexible and adaptive about social justice and its related research in education. These works can lead English educators to advocate for those who have been oppressed by educational systems and the terrain of concomitant social geographies, as they demonstrate how a newly evolving spatiality and temporality related to developing a grounded social justice consciousness orients the field by spatializing praxis throughout literacy events.

Can the Past Be Reframed or Rebalanced by a Space-time Structuration?

Spatiality and temporality open up new dimensions for considering how trans-disciplinary theories reveal the past as binary-laden and temporally fragmented as we interpret the present and predict the future. Spatiality becomes a new terrain of positing meaning that is not solely dependent on hegemonic discourse but that can generate new understandings of how change is accounted for in new contexts and even post-contexts.

The relationality of time/temporality as an additive to space, for instance, highlights for these researchers particular moments during specified contexts when injustices occur in a pairing described as a "spacetime structuration" (Miller, forthcoming). Through the efficacy that social justice work can have in the English classroom and schools at large by looking closely at space-time structuration, social justice can disrupt and interrupt current practices that reproduce social, cultural, moral, economic, gendered, intellectual, and physical injustices.

For instance, where current but dated laws still shape the populace's opinion and behavior around social issues such as ability, poverty, race, sexual orientation, and gay marriage rights, and even where those laws are no longer in place, not all attitudes and dispositions are quickly erased from our collective memories. Applying a spatial lens to specific time periods can help us make meaning of the power that dominant narratives had in shaping a populace. A teaching unit about social justice and injustice in classrooms then could be viewed as consequentially situated in particular geo-histories and gene pools as well as within the inhabitants who dwell in a particular locale. Teachers could show through readings, documentaries, videos, and even current policies and laws how injustices manifest the effect of any dangers of spatiality in any of these areas. Teachers might also demonstrate the power of inheriting social injustice power and how it can inform attitudes and identities in society. Teachers can demonstrate that if such injustices go unchecked or uninterrupted, they have great power to be operationalized structurally and rein-force cultural and ideological policies that perpetuate an unjust and unequal society. Unchecked and unexamined remnants also leave (in)visible social, cultural, economic, gendered, and personal scars that are reinscribed and that continue to be woven into educational geographies. Applying social justice and spatializing it into literacy event and research can have endless possibilities to shift emerging geo-histories.

Unpacking Context—the Space/Place and Time/Temporality Space-time Continuum

For researchers interested in time and space, contexts are specific spaces/places, accentuated by time, within a particular geography. Spaces/places as spatialized are not fixed or static; they shape and orient people's values, thoughts, behaviors, beliefs, and identities, while people also shape spaces/places and ascribe meaning to them. Spaces/places are also meant to hold "contemporaneous plurality" (Massey, 2005, p. 9) where a multiplicity of views can exist. On the basis of the time/temporality of an event, meaning is ascribed to a space/place through the dominant historical narratives (in /spaces/places) that are encumbered within specified sociopolitical, educational, cultural, and economic policies and laws. While such spaces/places during any space-time are always under construction, time/temporality is never irreversible. This means that while contexts are continually impacted by an inheritance of geo-histories of prior sociopolitical, educational, cultural, and economic policies and laws as individuals act on and seek to transform them whether through policy, environmental changes (clean air reform), buildings, developments, or the movement of new people or culture, time must be viewed as a by-product of a momentary event that identifies or punctuates a given context. Therefore, from a social justice viewpoint, time and space are oppositional because time hegemonizes place. This autopoeisis of past and present (and even those working in other spaces trying to create systemic change) space-time work in tandem to create layered experiences that rhizomatically (Miller & Norris, 2007) impact the inhabitants of a given geography. The layered effect happens concurrently and cannot be parsed linearly. In other words, the interrelatedness between person and place offers teachers an opportunity to make meaning about how evolving geo-histories could be recast as nonlinear and as nonhierarchical counternarratives. Such a recasting has the potential to challenge the way dominant narratives have been interpreted and have traditionally marginalized people on the basis of social categories connected to race, ethnicity, gender, gender expression, age, appearance, ability, national origin, language, spiritual belief, size (height and/or weight), sexual orientation, social class, economic circumstance, environment, ecology, culture, and the treatment of animals. In this light, the recasting of literacy events can turn classrooms into "real-time" experiences that have the potential to generate agency for students through a retelling of history. These authors take into consideration the dislocation of space from time/temporality and understand that literacy events are by-products resulting from collectives of dominant narratives over time.

That said, if we can agree that the spaces/places that surround us are socially constructed, that is, are sociospatial (Soja, 2010), and that the social inheritance that has befallen and informed identities are sociospatial, too, then we can surmise that they can be deconstructed and even dismantled through teaching and social and political action. Yet, through a commitment to unpack these historically situated geographies of injustice that have reproduced social, cultural, and gendered inequities, we must, at the same time, supply teachers (and inhabitants of geographies) and their students with neo-contemporary tools and discourses that help to resituate, replace, and recast the past while also repairing an education system that is on the verge of falling back into—if it hasn't already—a Marxist reproduction model. Spatializing social justice literacy research can inform shifts in policies that might, over time, have lasting value within various sociopolitical contexts.

Spacetime: Social Justice and Injustice

The binary relationality of justice to injustice helps us to bear witness and to observe the political activities mitigating acts of social justices and social injustices. In a particular space-time (Miller, 2008b) when social injustice occurs, it is often felt and witnessed and can incite response, and when social justice occurs, it often goes undetected and is experienced as the normalized morality. Currently, there is a growing momentum in education about spatializing social justice and its related research that is orienting our field toward an evolving spatial consciousness that Soja (2010) describes as a "spatial praxis" (p. 169).

Social Justice Research and Geo-History

Geographies have unjust histories that predate their contemporary inhabitants. Based on where we are born geographically, we inherit a politik of history that was instituted long before our habitation. These space-time geographies (see Figure 8.1), that is, the rhizomatic matrix (Miller & Norris, 2007) of the first space or literally the physical space, and the concomitant sociopolitical, educational, cultural, and economic policies and laws orient and shape people's values, thoughts, behaviors and beliefs. As we walk in the world from a nascent age, we acquire tools that help us navigate such myriad terrains by adapting, manipulating, and challenging and being challenged by the world around us. An inheritance of geo-histories, or the collective history of a given geography, bind a people (but not bound them) to now-unjust dated policies such as but not limited to prohibiting interracial relationships or the lack of rights for Black Americans, Asian Americans, Hispanic Americans, Native Americans, women, homosexuals, transgender people, the otherly abled, second-language learners, immigrants, and the poor and working class. These laws bare the core values and beliefs of a country that *once* believed that the "other" was lesser than, second-class citizens subject to hegemonic dominance, which has greatly affected humans and their mis/treatment of each other. While the remnants of these past state and national policies and their ensuing attitudes still linger in a collective wounding, and while they are still in the process of being

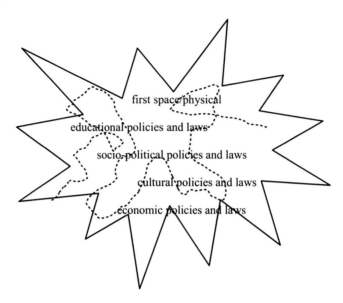

FIGURE 8.1 Rhizomatic Matrix

This rhizomatic matrix co-constructs the identity of the inhabitants of a geography during a given spacetime. The location of these factors that shape identity are arbitrary.

replaced by "more" just policies, guarantees of changes in behavior and attitude are far from being fully actualized nationwide. Because of these geo-histories that we have inherited and that we never made, many geographies of our country are still deeply entrenched in antediluvian attitudes that continue to perpetuate unfair and unjust social practices. Many of these attitudes filter into neighborhood schools and continue to inform the behaviors and attitudes of those being educated in this space-time (Miller & Norris, 2007). So while some progress toward social justice has been made for human rights in our country, social injustice is deeply embedded spatially, temporally and socially in the geo-histories of our country and presents a formidable challenge to educators to remedy, reconcile, and repair an educational system that is in need of immediate restructuring. By studying the space-time matrix of a geo-history, we can come to understand how people have been impacted by social justice and injustice.

Social Justice and the Spatial Turn toward Fourth Space

In recent research, the term "Fourth Space" (Miller, 2010) was coined to represent an agentive-concept based upon the groundbreaking work of the critical geographer Edward Soja, who translated Henri LeFebvre's work on "Third Space." Unlike Soja's (1996) first (real and concrete space), second (imagined space) (see Figure 8.2), and even Third Space (lived space where the real and imagined come together), Fourth

Space is an interzone, or a socially produced vertical space of interdependence between student and teacher and teacher and world. This space is located within the human psyche, a space of dormant agency, and can be enacted or triggered by experiences in classroom settings via an attic of the mind. Fourth Space is a space for agency (e.g., Zen and homeostasis) that rises above a whole society in which a deficient educational system and corporatized politics render teachers devoid of agency (Baumgartner, 2010). The physical or first space, which in the view of the teacher includes the classroom, the students, the school, involves concrete material that is deeply entwined within a complex history of power and hegemonic struggle. Challenges that are posed to a teacher's first-space spatiality through the teacher-student dialectical and that cannot be enacted because of possible redress and/or a teacher's fear of speaking truths that might be forbidden by policy can perceptually transport a teacher into Fourth Space. Fourth Space opens up for a teacher a hybridization of infinite terrain, of past, present, and future renderings. Through a Fourth Space embodiment, a teacher is transported "into" a space-time structuration that is maintained and sustained by the teacher alone—sort of an attic or private/privatized dwelling, if you will, where a teacher can eschew and traverse conventional models of expectation and consider possibilities for radicalization and even transformation for self and student alike before responding in the few seconds that the teacher calls "wait time" or "critical check-in out/times" (Miller, 2008a). It is a space of relocation that unifies for teachers what Spinoza called the body/mind dualism, which is often separated in first space. Here in Fourth Space (see Figure 8.3), in the teacher's inner sanctuary, during this brief check-out time, a teacher has seconds to stabilize by quickly reflecting, reconsidering, refusing, reconceptualizing, rejuvenating, and then reengaging with an emotional, cognitive, and corporeal response (Miller, 2010, p. 65). In private code, unseen to anyone, this space is a form of resistance, a space to enact social justice rightly. As teachers stabilize within this inner sanctuary, a response that is committed to the greater good and the preservation of human dignity, the struggle against hegemonic processes which have long endured, begins to weaken and lessen in its stronghold of education and humankind.

I offer the following discussion of space-time structuration as a case in point for thinking about how space and time operate as a system of power in English education classrooms. I offer this analysis of space-time as an invitation to think about how power operates in educational contexts and how recasting a literacy narrative can, in turn inform preserve and inform both a student's and a teacher's identity and agency.

The Scenario

A 10th-grade classroom is located in the rural South during 2010 in which there is a district policy against books that might promote or empower any traditionally marginalized group. A teacher, fully aware of the ban, ignores it and, instead, has

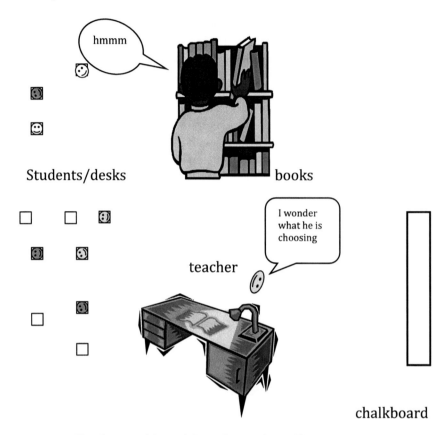

Students/desks   **books**

teacher

chalkboard

FIGURE 8.2 First Space and Second Space Activated in a Classroom

First-space examples in this scenario include the classroom, students' and teacher's desks, books, the chalkboard, the teacher, and the students. Second-space examples include the student selecting the text and imagining what is inside and the teacher's inner monologue about what the student is selecting.

Clip art used with permission from Microsoft.

a classroom library full of banned books. The teacher openly discusses with the students the district ban and what it could mean for the teacher if parents or district personnel were to object. She has told her students that the rationale for the district is that reading these texts might possibly incite such marginalized groups to become angry when they understand their oppression. In spite of the ban, a student decides he wants to read Alice Walker's *The Color Purple*.

STUDENT: (Goes over to the bookshelf and peruses it—visible to everyone, so this is known as **first space**. The student's thinking is not visible to anyone but the student as the student considers what book to read through an inner monologue—this event is in **second space**.)

Scene A   **Scene B**

FIGURE 8.3 Third Space and Fourth Space Activated in a Classroom

In Scene A the Third Space example occurs when the teacher asks the student what he selected to read and the student responds "*The Color Purple.*" In Scene B, the Fourth Space example is the teacher's response when he knows that the text is on the banned book list for the district but doesn't want to tell the student the politics behind the rationale that was given to him and must take a moment to reflect on how to respond to the student considering his fear of possible retaliation by the district.

Clip art used with permission from Microsoft.

TEACHER: (Thinks to herself, "I wonder what book he's looking at?" This event is also in **second space) (see Figure 8.2)**.

STUDENT: (Takes book off of shelf and walks to the teacher). "I'd like to read *The Color Purple.* I've wanted to read it forever." (This event occurs in the **Third Space**, where the real and imagined come together.)

TEACHER: "Well, it's a banned book. Let me think for a second." (The actual event occurs in **Fourth Space.**)

STUDENT: "I really want to read it. My mom read it and said it is one of her favorite books" (see Figure 8.3).

TEACHER: (Teacher is quiet while she reflects on how to respond.)

Discussion

This scenario, as examined through a space-time lens, sheds light on the importance of spatializing social justice in literacy research. The year of this event is significant, because while it is contemporary, it takes into account that while this school has a geo-historical narrative that still operates, students receive prejudiced messages about literacy events. When the teacher steps in and explains her position about the danger of banned books in the district, it provides the student a window of opportunity to critique and recast a narrative about oppression based on past and current temporality. A follow-up to this literacy event might take shape as a paper, project, readings, or even dialogue. Agency ensues through recasting the event by proposing a counternarrative.

To not address literacy events laden with adversity not only leaves us with blemished reputations nationally and worldwide but leaves youth all the more vulnerable to long-lasting psychosocial, emotional, and educational deficits that may impair their abilities to function at their best in our democracy. As critical educators and researchers, we can no longer allow for stakeholders at the top levels of government who determine policies that anesthetize our educational system. We must assume agency for remaking and co-opting space-time. We must claim classrooms, Fourth-Space ourselves, and apply social justice to remedy such disparities. Schools are in deep need of repair, and spatializing social justice research through literacy can inform movements of collective-social consciousness and responsibility. To leave any student behind, or to ban a book that has the potential to forever shift a person's identity is to privilege dominant cultures' beliefs and values about what it means to be "rightly" human while it simultaneously acknowledges defeat of social justice in education. The way we reshape and reframe our research and the literacy events in our classrooms simultaneously challenges the privileging of history over spatiality and temporality.

On the other hand, what about the implicit social injustice that is woven into the fabric of teaching or schooling practices through the absence of inclusive policies? How can teachers become agents of change by enacting Fourth Space and develop dispositions (Miller, forthcoming) dedicated to social justice for all students when it might cost them positions or status in their districts? This could be enacted by spatializing work across classroom borders, collecting data about ineffective standardized tests, showing the results of diminished time for curriculum on student achievement, not tolerating bias in school and in local charters, and strengthening a national voice that advances students rather than tests. Some of this work can be done in classrooms, during brown-bag lunches, at school board meetings, through national conferences, and by tapping senators and state representatives who can advance the cause of social justice reform in schools. In terms of professional development, this means making teachers partners in research, sharing articles and life experiences related to social injustice, tying continuing credits to courses in universities about social justice in education, and educating and updating principals, school board members, parents, and other community members about unfair practices that are still prevalent in schools.

Social Justice in the Horizon

What could social justice in literacy research look like in schools today? Agential Fourth Spaces recur throughout this edited text. Notably, agential Fourth Spaces are constructed and utilized by teachers, students, and researchers. Some chapter authors highlight the potential agency of teachers. Saldãna's memories of Mrs. Whitehouse (chapter 1), his high school English teacher, demonstrate how classroom space was transformed into a site for change and action as Saldāna carried his high school experiences with him throughout his adult and professional life. Likewise, the teachers described by Grigorenko, Beierle, and Bloome (chapter 4) drew upon collective memories to create opportunities for understanding, investing, and learning.

Other chapter authors have identified spaces for student agency. Guerra (chapter 2) describes how the simple act of reading his birth certificate invited him to navigate and negotiate the challenges of life in the Neither/Nor. Similarly, Pahl (chapter 3) presents "Declan Dancing," highlighting the out-of-school experiences that contribute to the school lives of children. Blackburn and Clark (chapter 6) present the possibilities offered by texts that tell the stories of LGBTQ youth. Drawing on technological affordances, Bass (chapter 9) describes how children, adolescents, and emerging adults are using new technologies as tools for representation, and Chisholm (chapter 10) explores possibilities offered by traditional and multimodal tasks in classrooms.

Finally, opportunities for agency in the Third Space are also available to researchers. Falchi and Siegel (chapter 5) describe how the temporal organization of school can limit meaning making for young children. The research of Crandall (chapter 7) and of Schwartz, Noguerón-Lui, and González (chapter 12) reminds educators that researchers have the power to reveal the inequities that accompany schooling for children whose cultural and lived knowledges have not been historically valued in schools.

As these authors see it, social justice can become an agent-generative tool/identity artifact that is both the embodiment or state of heightened moral and ethical consciousness and the extension of self for mediating identity (Leander, 2002) and for resisting the perpetuation of hegemonic-laden values and behavior that have kept people from rising to meet their full capability thresholds (Nussbaum, 2006). Once grounded in literacy research, social justice has power as a tool/identity artifact that can be revisited and continually renewed and experienced over space and in time to help policymakers, researchers, teachers, and pre-service teachers to make needed changes. Where geo-historically situated hegemony once prevailed as the omniscient arbiter for our society, social justice has the potential to become its successor; thus, from this vantage point, social justice has real-time relevance that can mark this time of change and inform a sociospatial consciousness.

Social justice related to schools, if afforded broad opportunities to develop panoramically (through policy, research, pedagogy, and praxis and as classroom method), can have value and efficacy over space-time. Such a restructuring can move us from spatial determinism and pivot our field toward developing a spatialized social justice consciousness in educational reform. Yet, though this would be ideal, we must also ask an important question: How do we sustain the efforts of change once they become woven into an evolving geo-history? It would seem that if our field is able to generate a social justice consciousness panoramically, social justice can become a mainstay in our field and possibly be spatialized into other disciplines in education (see Miller & Kirkland, 2010). Miller and Kirkland (2010) caution that, unless it influences policy, "social justice, like so many other catchphrases, will be as marginal as the populations for which we advocate" (p. 2).

Spatializing Social Justice—from and into—Other Fields

As we contemplate next steps for spatializing social justice research in English education, we can learn from various related fields, including democracy studies, sociocultural studies, critical pedagogy, critical theory, critical race theory, critical geography, cultural studies, disability studies, crip studies (studies that attend to cultures of disabilities and queerness), feminism, justice studies, media and communication, philosophy, political science, queer studies, sociology, spatiality/hybridity theories, and second-language theories. We might also consider the research from within our own field, such as the work conducted by the Conference on English Education (CEE) Commission for Social Justice. The *CEE position statement: Beliefs about social justice in English education* (CEE, 2009) and the *Resolution on Social Justice in Literacy Education* (CEE, 2010) offer concrete examples for how to spatialize social justice literacy research and practice, broadly speaking. We might also consider the recent work of Miller and Kirkland (2010), who highlight different ways of conducting social justice research through a "Threefold Theory of Social Justice" that forefronts reflection, change, and participation. The hybridization of any combination of the work from this volume's contributors along with other works referenced throughout have great potential for informing a future phase of social justice literacy work in schools. As research fields related to social justice begin to merge and challenged one another, we move toward a more powerful, sustained, and geographically dispersed collaborative of spatializing consciousness about social justice and literacy research.

The authors of this volume have offered their visions of literacy classrooms that honor and support students from all walks of life through various grounded space-time practices. What can we learn from them, and what *would* schools look like today if all people involved in schooling were on the same page about the inclusion and actualization social justice? We are challenged to continue to develop unique spatial and temporal analyses, fueled by commitments to social justice that highlight literacy events, that is, if we each believe that every student rightly deserves a school setting free from duress, where each student is afforded the same advantages as students sitting nearby and each student embodies the belief that it is the custodial work of all humanity to care for and accept others not because of their differences but because we are all part of a larger spatial consciousness that shapes and informs the inhabitants of all geographies. This change does not have to be a dream or waning fantasy—changes and small miracles are happening each and every day. Our field still has much work to do, and we cannot be agentive if we *only* hope. We must be teacher-generative-activists who truly embody change as we recast wrongs and thread social justice spatially and temporally throughout our collective literacy praxes. In other words, "The contract we enter into in schools must honor the sociocultural advantages and disadvantages of each of us. It must seek to offer the same educational, sociocultural, and psycho-emotional opportunities to all in order to help people meet and obtain a determined, but basic threshold that is mutually beneficial to each party who enters into the school space" (Miller & Kirkland, 2010, p. 5).

References

Baumgartner, B. (2010). Towards an ethics of selfhood: An essay on fourthspace, ontology and critical pedagogy. Unpublished manuscript, Indiana University of Pennsylvania.

Conference on English Education Executive Committee. (2009). CEE position statement: Beliefs about social justice in English education. Retrieved February 15, 2014, from www.ncte.org/cee/positions/socialjustice

Freire, P. (1970). *The pedagogy of the oppressed.* New York: Continuum.

Leander, K. (2002). Locating Latanya: The situated production of identity artifacts in classroom interaction. *Research in the Teaching of English, 37,* 198–250.

Massey, D. (2005). *For space.* London: Sage.

Miller, s. (2008a). Fourthspace—Revisiting social justice in teacher education. In s Miller, L. Beliveau, T. DeStigter, D. Kirkland, & P. Rice, *Narratives of social justice teaching: How English teachers negotiate theory and practice between preservice and inservice spaces* (pp. 1–21). New York: Peter Lang.

Miller, s. (2008b). Reeinvisioning preservice teacher identity: Matrixing methodology. In J. Flood, S. B. Heath, & D. Lapp (Eds.), *Handbook of research on teaching literacy through the visual and communicative arts,* vol. 2 (pp. 151–159). New York: Lawrence Erlbaum.

Miller, s. (2010). *Scaffolding and embedding social justice into English education.* In s. Miller & D. Kirkland (Eds.), *Change Matters: Critical essays on moving social justice research from theory to policy* (pp. 61–67). New York: Peter Lang.

Miller, s. (forthcoming). Learning from equity audits: Powerful social justice in English education for the 21st Century. In L. Scherff & E. Morrell (Eds.), *English education for the 21st Century: Teaching, teacher education, research, assessment, and advocacy.* Lanham, MD: Rowman & Littlefield.

Miller, s., & Kirkland, D. (2010). *Change matters: Critical essays on moving social justice research from theory to policy.* New York: Peter Lang.

Miller, s., & Norris, L. (2007). *Unpacking the loaded teacher matrix: Negotiating space and time between university and secondary.* New York: Peter Lang.

Nussbaum, M. (2006). *Frontiers of justice: Disability, nationality, species membership.* Cambridge: Belknap Press.

Soja, E. (1996). *Thirdspace: Journeys to Los Angeles and other real-and-imagined places.* Malden: Blackwell.

Soja, E. (2010). *Seeking spatial justice.* Minneapolis: University of Minnesota Press.

SECTION 3
Timespaces and the Future in Literacy Research

"Flashforward"

Once again we must beg Saldaña's forgiveness. In Chapter 1 Saldaña used the term "flashforward" to refer to times when he moved forward in his homage to Mrs. Whitehouse, his former high school English teacher. As we introduce Section 3, we repurpose this term to reference the future and our experiences of contemplating possibilities as we draw on the past and act in the present. In Section 3, we invite readers to consider the timespaces of the future. Education is inherently about the future. Teaching and learning are about preparing people for the future and providing them with tools that will contribute to a rich and fulfilling life. In this section, we reflect on not only people's hopes, dreams, and expectations but also the affordances and possibilities made possible by new technologies and new media. How are new technologies creating new possibilities for acting, interacting, and being? How are these new possibilities constructed and located in relation to both the ghosts of the past and the limits of the present? How and when are both new and old literacies invoked, replaced, revisited, remixed, and rejected as learners use these tools to create new ways of being and learning? In Section 3, we explore how timespaces of the future provide new opportunities for acting, interacting, learning, and, ultimately, living.

9

REMIXES: TIME + SPACE IN YOUTH MEDIA ARTS ORGANIZATIONS

Michelle Bass

Digital technologies enable people of all ages to create nontext-based representations of self and others, and adolescence has emerged as a stage of development of particular interest to literacy scholars, who study adolescents' experiences with these new technologies (Bruce, 2009). Digital media technologies, such as social networking sites (Watkins, 2009), fan fiction, and massive multiplayer online games (Black & Steinkuehler, 2009), and digital films (Bruce, 2009; Halverson, Lowenhaupt, Gibbons, & Bass, 2009) enable individuals to express multiple identities by creating an avatar in an online virtual environment or presenting a representation of self through a digital video production. Children, adolescents, and emerging adults are leading the way by using new technologies as tools for representation. The ability to create, re-create, and make meaning from processes and products afforded by these new digital media technologies has caused a shakeup of the esteemed field of literacy studies as scholars now have to ask: What counts as literacy in the 21st century?

Traditional markers of literacy are the ability to read and write in a given language, but in the 21st century literacy is no longer bound to text-based print. The modes of meaning making available have exponentially increased with the digital revolution; technologies have forced the literacy field to expand (Potter, 2011). Street (2003) suggests we think of literacies "as some complex of domains [e.g., visual, media, print] that varies with context so that the mix of domains depends upon cultural and contextual features" and does not see the need to add media as a caveat to the term and understanding of literacy (p. 81). Being able to understand how to make meaning from new literacies "requires appropriating skills in defining and refining goals, searching and selecting various documents, websites, and other sources for relevant material," and making connections between materials (Tierney, 2009, p. 293). To classify the new literacies as critical, one must "understand who produces media, how and why they do so, how these media represent the world, and how they create meanings and pleasures" (Buckingham, 2008, p. 17–18). To Buckingham's requirements, I would add the questions of where and when media are being produced.

The When (Time) and Where (Spaces) of Digital Literacy Creation and Consumption

While in some instances powerful learning using digital media technologies is taking place at schools where children and youth are able to develop identities and gain knowledge (Warschauer, 2011), many scholars (Hull & Greeno, 2006; Leander, 2009; New London Group, 1996; Vasudevan & Hill, 2009) believe that most schools are organized in less than optimal ways to allow these identities to form. In many cases, media outside schools are providing an education that may contradict and supplant school-based learning as "the currency of youth." Schools are doing youth a disservice when the education the schools provide does not incorporate media-based literacy practices. In-school environments have not changed sufficiently to accommodate "the evolution of new technologies, geographies, and communicative modes" that young people use in their out-of-school lives (Vasudevan & Hill, 2009, p. 5). Leander (2009) criticizes schools for forcing students to "shift from a world replete with multimodal text, remixing and mashing, and fluid novice-expert relations, to a relatively unidimensional formalized context centered upon only one form of static text and structured by particular adult-child authority and knowledge hierarchies" (p. 2). As a result of many schools' lack of inclusion, students are forced to leave their digital literacies at the school door.

After- and out-of-school environments do not have the same boundaries for participation and acceptance of digital literacy. In out-of-school environments, learning may involve youth media classes that use updated, technologically savvy curricula or incorporate unstructured learning opportunities, as in the case of youth making films at home. Aspiring filmmakers' audiences can be as global as their YouTube channel fans allow. These out-of-school learning environments have become rich spaces for examining knowing and thought via diverse literacies. Street (2009) suggests that researchers are therefore tasked with "making visible the complexity of local everyday community literacy practices and challenging dominant stereotypes and myopia" (p. 22). These new information-source technologies use "the visual, dramatic, musical, and performative arts to complement, reproduce, and supplement" each other (Lapp, Flood, Heath, & Langer, 2009, p. 4).

Youth can make representations of self on their own in nonstructured learning environments; however, it may be difficult for a researcher to capture all of these at-home art-making moments. Youth media arts organizations (YMAOs) have emerged as welcoming learning environments where researchers can explore "multimodal production that involve identity construction" (Halverson et al., 2009, p. 23). YMAOs can be affiliated with schools or run as afterschool programs; most cater to middle and high school-age students. These organizations are found across the United States in both urban (e.g., Philadelphia, Project H.O.M.E.; Chicago, Street Level Youth Media) and rural areas (e.g., Whitesburg, Kentucky, Appalachian Media Institute). The media created in these organizations include digital stories, sound recordings, and digital videos or films.

The Pew Internet and American Life program (Lenhart, Madden, Macgill, & Smith, 2007) reports that, more than ever before, youth from poor and urban communities are engaged with digital media, and many YMAOs primarily serve marginalized adolescents (e.g., youth from low-socioeconomic-status families, Native American youth, or African American youth). Through their participation in YMAOs, marginalized adolescents are taught to use digital technologies to craft representations of self for global audiences.

Creating digital films in YMAOs is a kind of participatory culture:

> A participatory culture is a culture with relatively low barriers to artistic expression and civic engagement, strong support for creating and sharing one's creations, and some type of informal mentorship whereby what is known by the most experienced is passed along to novices. A participatory culture is also one in which members believer their contributions matter and feel some degree of social connection with one another. (Jenkins, Purushotma, Clinton, Weigel, & Robison, 2007, p. 3)

Youth create representations of self and explore who they want to be in spaces where their contributions matter and they are able to connect with their peers. These new media environments provide young people with new ways "to be creative and innovative" while also providing "new opportunities . . . to acquire and synthesize information in a meaningful way" (Parker, 2010, p. 144).

In this chapter, I explore how interactions within time and space in youth media arts organizations (YMAOs) create remixes. I analyze products created by participants in Reel Works Teen Filmmaking, an out-of-school YMAO based in Brooklyn, New York. I then share a case study of one participant's journey from being a youth participant creating digital art to becoming the cofounder, teacher, and mentor of InProgress, an organization that works in and out of schools serving Native American, Latino, and other marginalized youth in communities around the St. Paul metropolitan area and on Northern Minnesota reservations. By studying products from one YMAO, I keep the space of digital production constant, with time presenting change. Conversely, when I explore the process of digital art creation over a person's life, the spaces and roles involved with creation change over time. These combinations of change over space and time resulted in remixes of the digital media content and personal roles in the respective YMAOs.

Remixing Digital Literacy

The New London Group (1996) discussed the importance of hybridity, "articulating in new ways established practices within and between different modes of meanings"

(p. 82). Knobel and Lankshear (2008) build off the idea of hybridity to describe remixing as endless hybridization, with each new mix serving as a meaning-making resource for the next remix. The term "remixing" originated in the music industry to,

> refer to using audio-editing techniques to produce "an alternative mix of a recorded song that differed from the original . . . taking apart the various instruments and components that make up a recording and remixing them into something that sounds completely different" (Seggern, n.d., p. 1; cited in Knobel & Lankshear, 2008, p. 22)

Knobel and Lankshear (2008) repurposed the idea of remixing to explore how youth made meaning and expressed ideas using digital technologies. Making a remix means that artists "take cultural artifacts and combine and manipulate them into new kinds of creative blends" (p. 22). Importantly, remixing is not borrowing but is "building upon a work that already exists and using it to make new meanings and express new ideas" (Parker, 2010, p. 145). Remix creators have to understand the craft they are re-creating and understand the original sources' use, necessary technical aspects, and aesthetic dimensions in order to effectively relate it to a new context (Knobel & Lankshear, 2008; Parker, 2010). Adolescents "re-create and redefine" themselves using their understanding of meaning making with digital technologies and, in doing so, acquire "new habits of expectation, meaning, and credibility; new ways of acting, interacting, and doing; and gaining the competencies to become part of this digital world" (Parker, 2010, p. 144).

Time over Space: Filmic Remixes

For my master's thesis, I wanted to examine the ways in which young people expressed identity through digital film. I was interested in exploring the ways in which filmmakers expressed their identities and in discovering any thematic similarities across films and/or within seasons. I chose Reel Works Teen Filmmaking, based in Brooklyn, New York, as the case organization for this analysis because the organization's directors communicated a clear mission to participants that they should explore issues of personal identity in their films (Mission statement, n.d.). They provided a clear structure (three-act, short-form documentary) with which to represent personal identity. I viewed and analyzed 90 films in the Reel Works Teen Filmmaking film corpus and viewed each of the films three times.

Reel Works has a mission to support youth in sharing their ideas and voice through film. The specific films I analyzed were from a program called the "Lab." Twelve youth are selected for this free 21-week afterschool program, which runs twice a year and "challenges Brooklyn high school students to create short documentary films about their lives" (The Lab, n.d.). I analyzed the entire corpus of Reel Works films produced in the lab since its inception in 2001, which included 90 films produced by 12 cohorts between fall 2002 and spring 2008.

On the Reel Works website, emphasis is placed on the fact that youth "must have a story [they] are passionate about and absolutely must tell the world!" (The Lab, n.d.). YMAO participants use their own lives and experiences to create their digital products. While creating their documentaries, Reel Works' youth participants "gain self-esteem, develop media literacy and master state-of-the-art digital filmmaking technology" (The Lab, n.d.).

The YMAO mission statement emphasizes the power of individuals to create their own unique story. Youth at Reel Works work with an individual mentor, who is usually a professional filmmaker, to create their films; youth are also required to attend workshops and meetings. This is not to say that the youth do not influence one another's filmmaking process. However, this peer-to-peer guidance has not been fully realized. As the executive director noted, "I'd like to see more peer mentoring. So one thing we try to do is have the master-class kids help new kids. (Interview, July 27, 2007). In open group meetings and in more formal settings, such as when participants pitch their ideas to Reel Works' financial supporters, peers provide feedback and suggestions regarding the content and focus of one another's films. In some films, youth interview Lab members about a topic. However, the focus of each film centers on each youth's ideas and voice and the identity the teen chooses to share.

There is an explicit structure to Reel Works films that is reflected in their pedagogy and discourse about the process. As the executive director of Reel Works recounts, the structure of the lab is like that of a movie: "It has a beginning, middle, and end to it" (Interview, July 27, 2007). In the Reel Works film equation, there should be a clear introduction, where the main focus of the film is introduced; a middle section, where the story is developed; and a conclusive third piece that wraps up the story. Over the course of their weekly lab meetings, youth watch films from previous seasons and discuss their strengths and weaknesses.

When I observed a workshop in 2007, focal topics included the quality of interviews as well as the purpose of the film and its essential question. Before viewing films from previous seasons, the executive director described the essential question as something that is always bigger than the topic that the filmmaker addresses in the film. He emphasized that the essential question should guide the youth as filmmakers and asked them to try to determine the essential questions addressed in the two films they viewed. With a strong pedagogical focus, supportive mentorship model, and structured workshop schedule, youth at Reel Works produced 7- to 10-minute identity-focused films.

I employed an inductive coding scheme (Braun and Clark, 2006), incorporating multiple viewings of the films as a way to search for patterns, and arrived at the following three main themes: facing loss, overcoming challenges, and making choices.

It quickly became apparent that there was overlap among the themes presented in the films. This could be attributed to the fact that the artists were all late adolescents from the same city dealing with the issues that young people everywhere experience. However, these youth were also working in the same space, Reel Works Teen Filmmaking, and, because of this spatial/temporal positioning, were exposed to previously crafted films as examples of what they could accomplish. This combination of sharing space and reviewing the same products resulted in a remixing of topics across films and across seasons.

Seasonal Topical Remixes

A clear example of the influence of one season on another was evident in the similarities between *The Man within Me* (2003) and *Out of the Picture* (2006). Both films examine young men who grow up without their fathers; in *The Man within Me* the filmmaker addresses how he sees himself as a young man who grew up without a father and how he fits into this community of men. In the opening of *Out of the Picture*, the filmmaker shares that his family recently moved to the United States, but his father was unable to join them. He does not speak about himself in the film but instead interviews three young men who have also grown up without their fathers in their lives.

The *Man within Me* presents a series of interviews with three men who grew up without fathers; one of the three men is the youth filmmaker. In *Out of the Picture,* the film opens with the filmmaker telling us that he has recently been separated from his father because his family has moved to the States from Grenada. He then wonders how not having fathers in their lives influences young men. This director does not put himself in front of the camera and instead interviews other young men who have grown up without fathers. One of his interviewees is the filmmaker of *The Man within Me.* While there are differences in interview styles and footage, the thematic similarity and the focus on a community of men who grew up without fathers shows how influential previous films can be for future seasons.

Digital Generation Remixes

The examination of the role of digital media in youth culture was another recurring pattern. Three films—*Danger Zone, VENT,* and *Rated R*—focused specifically on technology and how it was used to create identities. *Danger Zone* and *Rated R* are both framed as public service warnings about dangers related to the Internet. *VENT* is an exploration of the ways in which young people vent their anger and thus represent their identities. *Rated R* focuses on the choices youth make around watching violent videos on the Internet. *Danger Zone* is also about choices related to Internet use.

In *VENT* (2005), the filmmaker asks, "With violence all around us, is it any wonder that aggression dominates our free time?" One of the four teens she profiles about dealing with anger is a young woman who plays video games. She describes how video games allow her to have power, which she does not feel in her real life. She wonders whether her venting is beneficial and asks, "Are these methods of venting just a stage or truly representative of who we are?" The teen's answer seems to suggest the latter, "In 20 years and stuff, I'll still be playing. There will be new game systems. . . . You don't get to use guns every day, and in this game you can. And you're not even hurting everyone. You're just hurting, like, zombies." She makes a strong distinction: Her actions while playing video games do not translate to the real world.

Danger Zone (2007) is a film about online sexual predators. This film most closely resembles a public service announcement about the dangers of the Internet and social networking sites. The film presents interviews with adults who prosecute and prevent online predators, including a chief of a sex-crimes unit. The filmmaker also interviews peers about the dangers of social networking sites. The film is interspersed with anecdotes from teens about inappropriate dialogue and interactions with online predators.

Rated R (2008) examines the effect of Internet violence and why so many youth find it entertaining. Images and videos of violence from the Internet are displayed during the film. The director interviews her peers, including some of the participants in her Reel Works season, about their feelings regarding the entertainment value of violence. One youth answers, "[The] media has a lot to do with it." The director closes the film with a quotation from an interviewee: "Fascinating but ain't cool."

Body Image Remixes

While films might share an overarching story line, there was room for divergence. The following three films from different seasons are about young women struggling with their weight: *Fat Free, Comfort,* and *Skin and Bones.* The films share particular thematic coding choices and a message focused on overcoming challenges. *Fat Free* is the story of a young woman who constantly struggles with her weight and issues of self-esteem. Her film is presented as a video diary featuring photos of herself as a heavy child, footage of her working out at the gym, and before and after examinations of her stomach to see if she has lost weight. Ultimately, she shares that while her life may appear perfect—she graduated from high school and has a job in the city and a new Mercedes—her inner battle with her weight prevents her from truly enjoying life. *Comfort* focuses explicitly on the filmmaker's struggle to lose weight to avoid obesity-related complications that run in her family, such as diabetes. At the end, the filmmaker reports that she has lost weight and is trying to maintain her healthier lifestyle and feels more comfortable with herself.

With *Skin and Bones,* the director puts us face to face with her struggle with bulimia. The opening sequence ends with an image of the results of her latest binge in the bathroom. Unlike the other two films, this filmmaker includes an interview with her mother, who explicitly describes how she views her daughter as she struggles to gain weight. This film was thematically coded as focused on overcoming challenges associated with an eating disorder and the choices the director continues to make in her life. The film ends with her contemplating whether or not she will be healthy enough to leave home and attend college.

Space over Time: Role Remix

Through my research, I learned that many current organization instructors and leaders were once YMAO youth. I began to witness a remix of roles. Over time, the spaces and, subsequently, the roles of youth participants changed. Participants became mentors; in the case study explored later in this chapter, a former participant became a coleader of the organization. I became interested in the identity transitions of former youth participants. I was particularly interested in learning how participation in YMAOs might have influenced participants' major life transitions, specifically their educational transitions from middle to high school or from high school to college, as well as the occupational move from student to teacher. I was also open to learning about other important self-identified periods of transition.

Locating participants who had been youth members of the media organization and later worked for the organization was challenging. The executive directors of the four case study YMAOs were contacted and asked whether any of their current or former employees had been youth members. Only one former youth, Bao Thao, volunteered. At the time of the interviews, Bao was 28 years old and a married mother of two young sons. She had participated in InProgress as a youth and later shaped the program into its current organizational structure. At the time of the two interviews, she was an instructor and a mentor for in- and out-of-school programs and was also working on her own documentary films.

At our first meeting I used a modified version of Seidman's (2006) three-part life-history interview process to explore Bao's life history. The second meeting was focused on her experiences participating in and working with InProgress and her reflections on those experiences. Both session were planned as semistructured interviews but evolved into open dialogues between Bao and me.

Youth Participant and Student

Bao attended an alternative secondary school where graduation requirements centered on creative production evaluations rather than test scores. Media arts were introduced in her eighth-grade classroom by an "artist that came in to really teach us and show us . . . media arts stuff" by incorporating "social studies with video and writing with poetry" (Interview, April 2009). Bao was "given a video camera and had lots of stories [she]wanted to tell. . . . It was great, that first year was really just an introduction to video making" (Interview, April 2009). Her first video was a collaborative piece with classmates about gang violence.

Bao met the future codirector of InProgress, Cate, when she was the video production artist in her ninth-grade classroom. Cate also focused on video production, but in a more free-style approach; Bao reported that Cate said:

> Here's the video camera, do whatever you want to do with it. And everyone was just like, we don't know what to do it with it. And I remember she goes, here, just take it home and videotape, and, um, bring back the footage and we'll put something together for you. And I said, What? How am I supposed to do that? (Interview, April 2009)

Bao took the camera home and collected footage, which she thought looked good, but she was not sure it made sense. Bao recalled Cate saying, "You're really talking about a lot of different stuff here, aren't you? It's a pretty cool video." This caused Bao to really start looking at her work, and she realized, "Yeah, I am talking about a lot of stuff here." Cate encouraged Bao to attend an out-of-school workshop she was running for young people. There was one small problem: Bao had no way of getting from her home to the metropolitan-based organization.

> I took a look at her and I said no I can't, because it's so far away and I probably don't have a ride. And she said, what if I gave you a ride or what if I found you a ride, would you come? (Interview, February 2009)

Bao took the offer. As she explained, "This woman is willing to drive out here to pick me up." This made Bao think she should put more effort into making films. She worked with a mentor in the organization and made her first solo film which focused on her struggles with identity and culture as a young Hmong woman living in the United States. Bao described the film as a "self-portrait. An expression of how I felt. Um, being stuck, just in life in general" (Interview, February 2009). This film was shown at a local museum, and Bao received high praise from many gallery visitors.

> I was like, whoa. People are actually listening to what I have to say, and I didn't even have to, you know, speak a word. So I was like, um, I think from there on, I got really interested, um, using video as a voice for me. (Interview, February 2009)

Organization Cofounder and Leader

Using video as a voice was the catalyst for Bao's continued participation with Cate's organization. Bao began to work more closely with Cate to find other outlets for producing films. They quickly realized that there were many programs that worked with youth in the metropolitan area. One day during brainstorming, Bao expressed interest in bringing these programs together to form one organization. "We started talking about, um, who would become our board and how the organization would look like. And so, that's how InProgress got developed" (Interview, February 2009).

Cate and Bao quickly realized how important their organization could be for other young people who wanted to share their voices. "We realized that it's not about an organization, it's about the people that we work with, the artists that we work with. And from there on, it's who I am now" (Interview, February 2009).

Teacher and Mentor

Bao continued making her own films through high school, with many going into film festivals and being seen by audiences outside her organizational community. Following her high school graduation, she attended the local public university for a year but did not continue.

> That was not for me. I did not want to be taught how to make film for certain reasons and, um, I began teaching with Cate. And from teaching with Cate I learned more and more about what I really want to do for myself and my community and my culture and for my family. (Interview, February 2009)

Bao served as an instructor for many of the InProgress programs in the local schools. She and Cate introduced video and photography to students from elementary through high school. Echoing Bao's first experiences with video, they gave students cameras, saying, "Take the video camera and tell us a story" (Interview, April 2009).

Bao does not describe her work as teaching; rather, she thinks of herself as "sharing [her] experiences and carrying that or showing that to somebody else" (Interview, April 2009). She resists naming her role in the organization.

> I don't know if I'm coordinator or manager. I just see myself as the artist who is sort of, I don't know . . . I just see myself as the artist, the artist in the organization who's sort of giving my experience. Handing it down or mentoring artists who are coming in or providing opportunities and giving, um, getting, opening up doors and opening up opportunities for the other artists. (Interview, February 2009)

Many participants, like Bao, continue their engagement with InProgress after they create their first video pieces with the organization. Bao commented on the young people in their organization:

> They're here to contribute. They're here to take away from it and learn and give. And do wonderful things with it. And I'm really, I'm really excited and

just happy that it's here and that I'm able to contribute to it and be a part of it. (Interview, April 2009)

She recounted a story about a former participant who had recently called her to ask about how to start a film festival in his new hometown. She also shared with pride that a former youth member was now working as a Hollywood actor and had recently performed in a Clint Eastwood film.

For Bao, "InProgress is a part of me and who I am." It is especially important to her because of what she believes:

> [Young] people should have the opportunities that I [had]. And I want to be able to have those opportunities available and to create those opportunities for other young people. We have a lot of young people that participate now. (Interview, April 2009)

Storyteller

Bao is more comfortable embracing the role of storyteller. She encourages InProgress youth to incorporate their identities into their own work.

> We do media to really tell stories. And we understand that that is something that is really important. . . . It's more about storytelling, it's learning about who they are and what they want to be. It's also what they can do and what they want to do. . . . And they're in the middle, everything that they do with it and from it is within themselves. (Interview, April 2009)

Bao recognizes that the focus on storytelling makes InProgress different from many other youth media arts organizations, which are, as she explains,

> great at media making and introducing the media tools and getting them into the media field, but as far as you know, having them discover themselves and having them, uh, really learn how to tell their story from within, from their perspective, I think that's what In Progress does and that's something that we encourage. And, I think a lot of these young participants and artists that come back or are staying understand that and are trying to discover whatever that you're trying to discover within In Progress. (Interview, April 2009)

The importance of the storyteller role extends beyond Bao's work with In Progress. Bao has unofficially become her extended family's storyteller. What began as an in-class video production assignment evolved into a lifelong commitment to using digital film to share stories. Bao went from being a novice artist to being a teacher, mentor, and director for hundreds of other young artists. She has dedicated nearly 15 years to InProgress, and with each year and each new participant she continues to support new young artists.

Space + Time = Remix

YMAOs are only one kind of participatory culture where remixes occur. Classrooms also have the ability to serve as spaces for participatory culture. When digital technologies and literate practices are embraced in in-school learning environments, they "allow for a blurring of boundaries between informal and formal learning and harnesses the power of digital technologies for students to reflect on the participatory culture they live in" (Parker, 2010, p. 146). Teachers can promote a shift to bridge the gaps between life and school (Parker, 2010). Teachers need not fear their lack of digital literacy knowledge. Potter (2011) maintains that media literacy occupies a continuum, not a category:

> We all occupy some position on the media literacy continuum, there is no point below which we could say that someone has no literacy and there is no point on the high end where we could say that someone is fully literate— there is always room for improvement. (p. 21)

Grushka (2009) presents visual art education as a "platform for engaged and transformative learning, where students work between personal experiences, social realities and beliefs of family, peers, and significant others" (p. 239). She describes the importance of reworking representations of the world as a powerful way for understanding the complexities of identities and the evolving self, a sentiment that is reflected in the New London Group's concept of hybridity (1996) and Knobel and Lankshear's (2008) discussion of remixing. Grushka (2009) supports my belief in the importance of studying digital media production as a way of representing identity with her claim that "it is an essential aspect of being human to ask questions about the relationship between presenting representations, thinking, feeling, and the complexities of the experiencing phenomenon" (p. 239).

Zoss (2009) does not reprimand the field of secondary literacy studies for its lack of visual arts so much as she proposes the integration of the visual arts for both students and teachers by the addition of more "sign systems" rather than relying solely on language-based systems. Adding visual arts into the literacy curriculum allows teachers to teach adolescent students methods and skills for understanding the different kinds of texts they encounter in and out of school. These analyses on the affordances of digital technologies and tools for media literacy point to the fact that youth are not passive consumers of media but rather active agents in both consumption and production. Youth are using these tools to represent themselves to local and distal peers, known and unknown, and to the world.

Art making, such as digital film production, is fundamentally a representational practice, and youth are increasingly becoming members of (digital) art-making communities. If youth are the digital generation, marked by their ability to represent and express themselves digitally, then school personnel must embrace the possibilities of digital media technologies and the new literacies afforded by their use and consumption. Digital media products created by youth illustrate expanded ways of learning about how young people represent their identities and lived experiences.

Not allowing students to use these new resources could be disastrous to their "socio-technical designing," which Gee (2000) sees as the "highest and more important form of knowledge and skill" (p. 414). Inhibiting their ability to design products also inhibits students' consumer identities and their ability to successfully create, produce, and share their values and identities in a growing consumer market (Gee, 2000). The best youth-produced film may be available only on YouTube or another shared site like ListenUp! If youth do not have access to these sites or are unable to make intelligent interpretations about film, how can we expect them to be able to compete with their peers?

Digital media production has become an essential outlet for many adolescents as they contemplate and represent their changing identities and transition from adolescence to adulthood. The literature on out-of-school media production organizations shows the value of these opportunities for young people both in the creation of identity products and in the acquisition of the skills necessary to understand the digital works of others. Some young people come with a story they want to tell through their participation in a YMAO. The executive director of Reel Works explained that having a story already decided upon can be "predictive of kids' success" in creating a film that follows their prescribed pedagogy (Interview, 2007). Those participants who do not bring their own stories may do a remix of a previous participant's thematic focus. These filmmakers might take the previous season's films and manipulate the topical content to create a new, blended focus that is unique to them while still exploring the broader thematic idea.

Adolescents artists may be unsure of what they should and can say in new media spaces. Bao, a veteran storyteller by digital generation standards, recommends that "if you want to tell a story, tell your story first. Cause, that's the most important story and that's the story that you know and that you can tell best" (Interview, February 2009). And that story might be the inspiration for the next great remix.

References

Black, R.W., & Steinkuehler, C. (2009). Literacy in virtual worlds. In L. Christenbury, R. Bomer, & P. Smagorinsky (Eds.), *Handbook of adolescent literacy* (pp. 271–286). New York: Guilford Press.

Braun, V., & Clarke, V. (2006). Using thematic analysis in psychology. *Qualitative Research in Psychology, 3*, 77–101.

Bruce, D.L. (2009). Reading and writing video: Media literacy and adolescents. In P. Smagorinsky (Ed.), *Handbook of adolescent literacy research* (pp. 287–303). New York: Guilford.

Buckingham, D. (2008). Introducing identity. In D. Buckingham (Ed.), *Youth, identity and digital media* (pp. 1–22). Cambridge, MA: MIT Press.

Gee, J.P. (2000). Teenagers in new times: A new literacy studies perspective. *Journal of Adolescent & Adult Literacy, 43*(5), 412–420.

Grushka, K. (2009). Meaning and identities: A visual performative pedagogy for sociocultural learning. *Curriculum Journal, 20*(3), 237–251.

Halverson, E., Lowenhaupt, R., Gibbons, D., and Bass, M. (2009). Conceptualizing identity in youth media arts organizations: A comparative case study. *Journal of E-learning, 6*(1), 23–42.

Hull, G.A., & Greeno, J.G. (2006). Identity and agency in nonschool and school worlds. In Z. Bekerman, N.C. Burbules, & D. Silberman-Keller (Eds.), *Learning in places: The informal education reader* (pp. 77–98). New York: Peter Lang.

Jenkins, H., Purushotma, R., Clinton, K., Weigel, M., & Robison, A. (2007). Confronting the challenges of participatory culture: Media education for the 21st century. Retrieved February 15, 2014, from http://digitallearning.macfound.org/atf/cf/%7B7E45C7E0-A3E0-4B89-AC9C-E807E1B0AE4E%7D/JENKINS_WHITE_PAPER.PDF

Knobel, M., & Lankshear, C. (2008). Remix: The art and craft of endless hybridization. *Journal of Adolescent and Adult Literacy, 52*(1), 22–33.

The Lab (n.d.). Retrieved October 19, 2009, from http://reelworks.org/the_lab.php

Lapp, D., Flood, J., Heath, S.B., & Langer, J. (2009). The communicative, visual, and performative arts: Core components of literacy education. In J.V. Hoffman & Y.M. Goodman (Eds.), *Changing literacies for changing times: An historical perspective on the future of reading, research, public policy, and classroom practices* (pp. 3–16). New York: Routledge.

Leander, K. (2009). Composing with old and new media: Toward a parallel pedagogy. In V. Carrington & M. Robinson (Eds.), *Digital literacies: Social learning and classroom practices* (pp. 147–164). Los Angeles: Sage.

Lenhart, A., Madden, M., Macgill, A., & Smith, A. (2007). Teens and social media: Pew Internet & American Life Project. Retrieved February 15, 2014, from www.pewinternet.org/2007/12/19/teens-and-social-media/

Mission statement (n.d.). Retrieved October 19, 2009, from www.reelworks.org/mission.php

New London Group. (1996). A pedagogy of multiliteracies: Designing social futures. *Harvard Educational Review, 66*(1), 60–92.

Parker, J. (2010). *Teaching tech-savvy kids: Bringing digital media into the classroom, grades 5–12.* Thousand Oaks, CA: Corwin.

Potter, W.J. (2011). *Media literacy* (5th ed.). Los Angeles: Sage.

Seidman, I. (2006). *Interviewing as qualitative research: A guide for researchers in education and the social sciences* (3rd ed.). New York: Teachers College Press.

Street, B.V. (2003). The implications of the "new literacy studies" for literacy education. In S. Goodman, T. Lillis, J. Maybin, & N. Mercer (Eds.), *Language, literacy, and education: A reader* (pp. 77–88). Stoke on Trent, UK, and Sterling, VA: Trentham Books in association with Open University.

Street, B. (2009). The future of "social literacies." In M. Baynham & M. Prinsloo (Eds.), *The future of literacy studies* (pp. 21–37). New York: Palgrave Macmillan.

Tierney, R.J. (2009). Literacy education 2.0: Looking through the rear vision mirror as we move ahead. In Hoffman, J. & Goodman, Y. (Eds.), *Changing literacies for changing times* (pp. 282–304). New York: Routledge.

Vasudevan, L., & Hill, M.L. (2009). Moving beyond dichotomies of media engagement in education: An introduction. In L. Vasudevan & M.L. Hill (Eds.), *Media, learning, and sites of possibility* (pp. 1–12). New York: Peter Lang.

Warschauer, M. (2011). *Learning in the cloud: How (and why) to transform schools with digital media.* New York: Teachers College Press.

Watkins, S.C. (2009). *The young and the digital: What the migration to social network sites, games, and anytime, anywhere media means for our future.* Boston: Beacon Press.

Zoss, M. (2009). Visual arts and literacy. In P. Smagorinsky (Ed.), *Handbook of adolescent literacy research* (pp. 183–196). New York: Guilford.

10

THE ROLES OF TIME AND TASK IN SHAPING ADOLESCENTS' TALK ABOUT TEXTS

James S. Chisholm

In the past, classroom talk about texts has been dominated by the initiation-response-evaluation (IRE) discourse pattern (Cazden, 1988), in which the teacher *i*nitiates a question, a student *r*esponds to the teacher's question, and, to complete the sequence, the teacher *e*valuates the relative veracity of the student's response. Since discovering the predominance of the IRE in U.S. classrooms, researchers in English/language arts (ELA) have sought to understand both the causes and the consequences of talking about ELA content in this way. There is ample evidence to suggest that disrupting the IRE, using small-group, inquiry-based discussions, can promote students' learning by providing the opportunity for students to talk in order to learn, rather than to demonstrate already-learned understandings. The future of talk in ELA classrooms should reflect the dynamic and dialogic nature of the discipline, rather than a singular and static authority over preferred meanings in/of texts. To promote the kind of talk that will reflect the future of ELA, it is first necessary to understand the variables (e.g., time and task) that shape and contextualize student talk in the present. In this chapter, I consider the following questions in relation to excerpts from transcripts of students' talk about literature over the course of one 12th-grade ELA semester: How do different kinds of tasks (traditional, inquiry based, and multimodal) shape students' responses to literary texts? How does time contextualize students' responses to literacy tasks?

Although literacy researchers in the sociocultural and sociocognitive traditions have long pointed to the necessity for students to have the opportunity to construct meaning through classroom discussions that address authentic questions about texts (Nystrand, Wu, Gamoran, Zeiser, & Long, 2003), build on other students' ideas (Applebee, Langer, Nystrand, & Gamoran, 2003), and incorporate multiple perspectives on a given topic (Beach, Appleman, Hynds, & Wilhelm, 2010), such discursive interactions in secondary English classrooms have occurred rarely in the past (Nystrand, 2006). In part because of an apparent decrease in students' "time on task" during small-group, student-led collaborative activities, these potentially powerful contexts for inquiry are sometimes transformed into individual work accomplished in a group configuration (Nystrand, Gamoran, & Heck, 1993).

Scholars have demonstrated the myriad ways that talk in classrooms can leverage learning or preclude it from taking place. From ethnographic and longitudinal studies that reveal the deep relationship between talk and place, such as Heath's (1983) work in the Piedmont, to quantitative analyses of talk that draw on advanced statistical procedures (e.g., hierarchical linear modeling) to make sense of the timing of student and teacher talk in classrooms (Nystrand et al., 2003), the concept of talk remains an area of intense interest and inquiry in education research.

In this chapter, I examine the usefulness of a temporal language lens to make sense of talk as students completed (a) traditional, (b) inquiry-based, and (c) multimodal tasks. I argue that this lens offers a perspective on talk, collaboration, and learning through which researchers and teachers can view instructional activities for students in ELA.

The Role of Time in Contextualizing Students' Reponses to Literary Texts

Vygotsky (1986) situated the ontogenesis of learning in social interactions and the mediation of thinking in speaking. In this chapter, I draw on these central tenets of sociocultural theory and recent theoretical and empirical developments related to Bakhtin's (1981) concept of chronotope (Brown & Renshaw, 2006; Compton-Lilly, 2010; Lemke, 2004) to argue that both time and task informed three high school students' talk about literature in consequential ways.

In considering the ways in which time and task contextualized learning experiences for adolescents in this study, I examined one recognizable classroom event in which language and literacy learning can take place—small-group collaborative activities—at three different times during the semester (Week 7, Week 13, and Week 20). I chose to examine these small-group discussions at these points in time because they coincided with the culminating activities for three different literary texts that students had studied during their 12th-grade English semester. I also examined end-of-semester interview data in which participants considered their responses to three different literary texts as they engaged in collaborative instructional activities.

In an effort to disrupt misconceptions about small-group discussions (e.g., that students' "time on task" is limited and therefore unconstructive) and to add to our understanding of how this instructional context can provide robust opportunities for students' literacy learning, I conducted chronotopic discourse analyses of three students' talk during three small-group discussions and two interviews over the course of one academic semester.

Talking about Texts and Time in Space

In this section, I draw on two rich and overlapping sets of literatures relevant to understanding secondary students' talk about texts: (a) conceptual and empirical work done on time in school, and (b) classroom-based studies of small-group collaboration. I will provide a brief review of some of the relevant ideas from these bodies of literature before introducing the design of this research study.

Talking and Timespace

Bakhtin's (1981) concept of chronotope provides the background against which I situate my analysis of student talk in this chapter. Bakhtin's use of chronotope—timespace—in literary analysis has been taken up by researchers in education as a way to investigate the "meaning trajectories" (Lemke, 2004) that inform students' understandings of their literacy experiences in school and at home (Compton-Lilly, 2010) and the ways in which researchers and teachers can understand student participation in classrooms (Brown & Renshaw, 2006). These conceptual developments shed light on the ways in which classroom discourse can be interpreted. Studies of adolescents' talk about literary texts, for example, have often pointed to the participation structures that inform how literature is discussed (Cazden, 1988). Analyzing classroom discourse data using a chronotopic lens allows scholars the opportunity to investigate how time and space contextualize student talk and, in doing so, shape the participation structures themselves.

Brown and Renshaw (2006) have used the concept of chronotope to describe the organization of student participation in classroom instructional activities through the frames of "past experience, ongoing involvement, and yet-to-be-accomplished goals" (p. 249). I draw on Brown and Renshaw's (2006) operationalization of chronotope to examine student participation as a situated and dynamic process informed by the ways in which "past experience," "ongoing involvement," and "yet-to-be-accomplished goals" shaped students' talk about literary texts over the course of this semester-long study.

Talking in Small Groups

After 150 years of empirical work that focuses on talk in ELA classrooms (Nystrand, 2006), researchers continue to examine the affordances of small-group settings for promoting students' dialogic interactions with texts and one another. Fullerton and Colwell's (2010) recent review of the past 30 years of research on small-group discussions of literature demonstrated how small-group discussions could provide students with opportunities to explore ideas and develop arguments that can promote students' learning. Although these findings point to promising implications for practice, research reviewed in the Fullerton and Colwell (2010) study also identified situations in which small-group discussions actually precluded students' literacy learning. Group dynamic issues and power imbalances, as well as the phenomenon in which individual work is merely completed in a collaborative space (Nystrand et al., 1993), offer additional perspectives on the ways in which this space can be problematized.

Methods

Overview of the Study

Three students in one 12th-grade English course participated in this study. These students were selected as focal students from a larger study because of the diversity with which they participated during classroom instructional activities. One student engaged almost entirely in what some teachers might describe as "off-task" talk during his small-group, student-led collaborative activities (Mike). The second student profiled in this study spoke infrequently during whole-class discussions (Elizabeth). The third student participated enthusiastically and consistently during class discussions of literature (Natalie).

I traced each focal student's talk during small-group discussions at three different times during the semester (Week 7, Week 13, Week 20). During Week 7, students engaged in small-group discussions based on Shakespeare's (1623/1992) play, *Macbeth*. During Week 13, students studied Malamud's (1952) novel, *The Natural*. Goldman's (1973) fractured fairy tale, *The Princess Bride*, was the focus of discussion during Week 20. At the end of the semester, during Week 22, students completed semistructured interviews. For each small-group discussion and interview, I digitally video-recorded students, transcribed the video files, and coded student talk for the ways in which time and task contextualized students' utterances.

Instructional Context

Riverview High School (a pseudonym, as are all names used in this chapter) is a mid-size suburban high school in the eastern United States whose students consistently achieve SAT scores above the national average. Although Riverview enjoyed a reputation for "academic excellence," the "Academic English" students featured in this study did not necessarily represent the mainstream within the culture of the school. Two tracks of English classes "above" Academic English 12 existed ("Honors" and "A.P."), and one track existed "below" ("Developmental English"). The students in this "lower" track did not pass the state-mandated exam and were placed in a class devoted to developing basic reading skills.

Three focal students—Mike, Elizabeth, and Natalie—represented diverse per-spectives within the classroom. Mike, for example, was unsure about his prospects after high school. His participation during classroom activities seemed to depend on the setting in which the activity took place. During whole-class discussions of literature, he was quick to point out intertextual connections with popular media. Yet, during small-group discussions with Elizabeth and Natalie, Mike kept mostly to himself and ventured out less frequently into the group's conversation. Elizabeth considered herself an artist and engaged in mural project work "downtown." She was college bound and worked tirelessly on scholarship applications to area universities. Elizabeth considered herself both a "visual" and an "analytic" learner. Natalie was eager to graduate from Riverview High School. During small-group discussions, she often complained about the policies, procedures, and personnel of the school. During whole-class discussions, she participated enthusiastically by posing authentic questions and building on other students' ideas. Unfortunately for the research but fortunately for Natalie, she did graduate early, and I did not have the opportunity to study her participation during the *Princess Bride* data-collection cycle, nor was it possible for me to interview her at the end of the semester.

Transcript and Interview Sources

The data sources for this study included two transcripts of 30-minute interviews and three transcripts of 75-minute small-group discussions in which students completed (a) traditional, (b) inquiry-based, and (c) multimodal projects, respectively. Mike, Elizabeth, and Natalie completed one collaborative essay on *Macbeth*; one found poem—an inquiry-based project in which students transferred language from the novel to create a poem based on *The Natural* that addressed a central theme or interpretation of the original text; and one digital video based on *The Princess Bride*. During the end-of-semester interview, I asked students to elaborate on their experiences during all of the collaborative-learning and small-group discussion activities.

Using a Temporal Language Lens to Analyze Talk

To understand focal students' "meaning trajectories" (Lemke, 2004) and the ways in which timespace shaped students' talk during small-group discussions of literature, I transcribed, read, and coded each transcript for temporal language, such as "It takes too much time," and for markers of time, such as "In the beginning," "Meanwhile," and "After." I then reread all of the data sources. During the next cycle of data analysis, I created categories based on recurring patterns of temporal language codes and codes based on markers of time. For example, students used markers of time throughout these discussions to describe the *expectations of school* or to seek out quicker (i.e., easier) ways of completing the small-group projects. In the next iteration of coding, I drew on Brown and Renshaw's (2006) study of chronotopes and collaborative learning, including their system of categorization in which students' participation could be studied by considering the roles of "past experience," "ongoing involvement," and "yet-to-be-accomplished goals" (p. 249). The final process in my analysis involved rereading the data sources and identifying illustrative interactions on the basis of the categories identified in previous coding cycles. These analytic decisions allowed me to consider the roles of both time (past, present, and future) and space (small groups and interview settings) as students completed different types of instructional tasks (traditional, inquiry based, and multimodal).

Learning Within and Outside Traditional Chronotopes of Schooling

Mike, Elizabeth, and Natalie emphasized different chronotopes of schooling and literacy in their small-group talk as they completed instructional tasks based on three literary texts over time (see Figure 10.1). The nature of the task as a traditional academic task, an inquiry-based and unimodal (linguistic-only) task, or a multimodal task shaped the ways in which students talked about the literary texts under study. Analyses of my interviews with Mike and Elizabeth revealed how these two students identified the value of the traditional instructional tasks despite talk during those tasks that contradicted the notion that students perceived this task as valuable to their learning. Conversely, transcript analyses of student talk during the multimodal instructional task illustrated dialogic interactions with the text, yet students identified this instructional task as the least valuable in promoting their understanding of the literary text. I next consider possible reasons for these seeming contradictions.

	Mike	Elizabeth	Natalie
-Text	Brown & Renshaw Category	Brown & Renshaw Category	Brown & Renshaw Category
-Time	*Temporal Lens Coding Category*	*Temporal Lens Coding Category*	*Temporal Lens Coding Category*
-Task	*Transcript Example*	*Transcript Example*	*Transcript Example*
-*Macbeth*	**Ongoing Involvement**	**Ongoing Involvement**	**Ongoing Involvement**
-Week 7	Time and Participation Structures	Time and Expectations of School	Saving Time
-Collaborative Essay	*"Alright, I said nothing in awhile, so..."*	*"Alright. We're done doing the brainstorming now."*	*"Look up [online]: "Metaphor that explains Macbeth."*
-*The Natural*	**Ongoing Involvement**	**Ongoing Involvement**	**Ongoing Involvement**
-Week 13	Time and Expectations of School	Saving Time	Saving Time
-Found Poem	*"When's this class end?"*	*"I wouldn't waste my time; it takes like one hour to read 30 pages."*	*"Let's just compile a list."*
-*The Princess Bride*	**Yet-to-be-accomplished goals**	**Yet-to-be-accomplished goals**	
-Week 20	Time and Meaning/Composition	Time and Expectations of School	
-Digital Video	*"How are we going to say '5 years later'?"*	*"Are we showing it today? Ah! We have to wait until tomorrow?"*	

FIGURE 10.1 Categories for Focal Students' Chronotopic Responses to Three Literary Texts during Traditional, Inquiry-Based, and Multimodal Collaborative Instructional Tasks in Small-Group Discussion Settings over the Course of One Academic Semester

Time as Commodity

"Add some fluff and you're done." During the traditional, collaborative writing task based on *Macbeth,* students were asked to brainstorm their ideas in response to a list of prompts about Shakespeare's play. Students chose one prompt and constructed a group response to that prompt during the 75-minute block period. Mike, Elizabeth, and Natalie chose to identify a metaphor—using evidence from the text—that could describe Macbeth's actions from the beginning to the end of the play.

Students' talk throughout this task reflected their *ongoing involvement* (Brown & Renshaw, 2006, p. 249) in activities of various sorts. Students talked in temporal ways related to saving time and completing the project at hand. Over the course of their discussion, I identified 13 episodes in which students talked for three or more turns about a specific idea related to time. Of these 13 episodes, I identified three temporal categories that emerged during this small-group discussion: Saving Time (four episodes), Time and Participation Structures (two episodes), and Time and the Expectations of School (seven episodes). Students' utterances that dealt with "Saving Time," such as Natalie's suggestion to "Look up [on Google]: 'Metaphor that explains *Macbeth*'" perceived time as a commodity that could be saved or spent. Any utterances that related to finishing the collaborative writing project as quickly as possible were included in this category. "Time and Participation Structures" was the second temporal category that emerged during data coding and analysis. Mike's utterance fell into this category that related to how students participated in and through time: "All right, I said nothing in a while so . . ." Finally, "Time and the Expectations of School" emerged as another temporal category as reflected in Elizabeth's utterance "All right. We're done doing the brainstorming now." Implicit in Elizabeth's utterance is the notion that students could then move on to the next step in the collaborative writing process. Episodes coded as "Time and the Expectations of School" often identified the role of time as it related to course or class completion and graduation from high school. This linear orientation toward time supports scholarship on the ways in which traditional chronotopes of school shape how students learn in these environments (Compton-Lilly, 2010).

The following episode with Mr. Smith, the teacher, illustrates how the chronotopes of school influenced the small group's work (see Appendix A for transcript conventions):

MR. SMITH:	All right, have you decided how to break it up?
NATALIE:	Yeah.
ELIZABETH:	I started working on the bodies.
NATALIE:	I'm working on the intro, she's working on one of the bodies, he's doing conclusion, and then I'm probably gonna end up doing another body.
MR. SMITH:	I don't know if you can be working (xxx).
NATALIE:	Yeah you can.
ELIZABETH:	You just restate the thesis.

NATALIE:	We kinda just talked about what all we want to talk about.
MR. SMITH:	Okay. See what you can do then (*walks away from the group*).
ELIZABETH:	Explain his lionish qualities. Add some fluff and you're done. I think Mr. Smith thinks that this takes a lot more thinking than it really does. It's <u>doing</u> Mr. Smith, it's not thinking.
NATALIE:	Huh?
ELIZABETH:	It's not thinking Mr. Smith, it's <u>doing</u>. Thinking does not get words on here. (*eating*) These are the best chips in the entire world.

The small group's interaction with the teacher in this excerpt illustrates how an individual activity can be accomplished in a group space. Students worked individually on different sections of the paper, after which they combined the various sections to create a standard five-paragraph essay. Natalie identified in line 4 the sequence of events that students would take to complete the project (quickly). Elizabeth's utterances about the differences between thinking and doing in lines 10 and 12 present compelling data on how time, or the lack of it, can shape how students participate during a task. The task for these students became a trivial academic exercise that these students, by the 12th grade, had become skilled at mastering. The prompt did not lead students to engage with one another or the text with ideas; rather, students identified the formula that was called for to respond to the prompt, divided the amount of "doing" that needed to take place, and combined the results. Elizabeth's utterance in line 12, "Thinking does not get words on here," suggested that students perceived their engagement in this activity as mindless "doing," even though their participation in the activity could indeed constitute thinking and learning from another perspective.

The experience of time during this small-group activity as linear and the experience of the project as arduous and trivial shaped students' focus on saving time and conforming to the ways in which time and participation are organized and rewarded in school. Students have to do certain things during certain times of the school day. Traditional chronotopes of school (e.g., "time on task," "time as a commodity," and "time to course completion or graduation") permeated students' temporal language during this small-group discussion. Focal students' small-group interactions were characterized by their ongoing involvement in various school-related activities and by the ways in which they could "save time" working on the project so that they could "use" that time, inevitably, for other things—perhaps even for "thinking." Students actively sought ways to use their time more efficiently by curtailing their involvement with the collaborative composition during this traditional and linguistic instructional task. Ultimately, students perceived their participation as a "waste" of time, completed in order to meet the expectations of schooling. This perception seems to have prevented the focal students from engaging dialogically with the text or one another.

"**Just throw it together.**" Students completed another linguistic-based task during their small-group work on *The Natural* during Week 13 of the semester. This time, however, the task was an inquiry-based instructional activity rather than a traditional writing activity. Students were asked to choose one theme that they found most interesting and about which they knew the most as a group. Then, Mike, Elizabeth, and Natalie were asked to find at least three different passages in the text in which their selected theme was evident. Finally, students created a "found poem"—a poem that students composed by transferring language from the novel to fit the structure of a poem—in which they represented how their selected theme functioned in *The Natural,* using evidence from the text.

Again, *ongoing involvement* provided a general characterization category for student talk throughout their small-group task. "Saving Time" emerged once again as a temporal category that represented students' talk during three episodes related to this activity. When Natalie indicated that she hadn't actually read the text, Elizabeth suggested, "I wouldn't waste my time; it takes like one hour to read 30 pages." In a similar manner, while brainstorming possible approaches to creating the found poem, Natalie suggested, "Let's just compile a list." Both of these utterances highlight students' perceptions of time as a commodity that can be "spent" on things other than "thinking" or academic exercises—regardless of the type of thinking or doing such exercises might promote.

"Time and Expectations of School" emerged as another temporal category for student talk. During one episode of their small-group work, Mike questioned, for example, "When's this class end?" Although the text (*The Natural*) and the nature of the task changed from a traditional writing task (during the *Macbeth* activity) to an inquiry-based activity, time shaped students' talk in their small group in similar ways. Students brainstormed the quickest ways to complete the "doing" of the project and treated time in school as a restriction rather than a resource.

In the following excerpt Elizabeth and Natalie begin to transfer language from the novel to conform to fit the structure of a poem. The students exchanged ideas on what such a structure ought to actually look like before identifying a strategy that would allow them to "do" the exercise rather than "think" through meaning:

NATALIE:	My question is, does it actually have to rhyme?
ELIZABETH:	I don't think so, 'cause not all poems rhyme.
NATALIE:	Oh, this is a good one: "I wanted everything." So I'm thinking we need something to rhyme with Hobbs. Cobbs, Dobbs, Mobs. Roy Hobbs, not in the mob, cream of the crop, will go to the top.
ELIZABETH:	What does that say?
NATALIE:	"Again, please." It was after he threw the pitch and he swung and missed it. Roy Hobbs, not in the mob, cream of the crop =
ELIZABETH:	= it doesn't have to rhyme. =
NATALIE:	= He will go to the top.
ELIZABETH:	I'm just saying.
NATALIE:	Yeah, but it's a lot more fun. He will go to the top. Best there ever was.

ELIZABETH:	I think this one of yours and this one kinda fit together.
NATALIE:	"Cream of the crop" [and] "want everything"? . . .
ELIZABETH:	(*to Mr. Smith*) Does it have to rhyme?
MR. SMITH:	No.
ELIZABETH:	Okay. We can . . . I'm trying to think of the easiest way to approach it. . . . We can kinda like just find words like you did that are shorter that kind of fit together, kind of sequentially, but not really. 'Cause like, and just make like little three line things and just throw it together.
Natalie:	We need 20 lines. Not all of them have to be from the book.
Elizabeth:	They don't?

Elizabeth, in line 14, admits that she is trying to travel the path of least resistance. Although this might be a quite successful strategy for success in "doing school," it does not seem to provide the opportunity to learn deeply from and through meaningful interactions around texts. Later on in line 14, Elizabeth suggests that the group find the shortest words that can resemble a poem that can meet the teacher's requirement of 20 lines or more. "Just throw it together" (line 15) does not capture the kind of intellectual work that Mr. Smith hoped that the students would engage in during this small-group activity. Saving time and meeting the expectations of school shaped students' talk in ways that prevented dialogical interactions with the text and with one another.

As focal students considered ways in which they could save time, students drew on traditional and monolithic notions of poetry to conform their ideas to a particular structural feature of that genre: rhyme scheme. This structural rigidity, when considered along with the group's collaborative essay, which took as its form the five-paragraph theme, illustrates how some tasks can be completed by "doing school" rather than "doing work."

Time as Resource

"Do you have Kanye on your iPod?" At the end of the semester (Week 20), students were asked to complete a multimodal project in preparation for a whole-class discussion of Goldman's (1973) *The Princess Bride*. The instructions read: "Using the materials provided to you (digital video camera, acrylic paint and canvas, sculpting clay, and chalk and paper), demonstrate the growth or development of one particular character from the beginning of the novel to the end." The focal students, after much debate, decided to create a digital video.

The role of time in students' talk and students' perceptions of time shifted during this instructional activity. When students used temporal language or markers of time in this small-group discussion, it was to consider *yet-to-be-accomplished goals* that focused on meaning making and strategies toward composition. Mike, for example, asked, "How are we going to say '5 years later'" during the filming of the digital video that he and his peers created. With this question, Mike considered how to communicate the passing of time across semiotic systems (the linguistic to the visual). This question was not trivial, nor did it represent a complaint about the arduousness of the task. It was an authentic question about a visual composition. I coded three similar episodes during this discussion as "Time and Composition." "Time and Expectations of School" emerged again as a coding category for two episodes, but in these instances school time was not a restrictive container but a resource for publishing to authentic audiences. For example, Elizabeth asked Mr. Smith: "Are we showing [the video] today?" Mr. Smith shook his head to indicate "No." And Elizabeth sighed, "Ah! We have to wait until tomorrow?"

The following episode was coded as "Time and Meaning" and developed over the course of just two minutes. Students drew on various multimodal resources to think through this task. The interaction calls to mind Lemke's (2004) reflections on adolescents' skills in maintaining multiple attentional foci over short time spans, and how this is not leveraged in linear school time, in which students are often compelled to complete one activity before moving on to another:

EVAN: Was it 7 or 5 years after like Westley left? . . .

MIKE: I'll just say "some years later." A few years later.

MR. SMITH: The thing to think about—and be careful—are you retelling the story or are you demonstrating growth?

MIKE: Well, you're gonna see the growth. You go from that to that (*pointing to Evan and another student who happens to be on the football team*). I'm not making fun of Evan, but obviously, he's not as big as [the football player]. So, obviously he's grown in size. And he's going to be like more heroic. He's gonna be like "Hi, as you wish," and he's gonna come in and be like "Yeah, I run this." So he's like whispering and he's gonna come in and be loud and in charge.

EVAN: Should my character have a French accent?

MIKE: Yes, for sure. Without a doubt, you should have a French accent.

EVAN: I can't do a French accent.

MIKE: Say like "Oui, madame."

EVAN: "Oui!"

MIKE: Yes, "we," that's how you say it. There you go. You're amazing. My star. Who's gonna be the prince?

ELIZABETH: The prince? No, but, that doesn't even have Westley in it though.

MIKE: No, we'll have two scenes with them and then he would come back in. So this doesn't have to be that long. It's going to be like five, six scenes.

EVAN: (*in character*) "Buttercup, why don't you love me, Buttercup?"

MIKE: Hey do you have Kanye on your iPod?

Students experienced time in a different way during this interaction. Multiple modes of meaning were considered in order to plan the composition of the film. Everything from dialogue (line 4) to the sound of one's voice (line 8) to the music that would be played in the background (line 14) was all considered in quick succession and incorporated into the final product. Students' selection of Kanye West's "Heartless" during their digital reproduction of a critical scene in the text—when Buttercup agrees to marry Prince Humperdinck and not her "true love," Westley—evidences their multimodal and dialogic orientation toward this composition.

Students' perceptions of time as a resource during this activity changed, however, during the end-of-semester interviews. In response to a question about the activities that most successfully leveraged her learning during the semester, Elizabeth commented:

> I think the essay format helped me the best because I'm, I'm a really analytical person, so kind of being pushed to do things like that helps me. . . . Writing in essay format pushes me to get out my thoughts and back them up. So, I'm forced to think of reasons of why I think the way I do, which is more than just, "this is what I think" or "this is what represents." You have to analyze why you think the way you do and come up with examples from the text and everything. I think that helps me a lot more even though I really didn't like writing the essay [laughs].

Elizabeth's response is especially interesting given the fact that she made it a point to suggest that the collaborative writing activity she completed on *Macbeth* was "fluff" and required more "doing" than "thinking." Yet, she identified this as being the most helpful of activities.

Equally compelling, especially after Mike's talk during the digital video project— the one activity that seemed to engage him in every way—was the way in which he deemed the project "a joke" during my interview with him. Mike, like Elizabeth, identified the collaborative writing activity on *Macbeth* as the most powerful learning opportunity during the semester:

> [The digital video] was just more fun than it was actually a message. The poem, I didn't care for. And even though the paper is a little jumbled and unorthodox to say the least, it made a little more sense than most of the things. Like the poem was just like saying how Roy is great. "Roy's this, Roy's that, Roy's that best ever, blah." And then the video is just a joke. So, the paper, even if it wasn't in order, it stated like facts. It stated like comparisons. So if you just want a fact sheet, the paper did a good job.

Students' responses during the interview were very different from the ideas represented by their talk during their small-group collaborative activities. Students seemed to be responding monologically—to an authoritative voice—in an interview space that was designed to promote dialogue and an open conversation about learning and literature. Students identified the most typically traditional school activities as the most robust learning experiences. Mike and Elizabeth may, indeed, believe that the collaborative writing activity, ultimately titled "Macbeth Is a Lion," facilitated their understanding of the original literary text most effectively. However, discourse analyses of these students' talk across time and space support the claim that students' comments during the interview reflected another successful opportunity to "do school"—engage in a monologic pattern of classroom discourse with an authority figure. Nevertheless, students' talk during the multimodal instructional activity provided hope that future schools—and especially literacy classrooms— can be places where dialogue and engagement characterize time and promote, rather than restrict, learning.

Conclusion

Time contextualized talk in consequential ways for Elizabeth, Mike, and Natalie. Time restricted talk and participation during traditional and inquiry-based linguistic activities, which then seemed to inform how students talked about literature. At the end of the semester, when students completed their digital video project, time was used as a resource for making meaning. During interviews, however, focal students deemed the most traditional instructional activity the most helpful in facilitating their learning. Future research and practice in this area might develop students' meta-awareness of time in talk, as such an awareness might have altered focal students' perceptions of their own learning or the activities that enhanced or precluded that learning from happening.

Findings from this study raise additional important questions for future research on time and space in the English classroom. What are some of the consequences of rethinking chronotopes of school and literacy for secondary students? How can ELA teachers structure instructional activities that draw on adolescents' "multiple attentional foci" (Lemke, 2004) to design learning environments in which "people are so involved in an activity that nothing else seems to matter" (Csikszentmihalyi, 1990, p. 4)—the concept of "flow" that could characterize robust literacy learning experiences for students—even if they publicly denounce the pedagogical value of such activities?

References

Applebee, A.N., Langer, J.A., Nystrand, M., & Gamoran, A. (2003). Discussion-based approaches to developing understanding: Classroom instruction and student performance in middle and high school English. *American Educational Research Journal, 40*(3), 685–730.

Bakhtin, M.M. (1981). *The dialogic imagination* (M. Holquist, Ed.; C. Emerson & M. Holquist, Trans.). Austin: University of Texas Press.

Beach, R., Appleman, D., Hynds, S., & Wilhelm, J. (2010). *Teaching literature to adolescents* (2nd ed.). Mahwah, NJ: Lawrence Erlbaum.

Brown, R., & Renshaw, P. (2006). Positioning students as actors and authors: A chronotopic analysis of collaborative learning activities. *Mind, Culture, and Activity, 13*(3), 247–259.

Cazden, C. (1988). *Classroom discourse: The language of teaching and learning.* Portsmouth, NH: Heinemann.

Compton-Lilly, C. (2010). Making sense of time as context: Theoretical affordances of chronotopes in the study of schooling and school success. (Wisconsin Center for Education Research Working Paper No. 2010–11). Retrieved February 15, 2014, from www.wcer. wisc.edu/publications/workingPapers/papers.php

Csikszentmihalyi, M. (1990). *Flow: The psychology of optimal experience.* New York: Harper Perennial.

Fullerton, S.K., & Colwell, J. (2010). Research on small-group discussions of literature— past, present, and future: An analysis of three decades. In R.T. Jiménez, V.J. Risko, M.K. Hundley, & D.W. Rowe (Eds.), *59th Yearbook of the National Reading Conference* (pp. 59–74). Oak Creek, WI: National Reading Conference.

Goldman, W. (1973). *The Princess Bride: S. Morgenstern's classic tale of true love and high adventure.* New York: Harcourt.

Heath, S.B. (1983). *Ways with words: Language, life, and work in communities and classrooms.* New York: Cambridge University Press.

Lemke, J.L. (2004, April). *Learning across multiple places and their chronotopes.* Paper presented at the Annual Meeting of the American Educational Research Association, San Diego, CA.

Malamud, B. (1952). *The natural.* New York: Farrar, Straus & Giroux.

Nystrand, M. (2006). Research on the role of classroom discourse as it affects reading comprehension. *Research in the Teaching of English, 40*(4), 392–412.

Nystrand, M., Gamoran, A., & Heck, M.J. (1993). Using small-groups for response to and thinking about literature. *English Journal, 82*(1), 14–22.

Nystrand, M., Wu, L., Gamoran, A., Zeiser, S., & Long, D. (2003). Questions in time: Investigating the structure and dynamics of unfolding classroom discourse. *Discourse Processes, 35*(2), 135–198.

Shakespeare, W. (1623/1992). *Macbeth.* New York: Washington Square Press.

Vygotsky, L. (1986). *Thought and Language* (A. Kozulin, Trans.). Cambridge, MA: Michigan Institute of Technology Press.

Appendix A

Transcription Conventions

(xxx)	inaudible speech
= words =	immediately connected speech
words:	syllables extended in speech
<u>words</u>	emphasized speech
words	researcher's comments for clarification

11

"AFTER APPLE PICKING" AND FETAL PIGS: THE MULTIPLE SOCIAL SPACES AND EMBODIED RHYTHMS OF DIGITAL LITERACY PRACTICES

Kevin M. Leander and Beth Aplin

Literacy research has developed a relatively short history of asking how literacy practices and opportunities in out-of-school settings relate and, more often, fail to relate to practices and opportunities in school (Bigum, 2002; Dyson, 1999; Heath, 1983; Heath & McLaughlin, 1994; Schultz, 2002). While it is tempting to reinforce a divide between in-school and out-of-school learning, along with other familiar qualities that construct "school" and "out of school" as places (e.g., traditional vs. innovative, hierarchical vs. egalitarian, mandatory vs. voluntary), there are numerous ways in which this division breaks down in practice and should not be reified (Hull & Schultz, 2001). From the perspective in schools, a range of research has documented how we are never merely "in school"; instead, school is a nexus of social and cultural identities and literacy practices (Leander, 2002; Finders, 1997; Gutierrez, Rymes, & Larson, 1995; Yon, 2000). Further, if we look closer at out-of-school settings, some research has illustrated how practices in such settings may become highly school-like or pedagogized (Street & Street, 1991), unsettling the first impression that "doing school" and "being school-like" are social phenomena that are contained in institutional bricks and mortar.

Research on the relationship between in-school and out-of-school learning is important in that it enables us to better understand how learning in one setting supports or contradicts learning in another, how transfer functions, how identities are shaped across settings, and how learning in school may be transformed to become more engaging by drawing on qualities found in out-of-school settings. However, one of the assumptions that might operate behind such research is that setting or place is an engine that drives social practice. While this assumption might help us interpret why, for instance, institutional school settings house some practices (e.g., testing) more than others (e.g., video production), it does not provide a useful means to interpret how people assume agency to create unique relationships to different places. People are not merely "in" places but rather "with" places, not merely positioned but always taking up positions, and literacy is an important means through which relationships to place, space, and time are established. Nor does a place-based perspective on practice help us understand how individuals and groups bring places into relationship with one another through their social practices, using literacy to do so.

To further our understanding of these relations, in this chapter we consider how youth use literacy practices to organize the space-times of their individual and social lives. While we consider practices in different places (e.g., home and school, online and offline), we begin from the perspective that social practices are not determined by place. Rather, people assume and produce spatial and temporal relationships to places through practices of different types. We focus on digital literacy practices because such practices are prone to escape place-based logics of practice or, perhaps more obviously, disrupt such logics, while nevertheless occurring in clock time and being attached to material and social places (e.g., Hine, 2000; Miller & Slater, 2000). We investigate how two youth use digital literacies to alter, extend, transform, and manipulate the space-times of their lives. Relying on case studies of these youth, we ask the following questions: How do these youth use digital literacies to produce and organize space-time while in school? Second, how do these youth use digital literacies to produce and organize space-time while at home? Third, how do the space-time practices of these youth with digital literacies relate to the dominant practices of space-time that are operating in their school and their respective homes? Fourth, how (and why) do these youth create boundaries or traversals (Lemke, 2001) between home and school through their uses of digital literacies?

The case studies reported in this article are of "Richa" and "Mia" (pseudonyms). The analysis of ethnographic data makes evident how Richa extended the space-time of schooling into her home with her digital literacy practices. Richa made school an extension of home, first by appropriating and pursuing school goals while at home and then by creating a variety of boundaries in space-time that resembled those of school. In other terms, Richa's practices of space-time at home were heavily pedagogized (Street & Street, 1991). Mia's case is in sharp contrast in that she used digital literacies to construct a robust and traveling social network that traversed school and home situations. Mia's social network serves as a social space that is laminated, or co-present, with classroom practices on the one hand and with schoolwork at home on the other.

Study Background

The key informants for the present analysis are Richa and Mia, two ninth-graders who attend a private school for girls in grades 5–12, "Ridgeview Academy." Ridgeview Academy is located on a 38-acre campus in a suburban area of a large city in the mid-South of the United States. The student population of the school is 554 students; 5% of the students are minorities. Five years ago, motivated by the leadership of two school librarians and a former administrator, Ridgeview began a program of developing a wireless network in the entire school, which is currently completely functional and relatively stable. Three years prior to the time of our research (in 2002–2003), the school began to require parents to purchase laptops for their daughters attending the school. All students currently carry these laptops to their classes and homes daily. Laptops are maintained by a computer maintenance office on campus and are set up with a common set of software. Students in each grade are required to have the same PC laptop, although students who entered the school, say, in their ninth-grade year have newer models than those who entered in seventh grade.

Richa and Mia were observed at least once per week in both their English and their psychology classes from February to June 2003, and their course work from these classes was collected during these visits. Biweekly home observations of online literacy practices also began in February and continued through June 2003. Each home visit lasted approximately 1.5 to 2 hours and consisted of the researcher observing and asking questions about practice during online activity. Monthly follow-up home observations of Mia's online interaction were ongoing until June 2004. Richa and Mia were also formally and informally interviewed on several occasions throughout the study concerning their literacy practices; most interviews beyond the initial screening interview were discourse based, shaped around one of their (online or offline) texts or textual practices. Teachers, parents, an administrator, and other students were also interviewed as part of the study.

Ridgeview, Digital Practices, and Space-time

Ever since it implemented its laptop program, Ridgeview struggled with a number of contradictions between traditional schooling and ubiquitous Internet access. As one teacher put it, "We have opened Pandora's box." Even as Ridgeview has heavily invested in providing Internet access to its students, it has also structured, over three years' time, an array of implicit and explicit means of closing this access. In short, Ridgeview was a contradiction of social spaces: on the one hand it presented itself and technically structured itself to be an "open" wired social space for 21st-century girls, while on the other hand official school practices and discourses domesticated or pedagogized (Street & Street, 1991) potential openings of space-time provided by the wireless network. In official school practice, the wireless network was "rewired" or closed off and anchored in ways that reproduce traditional school space-time.

Several of the girls' individual practices during a library visit are indicative of the difficulty of structuring and enforcing a single space-time with the wireless network and the developed histories of information searching that the girls brought to the event. As the first girl we observed entered "American Poets" into the search engine Google, a second pulled a book from a library shelf and used the directory Yahoo to verify whether the author was American (a project requirement). A third girl attempted a power search of the online card catalogue on fairy poems, with no results, while a fourth, her partner, searched for fairy poems in Google. A fifth girl had brought a book of poems with her from her friend's locker and browsed through it. Another student spent some of her time looking through books on the cart shelves, while also talking with Ms. Schoenfeld about her possible theme. Mia used most of the searching time in the library to work on a report for her psychology class, including conducting research online. None of the students that we observed followed the sequential, ordered path across resources and space-time as ordered by the librarian and teachers, and only a minority used "power searching" or the online card catalogue.

Beyond commonplace notions of how school space is regulated by classroom walls and time is regulated by class periods, this example illustrates other features of the pedagogization (Street & Street, 1991) of space-time as it relates to digital literacies at Ridgeview:

- Defined plans precede resources and activity; actors know what they need or are seeking in advance.
- Sequential activity is dominant, and everyone follows the same sequential path.
- Asynchronous communication is primary to synchronous communication (e.g., e-mail or Web searching is more "schooled" than instant messaging).
- A single space is dominant (and under surveillance) for each task; "task" is monospatial, and "off-task" is partially defined as departure into another social space.
- Public social spaces, including the Internet, must be bracketed for student use; school needs to produce kindergartens of public spaces for students to understand them, learn within them, and be safe within them.
- Material print texts and print spaces (the built environment) are primary and are authorized, while virtual texts are unauthorized and supplemental.
- The Internet is a primarily a tool for information rather than a tool for communication. Information and Communication Technologies (ICTs) are primarily "ITs" in school.

Richa

At Ridgeview Academy, Richa was identified by students and teachers alike as smart and highly motivated academically and was also considered to be highly knowledgeable about computers. Richa's grandparents had emigrated from India, and, before moving to the South, she had grown up on the East Coast among an extended cultural network of Indian relatives and friends. Richa saw herself as culturally distinct from many of the norms at Ridgeview and, although she seemed well liked, struggled to find her place: "Part of what my culture says is that I shouldn't be like those blond people, so I'm not—I don't belong to their group." The "blonds" were a defined social group at Ridgeview, which Richa described as having a more "bouncy" attitude, while she was more of a "realist." In the eyes of others, Richa somewhat humorously suggested, she fit in with the "gothic scary group," who were "realists." Her social group was more on the fringe of Ridgeview, more cynical about the school scene, and more critically inclined toward social and political issues. Despite the marginalization of her identity at Ridgeview (and minorities in general), Richa was involved in extracurricular activities such as the school dance club, where she did modern dance and jazz, while she also practiced and learned Indian dance in an out-of-school Indian organization.

Richa's digital literacies at home. Richa spent extensive time involved in digital literacies at home for school-selected purposes, including projects that were not directly assigned by the school but were nevertheless associated with school goals. Richa noted that she frequently was busy with homework until 10:30 p.m. As an example of school-selected practices, Richa would take "framing" notes on her laptop while at home from her biology textbook, after discovering that the lectures in class followed the headings and subheadings of the textbook.

Richa was often observed conducting research on the Internet, using a mixture of the school-sanctioned Webliographer and its intranet-based Britannica and Google (which she increasingly used as she learned to determine for herself credible sources), more than any other school-selected practice. Richa would read through a source very quickly and decide if it was useful to her and then, after taking down the necessary bibliographic information, move between the source and her word processing document, creating and revising her own piece. For many assignments this process would continue over the course of multiple evenings, as she would simultaneously revisit research, drafting, and revising processes. Richa even searched for academic information when it was not a requirement of the assignment, and, while she was quite grade conscious, these searches also seemed to be motivated by intellectual curiosity. For instance, when she was writing a short story in French using simple and imperfect tenses, Richa accessed a name bank to find a French name that symbolized a red bird.

The terms "school-selected" and "self-selected" are problematized in Richa's case as she pursued school-related purposes in ways that moved beyond official school pedagogies and were in fact critical of them. For example, in the case of research, Richa was quite critical of the repeated lessons given in school on searching for information, such as was briefly described in the library scenario. She noted that even if one were to start with authorized websites, such as those listed in the librarian-reviewed Webliographer, by following links "it's kind of crazy because eventually you are going to get to something that is not right [authoritative], so the school system is kind of backwards." In this manner, even as Richa's space-time practices were well schooled, she was also critical of how teachers at Ridgeview closed off and controlled online space-time and underestimated student knowledge. She claimed to have learned to research by experience rather than by school lessons and asserted that the school seemed to teach the same lessons every year and to treat the students as if they were naive and could not make distinctions among sources of information. In developing her own practice of online research, Richa described moving from privileging books and a suspicion of online sources to having a comfort level with a general search engine:

> I am not very suspicious of whether other people are saying the wrong thing or not. I pretty much trust everyone now, so I just go on Google and find what looks like might be a credible source. I don't take a fourth-grader's little paper [as a credible information source], but I don't think with Britannica anymore.

Boundary maintenance as the pedagogization of space-time. Richa's boundary maintenance of space-time at home is an embodied habitus (Bourdieu, 1977) that supports, carries, and restructures the types of space-time boundaries upon which schooling is dependent. Schooling itself depends upon binaries of space and time, including "on task" and "off task," "in class" and "out of class," "school time" and "free time." In the following, we briefly consider four different, yet closely related practices of boundary maintenance: temporal distinctions, material spatial distinctions, parental maintenance, and cultural maintenance.

Richa sometimes spent her afterschool hours at Ridgeview doing homework and waiting for her parents to pick her up after their workdays had ended. On other occasions, she was at home slightly before 3:00, and she described the hour between 3:00 and 4:00 as a free time in her online practices. Self-selected digital literacies were supposed to fit within this or another designated time frame:

> This is usually my free time between 3:00 and 4:00. . . . I just need some time for my mind to relax before I start doing homework again, so [last year] it was for games and the year before that it was Neopets because I didn't have anything else to do. . . . So this year has been keeping up with celebrities, movies, and news because mostly the news today is very important I guess because we are going to start a war and I actually keep up with that. With the celebrities, movies and music, I can have something to talk about with my friends and because I have been following them for such a long time now and I watch so much TV it just seems imperative that I have to know everything about everyone.

Richa described a relatively routine practice of "keeping up" with entertainment and news information during her free time, going to CNN.com and then MTV.com "to make sure I have it all together," sequentially parsing her self-selected practices and engaging them in ways not unlike how she conducted her school-related research.

Richa also made fairly clean separations between the computers that she used for different digital literacy practices and thus, even though online space may be imagined to be contiguous, made distinctions in online literacy "events" depending upon which computer she was using. She did not use her laptop for instant messaging, claiming that the people in the Lion's Den (computer center) at school would "bite you" if you had AIM (America Online Instant Messenger) or other nonauthorized software on your laptop. On her home computer, one she shared with other family members, Richa noted that she talked to friends, kept up with news, checked her e-mail, and played games, which she described as "very useless stuff." Richa described how, even while traveling, she would bring along her laptop for schoolwork (e.g., research and writing), but, if she wanted to do instant messaging, she would use someone else's computer and log on with her screen name.

Mia

The following self-description of Mia is excerpted from an introduction to her poetry project:

> Mia is a fourteen year old girl who enjoys reading and writing poetry, art, acting, and playing tennis. . . . When she is not working for school, Mia enjoys spending time with her friends and doing things she loves. Self described as talkative and outgoing, she involves herself with many people and activities that provide her with a basis for life as well as her writing.

Mia's description suggests something of her breadth of interests, including literacy interests (e.g., poetry and acting). Even more so, the description reflects the centrality of social engagement in her life. Mia continually exuded a kind of social energy and was in the midst of many circles of social activity and communication. Mia's digital literacy practices were continuous across home and school situations and served to build and maintain a robust literacy-based social network. Mia constructed a traveling public social space. We focus in the following on the rhythms of Mia's digital literacies, describing them as social rhythms, contributing to an affective social life.

Mia's key digital literacy practice was to keep a Web log. Over the course of two years (September 15, 2002 to September 4, 2005), Mia wrote 307 posts (164 printed pages) to her Web log (or "blog"). These posts received 860 comments from others and 1,051 "eprops" (a simple "prop" or show of support for a post). These posts came at a more frequent tempo at the outset: her first 50 entries were written over one and one half months, while her last 50 were written over four months. Even at a slower tempo, though, what emerges in looking at the blog's history is the sense of a steady, constant rhythm of living and blogging or, rather, blogging as an integral part of the rhythm of life. While in late 2004 Mia had three gaps in posting of longer than 4 days (the longest being 12 days before Christmas), typically she recently posts in regular rhythm every 2 or 3 days, often at around the same times of day (noon, 1:45 p.m., 3:00 p.m., 7:45–9:00 p.m.,

9:30–10:30 p.m.). This rhythm of writing/living has changed over time; 2 years earlier, Mia would frequently also post around 9:30 a.m. The patterning of Mia's posting suggests how her writing/living rhythms, as an embodied practice, are implicit, habitual, and co-generative. While it would be possible to read the blog as simply a diary-like "response" to a life that Mia is "reflecting upon," in so doing we would make the practices and rhythms of literacy distinct from the practices and rhythms of living. Here, there is a subtle but important difference in that Mia lives a patterned life of affect *with* her blog rather than merely *representing* herself in it. The blog is a kind of speech act (Austin, 1955)—a performance of affect and identity that interacts with Mia's life and the lives of her readers in a patterned and rhythmic way.

Mia's digital literacies at home. Mia's digital literacy practices extended the social networks she participated in during school space-time into home space-time such that her social worlds were at least partially contiguous across embodied settings. Mia's digital literacies weren't saturated with school purposes as were Richa's, nor were they entirely separate from school discourse, identity, and purposes. Because many of those in Mia's online social network went to Ridgeview, her digital literacies at home involved regular writing and reading about in-school happenings and plans, school-related friendships and romances, and references to doing (or not doing) homework. In her digital literacies at home, it was typical for Mia to have several IM windows open, many of which would be with friends from school, while she also responded to others' blog entries or composed her own. About half of Mia's IMing and blogging also actively involved a social network from outside school, including a number of male friends. Then, Mia might quickly move to e-mail and open a message from an out-of-school friend on an upcoming social mixer, or from a teacher about a quiz on Friday, or from a club president about needing to submit tee-shirt money. Mia might then respond to an e-mail or two and then, after having been online for 45 minutes to an hour, turn to a school assignment, which she would approach as a task that she could accomplish quickly, in part because of her facility with online resources.

Mia's digital literacies in school. School-selected literacy events are relatively linear in composition compared to the cyclical rhythms of Mia's living and blogging that have been described previously. So, while one reading of Mia's blogging while in school might be that she is being subversive or interrupting schooling with blogging, an alternate interpretation is that the linear literacy rhythms of school practices were interrupting Mia's living/blogging activity. Mia addressed this interruption by distributing herself across simultaneous activity, polyrhythmically.

The students are preparing for the final. Ms. Schoenfeld starts with "Girls, we need to take a hard look at these poems." Mia has forgotten her poetry book today. She writes the list of poems on the back cover of her French workbook. The class gets going, and Mia logs in on her laptop.

Ms. Schoenfeld: "You need to know each one of these titles and who wrote it, and any questions about it."

Mia asks if all of their stuff needs to be in a folder or binder for the poetry project coming up due, and Ms. Schoenfeld responds that they can do it however they want. The teacher then goes over how to produce a "works cited" page. Mia reads a Xanga entry on someone else's Xanga. The title of the entry is "Thank God I'm an atheist." She laughs at what is written.

Ms. Schoenfeld: "Let us take a look—the other class is a little bit ahead of you." Six girls in the classroom have their laptops open. "Is there anybody who doesn't understand imagery?" Ms. Schoenfeld walks very close to Mia, who clicks to her home page and then to a Word document.

Mia types in the word "imagery" in a Word document. Mia then shifts back to Xanga and is now reading another Xanga posting by another author. Ms. Schoenfeld: "Who can describe an image from 'After Apple Picking' by Robert Frost?" Mia looks at Dana's book and gives her first answer of the day: "In the first four lines you get an image of an apple in an apple tree." Ms. Schoenfeld moves closer to Mia, and Mia is still on Xanga. "Good, very realistic one. Read those lines again because they are interesting lines."

The lines in front of Mia on her computer are "There is nothing more foul than dissecting a fetal pig." Mia looks over at Dana's book and reads the lines again from the Frost poem. Ms. Schoenfeld: "Frost especially likes to use the seasons of the year."

Mia has moved on to another Xanga site and then goes back to her own Xanga site. She is typing something in and occasionally glances at Ms. Schoenfeld. Most of the other girls are looking in their books. At 9:22, while the teacher continues the discussion of Frost, Mia posts the following Xanga entry,

> *strange how different kisses leave you. some leave you nervous and high strung, some leave you amazed and wondering, and then there are those that leave you when you wish they wouldn't.*

Ms. Schoenfeld: "What he is doing—is he looking in the mirror? Frozen water—again he tries to strengthen that image, of being old, tired, winter, freezing cold." Ms. Schoenfeld gets no response to her question and has Dana read the first five lines of the poem, then asks Mia to read the next few lines.

MS. SCHOENFELD:	Is there symbolic value to it?
MIA:	I was going to say that it stands for him but I think it stands for something bigger.
MS. SCHOENFELD:	Good intuition.

To summarize the last segment of the class, Ms. Schoenfeld calls on Mia at least twice more, continuing to relate back to Mia's former response ("I think it stands for something bigger"), and Mia offers her interpretation that the apple picking stands for death. Mia is still typing a comment in someone else's Xanga. She reads the following response that had just that moment been posted in response to her "kiss" entry by someone else in the school but not in this classroom,

> ahhh a profound post!
> melancholy if you must. . . .
> Posted 5/9/2003 at 9:29 AM by MissOhara

As the Frost discussion continues, Mia seems somewhat more engaged in Xanga but continues to attend to both activities. She changes the look of her Xanga home page to a blue background with purple lettering. Mia then stops fiddling with her new setup to read a few lines from the next poem under consideration. Next, Mia moves to Google and seems to be looking for pictures on the Web, perhaps to post to her Xanga. By the end of the school day, four more comments are posted to Mia's Xanga entry on kissing, laughing at her post and also identifying with it.

There are certainly a number of ways we might analyze this complex set of simultaneous interactions, considering, for example, Mia's multiple footings (Goffman, 1981) in the interaction or perhaps her astute procedural display (Bloome, Theodorou, & Puro, 1989) in school, all while engaged in other activity. We would like to interpret the interaction in a manner that requires us to reach beyond Mia's immediate activity to her literacy practices as rhythmic, embodied activity. If we consider Mia to be moving through space-time and not merely "emplaced" in one setting or another, she has developed over time a regular rhythm with her blog writing and reading that, as argued earlier, is fully integrated with her lived experiences and affective world. In other terms, her conscious experience of the world is not merely held inside her mind but is embodied, textualized in the blog, and distributed across the loose-knit community of those with whom she shares posts, comments, and eprops. The blogging space-time is practiced as an embodied rhythm that is quite regular and continually accessible at school through a wireless network and that ebbs and flows with events in her social world (e.g., kisses) and her feelings about them. The blog rhythm is cyclical, a form of repetition but with new "advents," new "dawns" (Lefebvre, 2004).

Mia's social-affective life is mediated by the blog, and the blog's affective life for others is mediated by Mia. We might think of this blog or network among Mia's blog and others as a certain kind of "affinity group" (Gee, 2003), and it can be partially explained in this way. Yet, in the case of Mia, it would be more representative to think about her blog as creating an affective space-time through the relationships among bodies, texts, persons, and routinized, yet shifting practices. The blog beats out a regular but shifting rhythm, following but also creating the ebb and flow of life for the writers involved. This kind of networked social affect is best captured in considering particular entries that collect a large number of responses. In these phases, the rhythm and tempo of Mia's blog are reset and intensified—like a series of drum riffs, the blog heats up and shakes emotions and relationships along with it. The following blog entry is suggestive of this kind of increase in intensity and affective energy. The entry is a poem by Mia, of which we have posted just a part for the sake of space. Mia worked on the poem during a school day when she was at home sick and posted it in mid-afternoon.

Monday, October 14, 2002

> i'd tell you that i'm sorry
> for the whole twisted while,
> sorry that i ruined it
> but i'm scared that you would smile.
> so instead of saying sorry
> i'll just let you know
> i'm happy in his arms
> since you let me go.
> sometimes lonely in the dark
> screaming out your name
> times like that i'd give a lot
> to have you mine again
> forgetting all the lonely tears
> smiling lies and tinted pain . . .
> Posted 10/14/2002 at 1:45 PM—email it

Mia's poem elicited the following 13 comments from her readers, numbered here for discussion, all of which came within 10 hours or so of her posting the poem.

1. Mia . . .
   Posted 10/14/2002 at 2:32 PM by diablo—delete—block user
2. :: sigh ::
   that should get the message through. thats really good Mia, get it all out dude!!
   latersness, I LOVE YOUUUUUUUUUUU!!!!!!!!!!!!!!!!!!!!
   Posted 10/14/2002 at 3:40 PM by shoney43—delete—block user
3. wow thats good
   Posted 10/14/2002 at 3:43 PM by fabman—delete—block user
4. A+, but since i do'nt really think the grammar is good, A-
   Posted 10/14/2002 at 6:24 PM by swizzle—delete—block user
5. no, the grammar is horrible, and some adjectives don't go with the nouns right. and there are also some thigns i disagree with. B-. alas, i am a hard teacher.
   Posted 10/14/2002 at 7:27 PM by swizzle—delete—block user
6. i told u that i loved u
   i told u everyday
   somehow u mustve taken it

some other kind of way
wish there was something i could do
or something else to say
but for now i'll be your scapegoat
until i fade away
Posted 10/14/2002 at 7:32 PM by sqrude—delete—block user

7. D–because it is incredible, but the rhyme scheme is messed up. It goes from rhyming to not. Alas, I, too, am a hard teacher
Posted 10/14/2002 at 7:33 PM by Hotfingersman—delete—block user

8. y do u think i'm smiling?
i guess that im not sure
y i dont act just like the awful
beast u make me for
so keep hurling out ur bitterness
untill i'll take no more
its sad we have to settle this
with a fucking "poem war"
Posted 10/14/2002 at 7:46 PM by sqrude—delete—block user

9. whoops, reread ur poem, realized that i skipped the last few lines when i read it, misinterpreted it, my bad, good poem, i enjoyed the recurring theme
Posted 10/14/2002 at 7:56 PM by sqrude—delete—block user

10. wow Mia!!! thats really really good.. i couldnt write something like that!! wow i write songs but they arent nearly that . . . hmm intelectual! u werent at school today! maybe ur sick.. if u are i hope u feel better! *jamie*
Posted 10/14/2002 at 9:29 PM by Mazzy332—delete—block user

11. Hey Mia that poem kicks ass but justin shut up hell up that poem kicked ass grammar doesn't matter, its called being expressive, ass, ok that poem was a lot then again u can do so don't talk, Big buddy
Posted 10/14/2002 at 10:56 PM by Kinglax—delete—block user

12. This is a really good one girl, keep writing and keep sharing em, specially to me—I'm gonna make you send me ALL of them! I like what I've heard so far—great job babe, and I'm looking forward to my "Mia Book". I hope you feel better, Tish
PS—Ohhh my god, the poem war is fucking hilarious! Nice responses Alex!
Posted 10/14/2002 at 11:54 PM by thisisTish—delete—block user

13. good poems from both teams
Posted 10/15/2002 at 1:10 AM by fabman—delete—block user

In terms of social space and embodied situation, four of the responses to Mia's poem were from school friends (1, 2, 10, 12), two of which were written during that same school day. Responses 6, 8, and 9 were written by Mia's former boyfriend, who lived in a different state, and other responses were written by friends in her home town but not at her school. One type of response (e.g., #2) that Mia receives to her poem is fairly common for her blog: affirmations of her feelings from others she knows well and affirmations of support or love for her. (More generally, this kind of practice is very typical in Mia's blog, where entire entries are given to expressions of affection for her friends and their qualities. Responses from friends include affective kudos, thankfulness, and requests from nonrepresented friends for her to write posts about them.) The commentary is carnivalesque in terms of its timing and divergent affective stances. Responses 3, 4, 5, 7, 10, 11, and 12 consider the poem as an aesthetic object, assigning it value or lack of value and even grading it as if it were a school assignment. Temporally speaking, the poem gets a compliment, then critique from others (4, 5, 7), and then some respondents either directly (11) or indirectly (10, 12) defend the poem from critics, implicitly guarding Mia's feelings in the poem and about the poem.

Conclusions and Implications

> Traversals are, I believe, the characteristic form that is becoming salient and significant in the transition to globalization; the form that will truly characterize the successor to modernism. (Lemke, 2001)

As a theorist of global semiotic processes, Jay Lemke imagines traversals as characteristic of late modernism, an entire class of "linkings, sequences, and catenations of meaningful elements" that cross (standardized) boundaries. In this chapter we have considered how digital literacies may be used to produce such traversals. Mia's embodied rhythms, her Web log and its individual texts, her online social network, and her laptop itself function as elements of traversal, all function in the production of space-time. At the same time, Richa's case makes evident, first, how embodied schooled practices can also traverse social situations, and, second, how a range of (modernist) practices of bounding and segmenting space-time might immobilize new technologies and other potential elements of traversal.

Figure 11.1 summarizes Richa's and Mia's digital literacy practices in and out of school with respect to the constitution of space-time and goal structures (self and school selected). This chart suggests Richa's and Mia's embodied literacy chronotopes, or embodied genres of space-time practice. In Richa's case, her school-situated practices are organized chiefly by school-selected goals and practices of space-time. The arrow in the diagram represents how school-selected goals and practices also inform Richa's practices at home; her disposition toward certain types of activity and her embodied habitus (Bourdieu, 1977) involving space-time bounding practices function as traversals of schooling across situations. "Body hexis" in Bourdieu is the dialectic of conforming the body in relation to other objectifications of the habitus (tools, goods, other dispositions). Through the mediation of the habitus, individuals learn gestures, postures, "a whole system of techniques involving the body and tools" that includes "a way of walking, a tilt of the head, facial expressions, ways of sitting and of using implements" (Bourdieu, 1977, p. 87). Body hexis reminds us that literacy practices involve ways of using the body in interaction with material goods and tools of various sorts (e.g., in traditional schooling, texts, paper, pencils of a particular, desks) and ways of positioning the physical body in relation to other bodies (e.g., the proper holding of the pencil). At Ridgeview, body hexis also included embodied orientations to the laptops, decisions about whether or not to carry them, and the overt and covert social organization of individuals around a screen image or other text. Moreover, as illustrated particularly in Richa's case, a schooled body hexis involves separations among authorized and unauthorized social spaces online or offline and appropriate (linear) rhythms of practice.

School practices evidently supported by Richa's family and culture, such that there was a collusion of goals and habitus. The horizontal arrow in the "at home" situation between "school selected" and "self-selected" practices (Figure 11.1) represents how this separation is complicated in Richa's case, in that she has evidently appropriated many school-selected goals and practices as part of her "self." However, although Richa embodies space-time in a manner that is generally consistent

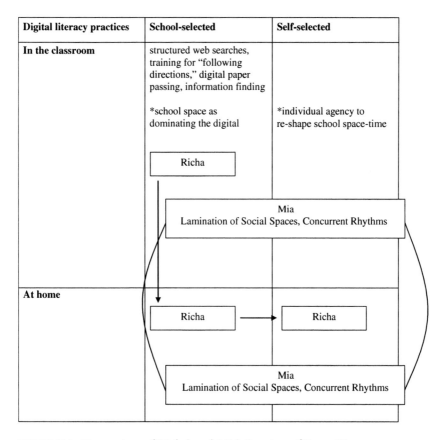

FIGURE 11.1 Comparison of Richa's and Mia's Practices of Space-Time

with schooled practice, she is nevertheless critical of some of these practices, critiquing the surface-level inquiry that schooling appears to encourage, along with its short time-scale, and also critiquing the ways in which teacher discourse and school boundaries infantilize youth knowledge of the Internet. At home, she also experiences and experiments with the desire to escape from the boundedness and linearity of schooling, even while she practices it.

In the case of Mia we have described how digital literacies may create their own embodied temporalities or rhythms. Figure 11.1 depicts the lamination of her school-selected and self-selected chronotopes in the situations of both home and school. Mia's disposition in both situations is that no single social space has dominance but that social-literate life is a matter of rotating in phase shifts among social spaces. It seems significant to recognize this as part of Mia's implicit practice; to merely interpret her as resistant and escaping from or being distracted from schooling would involve ignoring her active engagement in school activity and would also involve ignoring how her simultaneous engagements in multiple social spaces traverse school and home situations.

Relative to the rhythms of interaction in school, including those of classroom discussion and writing assignments, the rhythms of Mia's Web log are more cyclical, more periodic. This reading and writing involves repetitions, but repetitions with difference. Moreover, this patterning of social/literate life becomes thoroughly embedded into how Mia affectively experiences her life; writing does not represent life but is a way of living it. As part of detailing literacy practice as social, it seems important to attune to the rhythms of practice in that these rhythms signal how it is not only individual texts but also entire (social) literate practices that individuals become affectively engaged in. Practices that become cyclically rhythmic, like Mia's Web log, appear especially powerful for social life and literacy learning as cycles build upon past cycles and do not depend upon artificial external structuring

For some readers, this chapter could lead to a risky conclusion that wireless networks and digital literacies are distracting and damaging to school processes and goals. Indeed, such an implication is entirely sensible. Ubiquitous digital literacies would seemingly do little to support and improve the project of traditional schooling when we hold its social-spatial practices stable. But, we might also be willing play with the idea of "damage." For some youth, their self-selected digital literacy practices and rhythms do indeed inflict damage on school-sanctioned structures of space and time. Spatial and temporal boundaries, assumptions of monospatiality, temporal sequencing, surveillance, and safety are destabilized and challenged. How might schools and educational thought more generally respond to such a challenge—or damage—besides taming and closing off unruly social-spatial practices?

The case of Ridgeview Academy is informative in that the seeming intractability of schooled practices cannot be pinned on lack of resources (e.g., computer and network access), and we might turn instead to a lack of imagination to transform or "damage" the space-time of schooling. Following, we briefly note several moves toward a new imagination of literacy, space-time, and schooling that emerge directly from cases such as Richa's and Mia's:

- Pedagogical practices that depend upon simultaneity in online spaces, offline spaces, or online/offline traversals. As a simple example, embodied classroom discussions could be structured so that they invite the simultaneous interactions of distant others (e.g., experts, students from other cultures, different age groups, parents).
- Literacy projects that develop their own self-sustaining social-literate networks (such as Mia's blog) and develop their own embodied rhythms.
- Practices that explicitly depend upon, rather than rule out from the outset, information and textual resources that are considered "unauthorized" and that develop conversations and analyses about how canonical and noncanonical texts are related and valued.
- Digital pedagogies that emerge from and depend upon the knowledge/social practices that youth have already developed online (rather than treating youth as naive) and yet involve youth in the critique of naturally occurring practices.

Some of these practices, of course, might be easier to effect in schools than others in that their disruptions of space-time involve re-imagining not just school as a spatial-social system but how schooling relates to other spatial-social systems. These intersystem relationships are already present in the practices and bodies of youth such as Mia and Richa—emergent traversals vibrating across the paradoxical construction of wireless schooling.

References

Austin, J.L. (1955). *How to do things with words.* Cambridge, MA: Harvard University Press.

Bigum, C. (2002). Design sensibilities, schools, and the new computing and communication technologies. In I. Synder (Ed.), *Silicon literacies: Communication, innovation, and education in the electronic age* (pp. 130–140). New York: Routledge.

Bloome, D., Theodorou, P., & Puro, E. (1989). Procedural displays and classroom lessons. *Curriculum Inquiry 19*(3), pp. 265–291.

Bourdieu, P. (1977). *Outline of theory of practice* (R. Nice, Trans.). Cambridge: Cambridge University Press.

Dyson, A.H. (1999). Coach Bombay's kids learn to write: Children's appropriation of media material for school literacy. *Research in the Teaching of English, 33*(4), 367–402.

Finders, M.J. (1997). *Just girls: Hidden literacies and life in junior high.* New York: Teachers College Press.

Gee, J.P. (2003). *What video games have to teach us about learning and literacy.* New York: Palgrave Macmillan.

Goffman, E. (1981). *Forms of talk.* Philadelphia: University of Pennsylvania Press.

Gutierrez, K., Rymes, B., & Larson, J. (1995). Script, counterscript, and underlife: James Brown versus Brown v. Board of Education. *Harvard Educational Review, 65*(3), 445–471.

Heath, S.B. (1983). *Ways with words: Language, life, and work in communities and classrooms.* Cambridge: Cambridge University Press.

Heath, S.B., & McLaughlin, M.W. (1994). The best of both worlds: Connecting schools and community youth organizations for all-day, all-year long learning. *Educational Administration Quarterly, 30*(3), 278–300.

Hine, C. (2000). *Virtual ethnography.* Thousand Oaks, CA: Sage.

Hull, G., & Schultz, K. (2001). Literacy and learning out of school: A review of theory and research. *Review of Educational Research, 71*(4), 575–611.

Leander, K. (2002). Locating Latanya: The situated production of identity artifacts in classroom interaction. *Research in the Teaching of English, 37*(2), 198–250.

Lefebvre, H. (2004). *Rhythmanalysis* (S. Elden & G. Moore, Trans.). New York: Continuum.

Lemke, J.L. (2001). Towards a theory of traversals. Unpublished manuscript.

Miller, D., & Slater, D. (2000). *The Internet: An ethnographic approach.* New York: Berg.

Schultz, K. (2002). Looking across space and time: Reconceptualizing literacy learning in and out of school. *Research in the Teaching of English, 36*(3), 356–390.

Street, J.C., & Street, B. (1991). The schooling of literacy. In D. Barton & R. Ivanic (Eds.), *Writing in the community* (pp. 106–131). Newbury Park, CA: Sage.

Yon, D.A. (2000). *Elusive culture.* New York: State University of New York Press.

12

THE COMPRESSION OF TIME AND SPACE IN TRANSNATIONAL SOCIAL FIELDS: MOBILIZING THE AFFORDANCES OF DIGITAL MEDIA WITH LATINA STUDENTS

Lisa Schwartz, Silvia Noguerón-Liu, and Norma González

We have been made aware for some time in literacy research that issues of space and place are integral to our understandings of locations and relocations as we have theorized spatial metaphors that evoke images of movements across time and space. From Giroux's (1992) conceptualizations of border crossing, Bhabha's (2004) in-between and interstitial spaces, Lave and Wenger's Legitimate Peripheral Participation (1991), to Leander, Phillips, and Taylor's (2010) focus on geographies and mobilities of learning and Gutiérrez's "Third Space" (Gutiérrez, Baquedano-López, & Tejeda, 1999), these contributions make visible the learning and pedagogy that erupt not only in classrooms and schools but in the everyday and the local and in the global that is made local.

The circulation of people, material things, and ideas in such zones of passage constitutes some of the central social process of concern to us. How do the compression of time and space enable or constrain flows of signs, objects, and people? What continues to flow and shape and be reshaped? In these zones of encounter and contact, how are other spaces opened up for thinking across boundaries and frontiers? It is important to locate our work in the borderlands, a geopolitical entity fraught with heightened political visibility and antagonisms. We frame our research with reference to particular movements and circulations across a contested geographic space that is the U.S.-Mexico border. As the discourse of globalization focuses on flows, it is important to recognize that such flows can be discursively constructed and deconstructed in line with political ideologies and agendas.

Sadly, we and the youth and adults we work with are keenly aware of the ongoing polarizing debate on immigration, especially within the context of our home state of Arizona. The foreclosure of educational futures truncates students' aspirations and interrogates the democratic ideal of education as the great equalizer. One way to move beyond the time and space compression is to focus on capitalizing on the affordances of youth digital and multimodal meaning making (Hull, Zacher, & Hibbert, 2009; Ito et al., 2010) and on Latino students' funds of knowledge (González, Moll, & Amanti, 2005). Informed by these perspectives, our chapter aims to challenge deficit narratives about Latino students' academic identities and to examine the potential of collaborations that mobilize community resources within and across contexts in relation to learning, literacy, and identity. We shed light on the complexities of Latino students' negotiation of multiple languages and literacies in physical and virtual in-school and out-of school spaces. Beyond a "classroom-as-a-container" vision for learning (Leander et al., 2010), it is possible to explore ways in which Latino students overcome regulatory boundaries that restrict movement, means of communication, and opportunities for learning and self-advocacy.

Hybrid Frameworks: Circulating Concepts of Transnational Social Fields, New Literacies, and Social Networks

The case studies presented here share the social and spatial trajectories of students participating in academic literacy contexts. The studies combine and hybridize three main organizing concepts, *transnational social fields, new literacies,* and *social networks,* all increasingly shaped by the affordances of technology. These lenses focus on flows of information, resources, practices, and ideas across multiple geographies of learning. Participants in the research studies discussed herein, regardless of their actual physical movement across borders or generation status, live in and create transnational social fields. We draw on a definition of transnational social fields as "multiple interlocking networks of social relationships through which ideas, practices, and resources are unequally exchanged, organized, and transferred" (Levitt & Schiller, 2004, p. 1009) and recognize these fields as evolving through processes of history, migration, and movement of networked households in the U.S.-Mexico borderlands region (Velez-Ibanez & Greenberg, 1992). We are specifically interested in the how the circulation of resources in increasingly digitally mediated social fields (Lam, 2006) can be accessed in academic settings to develop students' new literacies.

We conceptualize new literacies as firmly couched in a cultural historical perspective that asserts the social, contextual, and historical in shaping literacy practices (Lee & Smagorinksy, 1999; Scribner & Cole, 1981). Significant to this perspective is a conception of literacy as a social practice evolving through time and space in multimodal and multidiscursive human activity (New London Group, 1996). The use of digital tools is envisioned not as a discrete skill or a particular type of literacy but rather as a way students can become conscious creators and producers of cultural spaces in processes of literate production, rather than solely consumers of media. Eschewing binaries and acknowledging the salience of hybridity are essential features of a new literacies approach that seeks to circulate agency through multiple systems of activity, across teachers', students', and researchers' social worlds and networks.

Informed by a new literacies approach, we emphasize the affordances of overlapping social, digital, and transnational networks. Our work aims to connect these multiple localities where learning and literacy practices occur. The mobilization of cultural and learning resources and mentoring and apprenticeship opportunities and the building of social capital and identity formation are all processes related to the connections and relationships in students' social networks. Applying a funds of knowledge perspective allows us to study the mutual transformation of practices through developing reciprocal relationships across networks. In addition, the focus on social networks has been central in the study of transnationalism and social capital in immigrant communities (Portes, Guarnizo, & Landolt, 1999). These concepts inform our analysis of practices moving across school and out of school spaces or across multiple households and the implications of these flows for the literacy practices of Latino students.

In the following case studies of two Latina learners, we focus on the circulation of practices, ideas, and resources across complex ecologies of learning. These students' trajectories are presented in data from two empirical ethnographic studies conducted in Arizona by two of the authors of this chapter. Schwartz conducted her research in a high school setting serving predominately Latino students, and Noguerón-Liu worked in a community center serving adult immigrant learners. In both studies, the authors collaborated with teachers as co-instructors designing learning experiences involving digital tools. Schwartz's study discusses how a second-generation high school student was supported in accessing and re-imagining her extended networks across multiple spaces by appropriating the social dimensions of new media for academic purposes. Noguerón-Liu's study focuses on mapping the multiple spaces and networks that supported the emergent digital literacy practices of a first-generation immigrant adult learner. Both projects were carried out in the spring of 2010, when Arizona became the eye of the storm in national immigration policy conversations, magnifying long-standing xenophobia and deficit discourses.

Expanding Practice: Appropriating the Social Affordances of the Digital in Academic Spaces

Schools overwhelmingly create false borders between practices circulating in students' social, digital, and transnational networks and those valued within the walls of classrooms. In this section, we present the case study of Beatriz, a second-generation Latina teenager participating in Schwartz's collaborative research with a high school writing classroom in urban southern Arizona. The study aimed to work with teachers and students to mobilize literacy practices across contexts and networks. Beatriz's learning trajectory illustrates the possibilities for appropriating the social affordances of digital tools, stemming from their use for communication and identification within peer, familial, and interest-based networks (Ito et al., 2010) and for expanding students' literacy practices across personal and academic domains.

The research involved Schwartz in co-teaching and conducting daily participant observation within the multiple online and offline spaces of a high school writing course. Students in the study were predominately Latino, first-, second-, and later-generation youth of Mexican heritage, and mainly in the 11th and 12th grades. Data were collected to illustrate tensions and synergies of migrating practices and objects across the multiple social and digital networks emanating from the lives of the students, teacher, and researcher. These data include video and audio recordings, field notes, social network profiles and communication, participation in wikis, self-assessments, and multimodal texts produced by students in digital classroom and popular media sites, as well as ongoing informal and formal interviews for focal students. Data analysis aligns with the participatory interventionist approach in the cultural historical tradition of expansive learning (Engeström, 1987), combined with a funds of knowledge framework, infused with Freirian (1999) praxis and new literacies pedagogy. Analysis centered on examining how key meditational tools supported students in accessing their social practices and networks to form reciprocal relationships between everyday and academic practices. Participant trajectories were formed to map evolving flows of practice.

Beatriz's trajectory, like those of many of her classmates, demonstrates her concern with facing significant economic and institutional constraints on future educational and employment opportunities after her impending graduation. Unlike many of her classmates, Beatriz was not a heavy user of new media when the class began. She used a cell phone but had neither Internet access nor her own computer at home. She went to the library or her *Tio's* (uncle's) to use the computer. For Beatriz and her family, MSN Messenger was the dominant tool for communicating with friends and relatives in Mexico and in California through chat and videochat in English and Spanish.

Beatriz revealed through an "identity" essay and interview that she considered herself a good student, but in her senior year she was often absent multiple days in a week, and this was affecting her grades. Her demeanor at the onset of the class when she was prompted to participate was often withdrawn and unresponsive or irritable. Beatriz shared through the identity essay that she had fond memories of her family from when they lived in California, but now she felt distant from her familial networks, and in class she exclaimed that her parents could not help her with the challenges of applying for college. She wrote in the identity essay that she kept her "school self" and her "home self" distinct. Forms of mediation, like the identity essay, provide a frame for discussing how new literacy practices hybridized across networks in Beatriz's learning trajectory. The following section maps Beatriz's trajectory through classroom activity mediated by an emphasis on the social dimension of digital tools.

Beatriz: Hybrid Zones of Participation

As a means to re-imagine the home and school and the online and offline divides, academic activity was shared in the semipublic spaces of classroom social network sites and wikis. In the writing classroom, collaboratively creating a "ning" online social network site helped to begin the development of hybrid zones of participation, different from the restrictive spatial-temporal and social and discursive norms of many classes. The ning site made visible multiple aspects of students' identities, social practices, and literacies in the different spaces of their lives. In conversation about the possibilities for students to codesign the content of the class ning social network, Beatriz voiced an interest in information about college and future plans and was encouraged to use the ning as a space to discuss the topic. Despite her initial lack of familiarity with the social network genre, she decided to create a discussion post, titled "Life after high school. . . ." She asked her peers to address the question "What will happen after high school?" and solicited them to invite others to share and to post information about colleges. Beatriz's attempt to connect with her classmates and classroom activity through her own interests demonstrated a shift in her participation toward considering that, through her classroom networks, she might be supported in her concerns about the future.

After learning about Beatriz's preoccupations through her work in the ning and identity essay, Ms. Smith, the writing course teacher, promoted the continuation of the topic "life after high school" for the second essay. For this essay students conducted collaborative research in which they developed questions related to concepts of identity, drawn from multiple disciplines and their own theorizing, to use when interviewing people in their networks. Students were encouraged to use digital means to access their interviewees, and they shared interviews, analysis, and paper writing in a collaborative wiki. Beatriz was instrumental in crafting her group's collective question: How does who we are affect our decisions for the future? The topic was a common thread within her group, named "The Graduates," indexing the students' orientation toward this milestone.

Beatriz formulated individual subquestions about school. She interviewed her younger sister, a friend's mom from Mexico who had recently returned to school, and a cousin in California who was working to save money to follow her dream of returning to college. Here is an excerpt of her cousin's interview, done in Messenger and shared on her group's wiki:

BEATRIZ SAYS: *Oh what up dudes jajajaja. . . . I thought you didnt get my message hahaha . . . Hey my mom says hello jaja.*

★GABRIELA★ SAYS: Lol I did but then I was shit I forgot! So I was like I cnt meet Beatriz now caz jr took the car but like then I remembered I have messager on my phone lol. Tell her I said hi back!!! :)

After Beatriz explains the project and asks one of her first questions, the interview continues:

BEATRIZ SAYS: *Ok now tell me what your interested in for the futere ...*
                      for example plans you might have for schooling, jobs etc.
★GABRIELA★ SAYS: Am going back to college in the fall, yay am excited!
                      I pick a school already! ... am working right now in
                      getting in shape n studying so I can pass the LAPD
                      test! Dude I just start doing TAEBO Am freaking
                      sore I just wanna die lol +o(:D

The exchange demonstrates hybrid social and academic objectives emerging through activity that Beatriz related was "a lot of fun." The interview for class research aligned with Beatriz's existing social practice of instant messaging her friends and relatives, her concerns with graduation, and her access to extended social and digital networks through the use of her *Tio's* (uncle's) computer to do the interview.

Emphasizing the social affordances of digital tools used for academic assignments that engaged Beatriz's interests supported her in reorienting her stance toward both classroom activity and her own networks. The use of digital tools also mediated collaboration with others. Members of her research group, despite many absences, worked together in class and remotely to share their findings and opinions. Thinking together in their rough draft on the wiki, they wrote:

> Most of our friends who interviewed were thinking well ahead for the future. We found that most or all of them were positive about their future. Most were looking forward to college, while some were already in there careers and enjoying them. (Beatriz) ... if you think that your not going to do anything in life you might give up and not even try ... (Edgar) ... would like to add that having positive thinking is what keeps us motivated . . . (Yvonne) It made me feel really good reading all the interviews ... it seems to me that we all want a better future. We are doing what ever it takes to get a higher education.

Through the essay, the students hybridized academic and personal agendas mediated through the use of the wiki. With Beatriz often taking the lead, this joint activity constructed a place for the group to collaborate across time, space, and their extended networks. Together they voiced a positive vision for and recognition of the interrelatedness of their academic and personal futures.

In a final interview Beatriz stated that the collaboration was a new and "interesting experience, in terms of thinking, different opinions and different ideas, it was a challenge." She related that exploring the self and the self in relation to others made her think and presented a new way of writing. It is significant to share Beatriz's reflections on class assignments because they point to the importance of the social organization of appropriating digital tools. Leveraging the social affordances of the digital with the resources represented by her concerns and networks is what made it possible for Beatriz to expand her new literacy practices across contexts and reorient her position toward connecting her multiple selves and aspirations.

Expanding Learning Sites: Developing Digital Literacies in Transnational Spaces

In the next section, we present the case study of Joselyn, a participant in Noguerón-Liu's study. Joselyn's learning trajectory maps the ways she mobilized a variety of social, linguistic, and material resources across online and offline spaces. These resources supported her own appropriation of new digital literacy practices, as well as her existing transnational ties. In a qualitative study, Noguerón-Liu followed adult immigrant learners' participation in digital literacy practices in a community center over nine months. Using ethnographic techniques, she conducted participant observation, interviews with focal participants and family members, writing of field notes, and collection of computer-screen activity. Data sources related to Joselyn were coded thematically using grounded theory methods (Strauss & Corbin, 1998), with the following purposes: (a) categorizing digital literacy practices observed in the classroom and reported in interviews; (b) constructing a chronology of events related to digital literacy socialization in her life history; and (c) describing the contexts of socialization and their relations to other technology users in such contexts.

Joselyn's case study is particularly grounded in two of the space-time metaphors proposed by Leander et al. (2010): learning-in-place and learning networks. We describe the nature of the spaces where Joselyn participated in digital literacy practices and the ways virtual and transnational locales shaped her learning process. We then focus on the social networks that Joselyn drew from in her use of communication and media production technologies.

Joselyn: Emergent Practices across Sites and Networks

At the onset of the study, in August 2009, Joselyn joined a basic computer skills course at a community center in a metro area in Arizona. Prior to migration, she had attended school in Mexico, completing two years of college toward a business degree. She had lived in Arizona for 10 years; at age 30, she mostly stayed at home to take care of two young daughters. In spite of having a desktop computer at home, she reported fearing to use it because of uncertainty and lack of familiarity with the software.

The computer courses at the center were made possible through a binational agreement between a Mexican university and a U.S. state university. This agreement allowed Arizona students to enroll in online adult education courses in

Spanish, while receiving face-to-face instruction from local bilingual tutors. Hence, Joselyn's classroom became a site positioned and shaped in relation to other spaces; as Leander et al. (2010) explain, this nexus of relations to different sites transcends visions of this learning space as bounded and isolated. This classroom space incorporated activities and practices connected to institutions in local and remote locations, beyond national boundaries (Levitt & Schiller, 2004). In addition, this site displayed the complex dynamics between transnationalism from "above" and "below" (Guarnizo & Smith, 1998). At a macro social scale, a binational institutional agreement responded to efforts to provide educational opportunities for Mexicans residing in the United States; at a micro social level, Joselyn's own migration history, strong Spanish literacy skills, and transnational affiliations made these courses a viable option through which she could acquire learn computer skills.

Within these macro and micro scales, a meso-level approach allows us to view classroom practices and affordances in relation to other sites. Local instructors carried out transcultural work to support students' understanding of content produced in Mexico and accessed online. At the center, Joselyn was able to read online tutorials in Spanish and established communication with a distant tutor in Mexico, while receiving step-by-step directions from her local instructors. Hence, in every class, Joselyn negotiated the meaning of a "virtual" classroom (the online platform created in Mexico) and the face-to-face instruction taking place offline. The transnational dimension of the classroom space was also evident in Joselyn's household. Many of Joselyn's family members (such as her mother and siblings), as well as her husband's relatives, were living in the same city in the United States. However, they maintained strong ties with relatives living in Mexico and relied on phone calls and travel to support these connections. Joselyn's experiences in the center made her aware of the affordances of new technologies of communication to reach her distant relatives and to strengthen already-existing relations with remote locations, such as her hometown and her husband's hometown.

At the center, Joselyn also became part of a large transnational network of students enrolled in the online platform. She was able to view other students' and distant tutors' messages via the platform, as the local instructor explained the affordances of e-mail within this site and proper communication practices as "virtual" students. Her simultaneous participation as both a virtual and a traditional student resulted in her assignments having multiple audiences: for instance, slide shows or Microsoft Word documents she produced as part of her classwork were viewed by peers, her local instructor, and her distant tutor. At the same time, Joselyn got to know other students in the classroom site who shared her cultural and migration background and interest in new technologies. These frequent day-to-day interactions allowed Joselyn to build a social network of peers who were making sense of online communication together and who helped her build a list of "contacts" in her brand new e-mail and Facebook accounts.

Joselyn's extensive network of relatives was instrumental in her appropriation of digital literacy practices, in particular, online communication and media production practices. Her older sister María attended the class with her, and they "practiced" creating documents together in María's household, where they also recruited Maria's teenage son's support for troubleshooting and program installation. What started as e-mail and Facebook communication between Joselyn and her sister extended to involve Joselyn's adolescent nieces. As Joselyn shared:

> *Tenemos un Facebook con las sobrinas de aquí, de un correo que me mandaron, le responde a alguna request. . . . Con ellos [usamos] comunicación de correo electrónico, "como estás," o "va a haber algo aquí," o "vamos a ir a algún lado," ponernos de acuerdo ahí. O incluso a veces estoy así en línea, y mi hermana está en línea, y la encuentro, y nos ponemos "como estas," y pues nos ponemos a platicar.*
>
> We have a Facebook with our nieces from here, from an e-mail they sent me, I responded to a request. With them [we use] e-mail communication, "how are you," or "is there going to be anything here," or "are we going somewhere," we agree on what to do in there. Or even sometimes, I am online, and my sister is online, and I find her, and there we say "how are you," and then we start talking.
>
> (Interview, April 15, 2010)

Hence, Joselyn's appropriation of e-mail and online social networks was fostered by her online interaction with adolescent nieces. In addition, these same tools were used to reach relatives who were distant and living in Mexico. Like Beatriz in Schwartz's study, Joselyn identified MSN messenger as popular among Mexican users, and she used this account to reach her sisters-in-law, who lived in her husband's hometown. With the aid of her adolescent nieces, Joselyn also started to create slideshows documenting family events (such as birthday parties) to share with her relatives in Mexico. The addition of media sharing and instant messaging to her repertoire of communication practices allowed Joselyn to transform the nature of her transnational practices.

Joselyn was able to connect with social networks across spaces that are traditionally viewed as geographically bounded. She was mentored in various digital literacy practices by instructors in a formal classroom and by relatives in the extended cluster of households that shared family resources—including digital tools and the expertise of younger family members. These interactions took place in offline and online domains, creating multiple opportunities for Joselyn's socialization into ways of talking and being in digital spaces. And last, these networks of peers, tutors, and relatives extended beyond national borders, reproducing and strengthening the transnational social fields in Joselyn's everyday practices.

Lessons Learned: Reframing Classroom Geographies

By looking closely at the practices, positions, and relationships in these two students' trajectories, we are able to see the richness of support for their learning across multiple localities. Activity documented in the research reconfigured normative classroom geographies and reframed classroom spaces as located within students' social and digital networks and transnational social fields. This flexibility opened up possibilities for appropriating resources circulating in these arenas for engagement in new literacy practices. Both studies detail partnerships that cut across and reshaped traditional divisions represented in classroom environments: from the binational program in Noguerón-Liu's study to the collaboration among students, teachers, and researcher in Schwartz's work. Each classroom combined digital tools and an orientation toward collaborative and digital fluencies emphasized in a new literacies–informed pedagogy. Resources made available to students in these expanded contexts included the use of Spanish, an array of digital tools, and the collective aspirations and strategies of the students' extended networks to reframe and construct educational futures.

In both studies, hybrid zones of participation developed through digital media use that made visible and valuable the "stuff" of students' everyday experience for analytical and personally responsive academic inquiry. In Noguerón-Liu's study, Joselyn's sense of self as a strong user of Spanish literacy and her interest in maintaining family connections and maximizing the use of new technologies led her to mobilize the knowledge acquired in the classroom to achieve her social and personal goals. Within Schwartz's study, the learning trajectory of Beatriz illustrates how digital tools appropriated as eminently socially and culturally mediated artifacts and spaces afford possibilities for reconnecting students to the resources circulating in their extended networks. These cases point to the potential of digital and transnational spaces to connect across falsely dichotomized contexts and provide opportunities for students to develop new identities as learners.

An important component of this discussion is to highlight that even students, like Beatriz, who successfully make it to their senior year in high schools suffering from high dropout rates, are at risk of losing their momentum if schools fail to address students' struggles emanating from an increasingly hostile social and economic climate for Latinos in the United States. This work serves to show how an emphasis on the social affordances of the digital and the transnational can be appropriated to join academic and everyday concerns. In these expansive spaces, the development of new multidiscursive literacies that support youth as learners can help leverage resources across their social and academic networks.

Our findings are also relevant to the discussion of the nature of access to digital tools for minority students, often framed from a deficit, "digital-divide" perspective. Beatriz and Joselyn relied on shared family funds of knowledge and material resources to access what they needed to communicate online. Beatriz utilized her uncle's computer, while Joselyn relied on her nephews and nieces for mentoring and troubleshooting. Beatriz conducted an interview via instant messaging for an academic research paper, while Joselyn applied media creation skills learned at the center to create digital family albums. Both students engaged in computer-mediated interactions with purposes that bridged social and academic practices. In their work with digital media, Beatriz and Joselyn built the transnational social fields in which relationships with remote relatives and contacts were maintained and transformed.

Of significance is that, for both Beatriz and Joselyn, family and personal practices were reshaped by their mobilization of digital tools and goals acquired in formal school settings. Sharing the voices of her interviewees in a collaborative wiki, Beatriz re-imagined family and friends as sources of valuable information and inspiration about how her identity might affect her decisions for the future. For Joselyn, her appropriation of digital tools and interactions in online spaces allowed her to reconfigure and reinforce her existing family ties and gain confidence as a technology user.

Conclusion: Zones of Possibility for Latino/a Learners

As identities and networks develop across space and time, these analyses point to the ways in which classroom and family practices with new media shaped the learning trajectories of first- and second-generation Latinas. Framing the possibilities of classroom practices within social and digital networks and transnational social fields has relevant implications for practice in the teaching of culturally and linguistically diverse students and for the integration of digital tools in academic settings. Both studies present cases emphasizing the importance of appropriating digital tools through pedagogies that work to hybridize practices and relationships across social worlds. In high school and adult education settings, Beatriz and Joselyn engaged in online environments that promoted the visualization of their academic futures from positions valuing their extended networks. They were able to reconfigure mediational means available to them in both in-school and out-of-school spaces. At the intersection of digital and geographical borderlands, the learning trajectories of Beatriz and Joselyn exemplify their agency in actively connecting multiple localities, goals, and relationships through their use of digital tools.

In addition to validating resources derived from diverse contexts, these case studies have important implications for classroom practices that engage minority women in the appropriation of new technologies. In the classroom contexts described earlier, female instructors and researchers participated in the design of units and lessons; social networks of female peers and family members engaged in communication with focal participants. The interstitial and connective spaces that developed within these partnerships provided a context where Latina students were able to integrate and expand their identities and literacy practices through learning new skills and forming new subjectivities.

The popular imagination and public opinion shaping our definitions of "technology user" or "digital literacy competence" may be changing as new media become increasingly ubiquitous in daily lives. However, digital-divide and deficit narratives do not normatively serve to foster a vision of Latinas as tech-savvy future professionals in technology-related fields. The examples shared within this chapter serve to offer views of Latinas as confident and creative users of new media. With statistics showing a rise in Latino students' enrollment in college (Fry, 2011), a precipitous drop in Hispanic household wealth (Taylor, Kochhar, & Fry, 2011), and a low number of Latinos employed in the field of information and communications technology (Dockerman, 2011), mobilizing funds of knowledge derived from the social, digital, and transnational networks circulating in immigrant households may well serve as a pathway for Latina students' academic and career development in relation to IT expertise.

The analysis in this chapter points to the potential of mobilizing knowledge beyond classrooms or nation-states as containers. In these research projects, flows of ideas, resources, and identities across K-12 contexts, higher education, households, and communities allowed the reconfiguration of classroom spaces and educational possibilities. In both studies, university–school collaborations created new openings for negotiating exchanges of information across multiple sites. These processes emphasized the circulation of Latino students' funds of knowledge through digital means and the existence and evolution of transnational social fields as resources and realities for Latino students. As researcher-practitioners, we also crossed boundaries and created new positionalities for our work with Latino students. We engaged theoretical lenses and participatory approaches that make visible the richness of negotiating the complex learning ecologies of students, teachers, and researchers circulating in border zones. Developing new literacies within the hybrid zones of participation that emerged from these contexts worked to create new possibilities for expanding, rather than compressing, time and space in literacy research and classroom activity.

References

Bhabha, H.K. (1984). *The location of culture*. London: Routledge.

Dockerman, D. (2011). Statistical portrait of Hispanics in the United States, 2009. Pew Hispanic Center. Retrieved February 16, 2014, from www.pewhispanic.org/

Engeström, Y. (1987). *Learning by expanding*. Helsinki: Orienta-konsultit. Retrieved February 15, 2014, from http://lchc.ucsd.edu/mca/Paper/Engestrom/Learning-by-Expanding.pdf

Freire, P. (1999). *Pedagogy of the oppressed*. New York: Continuum.

Fry, R. (2011). Hispanic college enrollment spikes, narrowing gaps with other groups. Pew Hispanic Center. Retrieved February 15, 2014, from http://pewhispanic.org/reports/report.php?ReportID=146

Giroux, H. (1992). *Border crossings: Cultural workers and the politics of education*. New York: Routledge.

González, N., Moll, L.C., & Amanti, C. (2005). *Funds of knowledge, theorizing practices in households, communities, and classrooms*. Mahwah, NJ: Lawrence Erlbaum.

Guarnizo, L.E. & Smith, M.P. (1998). The locations of transnationalism. In M.P. Smith & L.E. Guarnizo (Eds.) *Transnationalism from below* (pp. 3–34). New Brunswick, NJ: Transaction Publishers.

Gutiérrez, K., Baquedano-López, P., & Tejeda, C. (1999). Rethinking diversity: Hybridity and hybrid language practices in the third space. *Mind, Culture, & Activity, 6,* 286–303.

Hull, G., Zacher, J., & Hibbert, L. (2009). Youth, risk, and equity in a global world. *Review of Research in Education, 33*(1), 117–159.

Ito, M., Baumer, S., Bittanti, M., Boyd, D., Cody, R., Herr-Stephenson, B., et al. (2010). *Hanging out, messing around, and geeking out: Kids living and learning with new media.* Cambridge, MA: MIT Press.

Lam, W.S.E. (2006). Re-envisioning language, literacy, and the immigrant subject in new mediascapes. *Pedagogies, 1*(3), 171–195.

Lave, J., & Wenger, E. (1991). *Situated learning: Legitimate peripheral participation.* New York: Cambridge University Press.

Leander, K., Phillips, N., & Taylor, K. (2010). The changing social spaces of learning: Mapping new mobilities. *Review of Research in Education, 34,* 329–394.

Lee, C.D., & Smagorinksy, P. (Eds.). (1999). *Vygotskian perspectives on literacy research: Constructing meaning through collaborative inquiry.* New York: Cambridge University Press.

Levitt, P., & Schiller, N.G. (2004), Conceptualizing simultaneity: A transnational social field perspective on society. *International Migration Review, 38,* 1002–1039.

New London Group. (1996). A pedagogy of multiliteracies: Designing social futures. *Harvard Educational Review, 66* (1), 60–92.

Portes, A., Guarnizo, L., & Landolt, P. (1999). The study of transnationalism: Pitfalls and promise of an emergent research field. *Ethnic and Racial Studies, 22*(2), 217–237.

Scribner, S., & Cole, M. (1981). *The psychology of literacy.* Cambridge, MA: Harvard University Press.

Strauss, A., & Corbin, J. (1998). *Basics of qualitative research: Techniques and procedures for developing grounded theory* (2nd ed). Thousand Oaks, CA: Sage.

Taylor, P., Kochhar, R., Fry, R. (2011). Wealth gaps rise to high levels between Whites, Blacks and Hispanics. Pew Social and Demographic Trends, Washington, D.C.: Pew Research Center. Retrieved February 16, 2014, from http://ehub29.webhostinghub.com/~busine87/assignments/business_statistics_-_wealt.pdf

Velez-Ibanez, C., & Greenberg, J. (1992). Formation and transformation of funds of knowledge. *Anthropology & Education Quarterly, 23,* 313–335.

AFTERWORD: THE TIME-SPACE DOUBLE HELIX OF RESEARCH

Jennifer Rowsell

For inspiration to write this afterword, I returned to some beloved data from a longitudinal high school study that I keep in a box, and there I found a crumpled sheet of paper with a paragraph before which I wrote, "time, space, and felt memories." Figure 13.1 shows a scanned version of Kyle's writing.

The actual text as Kyle wrote it:

> *The loose glass panel on the screen door seems as if the slightest push would cause it to come lose and shatter over the dining room floor. As I walk into the dimly lit room, an orange glow from the Christmas lights of years past invades my vision and a strong fog of cigarette smoke stings my nostrils. Oddly, this scene reminds me of my childhood, albeit I have never been to this place before. My grandmother's house has a similar presence. The dog barking at my feet feels initimidated by my stature, and begins to bark. A mutual friend (with the owner of the house) tells me to sit, so as not to frighten the dog any longer. I sit down slowly, and surely enough, the dog refrains from barking. Some time passed and the owner of the house returns home, slightly surprised to see her friends all at her house without her direct consent. I move out of the way so that she may pass through the loose screen door and enter the room. She, our mutual friend, and a friend of hers all move into the kitchen, which is more or less a sectioned off area next to the dining room, only differentiated by a small wall with a counter that connects the two. I scoot across the floor, to make sure that the dog is not frightened, and enter a space between the kitchen and the bathroom where a chair exists that I could sit on without offending the dog. I notice that there is a wall leading from the dining room into the children's rooms that is covered in writing. You can almost date the artwork depicted here, you can see how over the many years the children have lived here they have written many things that are permanent, and thus still exist. After the group of friends are finished gathering their food and drinks, they*

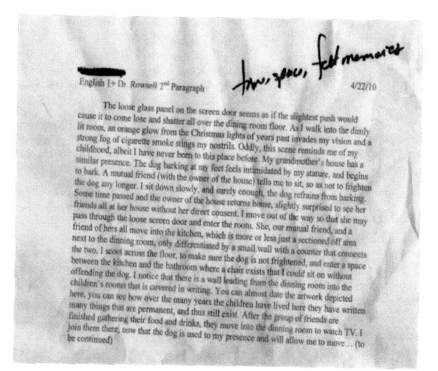

FIGURE 13.1 Kyle's Writing

Photograph by Jennifer Rowsell.

move into the dining room to watch tv. I join them there, now that the dog is used
to my presence and will allow me to move . . . (to be continued). April 22nd, 2010.

The descriptive paragraph has the qualities of writing that capture my imagination: it is specific; it invites senses; and it elicits memories. After finding it, I remembered that the writer, fourteen-year-old Kyle, had crumpled it up during English +
class because he considered it "not good enough for the assignment" (the assignment
was to write a paragraph that captures a moment in time). Reflecting on it, I recall
uncrumpling the paper because I liked Kyle's writing and, more to the point,
because I appreciated that a moment *could* have been lost . . . but it wasn't.

What could have been lost is a phrase that is fitting for what Compton-Lilly and
Halverson's edited book does for the literacy community: it saves memories and
preserves agency in elegant and eloquent ways. Chapter after chapter, the book
exposes some fundamental truths about time and space, such as: (1) showing how
memories accumulate and become embellished over time; (2) demonstrating how
manifesting meanings, sensations, and associations intensifies with time; (3) illustrat-
ing how spaces create and solidify retrospective narratives; and (4) demonstrating

how time and space go into the recesses of our unconscious, yet continue to exert power and force on our lives. In short, the collection reminds its readers that we are always "in a process of becoming across time and space" (McLeod & Thomson, 2009). Sometimes, in fact often, we forget this as researchers.

After all of these rich accounts of time and space in the lives of others, let's take a moment to step back and think about how time and space impact the researcher and the researched. Deeply rooted in each chapter is a commitment to exploring the entanglements of time and space across diverse contexts from different angles and optics. Modernist, postmodernist, social justice, LGBTQ connections, chronotopes, funds of knowledge, rhizomes, timescales—theoretical strands are threaded into the lived relationships and histories experienced by research participants and their researchers, and they are *both* in the process of becoming across time and space. In this way, there is a double helix of memories: as researchers analyze time and space in participants' lives, so too researcher-researched time and space unfold. Analyzing space and time to derive knowledge and meaning about literacy might appear as intrinsic to data, but actually, stories of the researched are entwined with stories of the researcher. To draw on Wacquant (2005), knowledge and meaning in research is created by "the mindful *body of the analyst*" as "an indispensable tool for research" (Wacquant, 2005, p. 466). As Bourdieu, Chamboredon, and Passeron (1991) and others (Law, 2004) pointed out some time ago, our research practices generate the knowledge and meanings that we discover.

Building on the work of McLeod and Thomson (2009), scholars in Compton-Lilly and Halverson's edited collection attend to how time and space play out in research: (1) there is *biographical* time—time that unfolds for both the researcher and researched in reflexive ways; (2) there is *research time*—the amount of time spent in a site; and (3) there is *analytic time*—the work of thinking and writing about relationships grounded in theory. All three strands are evident in chapters but are foregrounded more in some than in others. In the chapters by Saldaña, Guerra, and Crandall, there are strong biographical, reflexive undercurrents inflecting research time and space. In those by Pahl, Falchi and Siegel, Blackburn and Clark, Bass, and Leander and Aplin, there is the strength of research time informing what unfolds in terms of literacy practices over space and time (i.e., both time that has elapsed and number of years in a particular site). In the contributions by Grigorenko, Beierle, and Bloome; Miller; Chisholm; and Schwartz, Noguerón-Liu, and González, there is the leveraging of theory and analytical lenses to extract time and space out of instances of practice. The front story of every chapter is to develop and enhance accounts of time and space in literacy research, and the back story of every chapter is how we become and change as researchers across time and space. *This* is the story that intrigued me. As all of the spotlighted researchers walked alongside their participants, their own memories and felt experiences transpired and sedimented into the research and their researcher identities.

Circling back to Kyle's text, like Johnny Saldaña's time travel in the first chapter, I *flash back* to a high school in the United States and to Kyle's towering figure over me as he crumples up his text in the brightly lit English + classroom. I *flash sideway* to think about how the text was "lost" over the intervening years and then, through serendipity, found again. I *flash forward* about the lessons I can learn about time and space as a researcher. More specifically, I forgot as a researcher that I experience the process of time and space and that body, senses, memory, and felt experience play as much of a role in the process as field notes, instruments, and textual knowledge and theory. Mauthner and Doucet (2004) describe a more enlightened perspective on research that takes account of this double helix of time-space:

> Commitment to a postfoundational epistemology and to a reflexive social science demands not only that we recognize the contexts of knowledge production, but also the "subjectivities through which our research materials are produced" (Pink, 2004, p. 397), and "the embodied and experiential ways in which we come to understand the world" (Mauthner & Doucet, 2008, p. 980).

Although it is not explicitly stated, every author in the collection experienced a double helix of becoming with their participants. Time and space, as they are seen in nuanced and inflected ways in the book, expose fundamental truths about life and learning that are indeed not too abstract, too intellectual, or too philosophical to be the subject of a book about education or literacy. In fact, extracting time and space allows us to recognize and maybe even appreciate our evolving commitments to the field.

References

Bourdieu, P., Chamboredon, J. C., & Passeron, J.C. (1991). *The craft of sociology*. Berlin: Walter de Gruyter.

Law, J. (2004). *After method: Mess in social research*. Abingdon: Routledge.

Mauthner, N., & Doucet, A. (2008). "Knowledge once divided can be hard to put together again": An epistemological critique of collaborative and team-based research practices. *Sociology, 42*(5), 971–985.

McLeod, J., & Thomson, R. (2009). *Researching social change*. London: Sage.

Pink, S. (2004). Visual methods. In C. Seale, G. Giampietro, J. F. Gubrium, & D. Silverman (Eds.), *Qualitative research practice*. London: Sage.

Wacquant, L. (2005). Carnal connections: On embodiment, apprenticeship, and membership. *Qualitative Sociology, 28*(4), 445–474.

AUTHOR BIOGRAPHIES

Beth Aplin is a middle-school teacher in the Metro Nashville Schools. She loves her work and sees herself as teaching both math and lessons about life.

Michelle Bass graduated from the University of Wisconsin–Madison in May 2012 with a PhD in Educational Psychology. She is currently pursuing a master of science degree in information from the University of Michigan School of Information. She works at the Taubman Health Sciences Library as a University Library Associate and works on many library projects and initiatives, including providing instruction for health sciences students and collaborating on systematic review searches.

Marlene Beierle is currently a Professor in the Department of Outreach and Engagement at the Ohio State University. Her research interests center on ethnographic studies of classroom cultures and how teacher/student and student/student dialogic interactions support and/or constrain opportunities for literacy learning.

Mollie V. Blackburn is a Professor of Teaching and Learning at the Ohio State University. She is the author of *Interrupting Hate: Homophobia in Schools and What Literacy Can Do about It* and a coeditor of *Acting Out!: Combating Homophobia through Teacher Activism* and *Literacy Research for Political Action*. Her scholarship has received an award from the Queer Studies special interest group of the American Educational Research Association, among others.

David Bloome is EHE Distinguished Professor of Teaching and Learning in the Department of Teaching and Learning of the Ohio State University College of Education and Human Ecology. His research focuses on how people use spoken and written language for learning in classroom and nonclassroom settings and how people use language to create and maintain social relationships, to construct knowledge, and to create communities, social institutions, and shared histories and futures.

James S. Chisholm is Assistant Professor of English Education in the Department of Middle and Secondary Education at the University of Louisville. He studies adolescents' multimodal literacy practices and inquiry-based discussions of language and literature in high school English classrooms. His research has appeared in the *Journal of Literacy Research*, the *Journal of Adolescent & Adult Literacy*, and the *60th Yearbook of the Literacy Research Association*.

Caroline T. Clark is Professor of English Education and Adolescent Literacies and Chair of the Department of Teaching and Learning at the Ohio State University. Her scholarship focuses on language and literacy practices across formal/school and informal settings and collaborative research with teachers and young people for social action. Together with Mollie V. Blackburn, she facilitates a teacher inquiry group committed to supporting LGBTQ students, teachers, and families in schools.

Catherine Compton-Lilly is an Associate Professor in Curriculum and Instruction at the University of Wisconsin–Madison. She teaches courses in literacy studies and works with professional development schools in Madison. Her interests include examining how time operates as a contextual factor in children's lives as they progress through school and construct their identities as students and readers. Dr. Compton-Lilly is the author/editor of several books and has published widely in educational journals.

Bryan Ripley Crandall is an Assistant Professor in the Graduate School of Education and Allied Professions and Director of the Connecticut Writing Project at Fairfield University. He taught high school English for more than 10 years in Louisville, Kentucky, where he began volunteering with refugee relocation services. His research interests include adolescent literacies, technology, professional development, urban schools, and ways to support students with limited and interrupted formal education.

Lorraine Falchi is a Director at La Escuelita, a dual-language preschool. She engages in ethnographic research to understand and analyze young emergent bilinguals' multimodal and multilingual literacy practices in context. Her research is published and presented in a range of journals and conferences. She holds a doctorate in curriculum and teaching from Teachers College, Columbia University. Dr. Falchi teaches courses at universities and has taught preschoolers to upper elementary children.

Norma González is a Professor in the Department of Language, Reading and Culture at the University of Arizona and is affiliated with the Second Language Acquisition and Teaching program. She is an anthropologist of education, and her

PhD is in sociocultural anthropology. She is the incoming President of the Council of Anthropology and Education. Her research focuses on language processes in the U.S./Mexico borderlands, immigration and education, language ideologies, and household ethnographies.

Margaret Grigorenko is Associate Professor of Education and Associate Dean of Education at Cedarville University. Her research focuses on how language is used in schools in ways that impacts students' ability to access academic content and to show what they know. In particular she focuses on students who have difficulty meeting school reading expectations and students whose home language is not mainstream English.

Juan C. Guerra is Associate Professor of English at the University of Washington, where he teaches courses on language variation, language policy, rhetoric, literacy, and first-year writing pedagogy. His research and scholarship are highlighted in two books: *Close to Home: Oral and Literate Practices in a Transnational Mexicano Community* and an edited collection, *Writing in Multicultural Settings*. His current work focuses on the rhetorical and discursive tools that disenfranchised students use to navigate the varied social spaces of their everyday lives.

Erica Halverson is an Associate Professor at the School of Education at the University of Wisconsin–Madison, where she researches how digital storytelling affects teens' identity formation and literacy. In 2010 she received the Jan Hawkins Award from the American Education Research Association.

Kevin M. Leander teaches in the Department of Teaching and Learning at Vanderbilt University. He is interested in developing methodologies for interpreting how semiotic resources are used to produce and relate to the multiple space-time contexts of a given classroom interactions. Kevin argues that classroom interactions are as much "about" who participates in them as they are "about" the topics that they claim to engage. To understand these identity and learning relations, he articulates a critical perspective on identity and culture along with a mediational perspective on learning, informed by cultural-historical activity theory.

Allan Luke is an emeritus professor at the Queensland University of Technology. His research has focused on arrange of topics, including early literacy, accountability and assessment, and comparative pedagogies.

sj Miller is Associate Professor of Literacy at the University of Colorado Boulder. sj has published widely in journals and presented at national conferences on a variety of topics related to teaching young adult literature, anti-bullying pedagogy, challenging the gender binary, multimodal applications of popular culture in secondary classrooms, and cultivating socio-spatial justice dispositions with secondary preservice English teachers. sj's work influenced the newly-vetted CAEP Social Justice Standard 6.

Silvia Noguerón-Liu is an Assistant Professor in the Department of Language and Literacy Education at the University of Georgia. Her current research explores the language and literacy practices of immigrant families in new Latino diaspora contexts and the ways such practices are shaped by transnational flows and participation in digital media production and consumption practices.

Kate Pahl is a Reader in Literacies in Education at the University of Sheffield, UK. She is currently engaged in a number of projects funded by the AHRC Connected Communities program with a focus on coproduced research in community contexts. She is the author, with Jennifer Rowsell, of *Artifactual Literacies: Every Object Tells a Story* (Teachers College Press, 2010). Her forthcoming book, *Materializing Literacies in Communities,* will be published by Bloomsbury Press.

Jennifer Rowsell is Professor and Canada Research Chair in Multiliteracies at Brock University's Faculty of Education, where she directs the Centre for Multiliteracies. She has cowritten and written several books in the areas of New Literacy Studies, multimodality, and multiliteracies.

Johnny Saldaña is the Evelyn Smith Professor of Theatre in the School of Film, Dance, and Theatre at Arizona State University. He is the author of *Longitudinal Qualitative Research: Analyzing Change through Time; Ethnodrama: An Anthology of Reality Theatre; The Coding Manual for Qualitative Researchers; Fundamentals of Qualitative Research;* and *Ethnotheatre: Research from Page to Stage* and is coauthor of the third edition of Miles & Huberman's *Qualitative Data Analysis.*

Lisa Schwartz is a Postdoctoral Scholar and Research Director at the University of Colorado at Boulder. In her research she co-creates and examines digitally mediated hybrid spaces that support youths' and educators' movement of semiotic resources across in-school and out-of-school contexts in order to develop academically and personally meaningful inquiries. Her current work leverages both the new media repertoires and everyday science, technology and design literacies of youth from nondominant communities for expansive learning.

Marjorie Siegel is Professor of Education and Chair of the Department of Curriculum and Teaching at Teachers College, Columbia University, New York, where she teaches in the Literacy Specialist and EdD programs. She has conducted ethnographic research on transmediation and collaborative action research on reading mathematics. Her current research interests include children's experiences with mandated literacy curricula and the analysis of multimodality in school settings.

INDEX